Understanding differences
between divorced and intact
families

Understanding Families

Series Editors: *Bert N. Adams, University of Wisconsin*
David M. Klein, University of Notre Dame

This book series examines a wide range of subjects relevant to studying families. Topics include parenthood, mate selection, marriage, divorce and remarriage, custody issues, culturally and ethnically based family norms, theory and conceptual design, family power dynamics, families and the law, research methods on the family, and family violence.

The series is aimed primarily at scholars working in family studies, sociology, psychology, social work, ethnic studies, gender studies, cultural studies, and related fields as they focus on the family. Volumes will also be useful for graduate and undergraduate courses in sociology of the family, family relations, family and consumer sciences, social work and the family, family psychology, family history, cultural perspectives on the family, and others.

Books appearing in **Understanding Families** are either single- or multiple-authored volumes or concisely edited books of original chapters on focused topics within the broad interdisciplinary field of marriage and family.

The books are reports of significant research, innovations in methodology, treatises on family theory, syntheses of current knowledge in a family subfield, or advanced textbooks. Each volume meets the highest academic standards and makes a substantial contribution to our understanding of marriages and families.

The National Council on Family Relations cosponsors with Sage a book award for students and new professionals. Award-winning manuscripts are published as part of the **Understanding Families** series.

Multiracial Couples: Black and White Voices
Paul C. Rosenblatt, Terri A. Karis, and Richard D. Powell

Understanding Latino Families: Scholarship, Policy, and Practice
Edited by Ruth E. Zambrana

Current Widowhood: Myths & Realities
Helena Znaniecka Lopata

Family Theories: An Introduction
David M. Klein and James M. White

Understanding Differences Between Divorced and Intact Families
Ronald L. Simons and Associates

Adolescents, Work, and Families: An Intergenerational Developmental Analysis
Jeylan T. Mortimer and Michael D. Finch

Ronald L. Simons
& Associates

Understanding Differences Between Divorced and Intact Families

Stress, Interaction, and Child Outcome

UNDERSTANDING FAMILIES

NEW ENGLAND INSTITUTE
OF TECHNOLOGY
LEARNING RESOURCES CENTER

SAGE Publications
International Educational and Professional Publisher
Thousand Oaks   London   New Delhi

For information address:

SAGE Publications, Inc.
2455 Teller Road
Thousand Oaks, California 91320
E-mail: order@sagepub.com

SAGE Publications Ltd.
6 Bonhill Street
London EC2A 4PU
United Kingdom

SAGE Publications India Pvt. Ltd.
M-32 Market
Greater Kailash I
New Delhi 110 048 India

Printed in the United States of America

Library of Congress Cataloging-in-Publication Data

Simons, Ronald L.
    Understanding differences between divorced and intact families:
Stress, interaction, and child outcomes / Ronald L. Simons and
associates.
        p.   cm.—(Understanding families; v. 5)
    Includes bibliographical references (p.   ) and index.
    ISBN 0-8039-5161-2 (cloth: acid-free paper).—ISBN
0-8039-5162-0 (pbk.: acid-free paper)
    1. Family—United States—Psychological aspects.   2. Single-parent
family—United States—Psychological aspects.   3. Children of
divorced parents—United States.   4. Adjustment (Psychology) in
children—United States.   5. Single parents—United States.
I. Title.   II. Series.
HQ536.S4977   1996
306.85—dc20   96-4471

This book is printed on acid-free paper.

96   97   98   99   00   01   10   9   8   7   6   5   4   3   2   1

Sage Production Editor: Gillian Dickens
Sage Typesetter: Andrea D. Swanson

This book is dedicated to our marital partners.
Their love and support have made work,
as well as life in general,
easier and more enjoyable.

Contents

III. FAMILY INTERACTION

IV. CHILD OUTCOMES

Preface

During the past 8 years, I have had the good fortune to be part of an exciting research team concerned with the effect of socioeconomic factors on family processes and child development. This group of sociologists consists of Rand Conger, Fred Lorenz, and Les Whitbeck at Iowa State University and Glen Elder at the University of North Carolina—Chapel Hill. Our collaboration grew out of a mutual concern with the effect of economic hardship on family interaction and child adjustment. In the late 1980s, we launched the Iowa Youth and Families Project (IYFP), a study of several hundred two-parent families living in North Central Iowa. This study was begun, at least in part, to assess the effect of the Midwest agricultural crisis on rural families. A few years later, we initiated the Iowa Single-Parent Project (ISPP), a study of stress and adjustment among single-parent families living in small towns and rural areas. The analyses presented in this book are based on the families from these two projects.

The members of our research team possess somewhat different (albeit complimentary) research interests; this has allowed us to establish a fruitful division of labor in which each of us takes responsibility for providing leadership with regard to a particular set of research topics. Although I am the person with primary responsibility for issues involving the effect of family structure on child development, the research agendas of the other investigators are at least indirectly related to this subject. I have tried to structure this book so as to capitalize on the strengths of our research team.

The book begins by positing a general model of the manner in which parental divorce affects child development. This model represents an extension of our earlier work on economic pressure, parental behavior, and child outcomes. It emphasizes the ways in which family structure differences in stress and parental adjustment account for the fact that children of divorce show more conduct and emotional problems than those from intact families. The subsequent chapters test the various components of the model. The first author listed in each chapter represents the team member with the most expertise on that particular topic. In many instances, a postdoctoral fellow or graduate research assistant is listed as a coauthor.

The resulting product is difficult to classify. In some ways, it is an edited volume; in other respects, it is not. Separate authors are listed for each chapter. But the book is organized around a specific theory of the effect of divorce on child adjustment and the various chapters build on each other in testing the dimensions of this theory. Thus, although at first glance the book may look like an edited volume, I hope it reads like a coherent research monograph.

Both the IYFP and ISPP have been very labor-intensive activities. Hundreds of people have contributed to the success of these two projects. This includes the study families, who spent hours completing questionnaires and engaging in videotaped interaction; the many field staff, who visited the families in their homes; the trained observers, who scored the videotapes of family interaction; and the research associates and assistants, who assisted in the data cleaning and analysis. This work was possible because of the generous financial support provided by several organizations. They include the National Institute of Mental Health (MH43270, MH48165, MH00567), the National Institute of Child Health and Human Development (HD27724), the National Institute on Drug Abuse (DA05347), the Bureau of Maternal and Child Health (MCJ109572), the John D. and Catherine T. MacArthur Foundation, Iowa Methodist Health Systems, and the Iowa Agriculture and Home Economics Experiment Station (Project No. 2931).

Finally, I would like to thank David Klein and Bert Adams, the editors of this series, and Mitch Allen, executive editor at Sage, for their thoughtful suggestions and kind encouragement.

Ronald L. Simons

PART I

INTRODUCTION

1

The Effect of Divorce on
Adult and Child Adjustment

RONALD L. SIMONS

A s both social scientists and lay people are aware, the American family has changed dramatically during the past 30 years. A structural transformation has taken place involving a significant decline in the proportion of families composed of children living with their natural parents, coupled with a striking increase in the number of single-parent and stepparent families. These changes largely have been the result of a rapid rise in the divorce rate that began during the 1960s and did not level off until the mid-1980s—whereas the probability of divorce for a white female was 20% in 1960, it rose to 45% by 1980 (Espenshade, 1985; Schoen, 1987). Projections indicate that between one half and two thirds of recent first marriages end in divorce (Bumpass, 1990; Martin & Bumpass, 1989; Norton & Moorman, 1987). These high rates of marital breakup have had a major effect on the living arrangements of children. In 1960, for example, 73% of all children lived with their natural parents, whereas this figure was projected to be 56% in 1990 (Hernandez, 1988). Bumpass and Sweet (1989) estimate that 44% of children born between 1970 and 1984 will live for a time in a single-parent family, and Furstenberg and Cherlin (1991) project that 60% of children born in the 1990s will have this experience.

Social science, particularly the discipline of sociology, is concerned with the effects that variations in social arrangements or social structures have on human behavior. Given this focus, it is little wonder that social scientists have devoted a great deal of attention to investigating the consequences of these remarkable changes in family structure. Much of this research has examined the social and psychological functioning of children and adults living in single- versus two-parent families.

Most social scientists are political liberals who are strongly committed to social values involving tolerance of diverse lifestyles and gender equality (Glenn, 1993). Given these value commitments, researchers during the 1970s and early 1980s viewed high divorce rates and a rapid rise in the number of single-parent families as an indicator of society's movement toward a more equitable, open atmosphere. These social changes were seen as an indication that unhappy couples no longer felt obligated to stay together and that women were free to escape oppressive marital relationships and seek more satisfying lives. Such normative changes were seen as healthy for both adults and children. Divorce allowed adults to terminate hopelessly troubled marriages, and children avoided the burden of being raised in an atmosphere of parental conflict. Family scholars asserted that structural changes in the family should not be viewed with alarm, as they were more a sign of institutional evolution than of social disorganization (Bane, 1976; Herzog & Sudia, 1973; Levitan & Belous, 1981).

Of course, it was apparent that dissolving a marriage was a psychologically distressing event for both parents and children. It was assumed, however, that this emotional turmoil was temporary and would dissipate as family members adjusted to their new living situation. Furthermore, although divorce was a stressful transition for the parties involved, it was considered to be an event that produced as many positive as negative consequences. An example of this optimistic view is provided by the discussion of children's adjustment to divorce presented in the 1971 edition of Ira Reiss's popular textbook on families. Reiss argues that

> there is little basis for concluding that divorce inevitably does lasting psychological damage to children. . . . It may be that divorce produces more imaginative, more self-reliant types of personalities because of the

lack of two parents as guides. We must not assume that if divorce has any consequences on children they must be "detrimental." (p. 300)

Thus, during the 1970s and early 1980s, social scientists assumed that there were specific strengths and weaknesses associated with different family types but that, in general, the alternative structures were equally viable environments for child and adult development.

Results from several cross-sectional and longitudinal studies became available during the 1980s that challenged this view of the structural changes taking place among American families. First, there was evidence that single parents not only have higher rates of emotional (Stack, 1989; Travato & Lauris, 1989; Tschann, Johnston, & Wallerstein, 1989) and physical (Kisker & Goldman, 1987; Mergenhagen, Lee, & Gove, 1985; National Center for Health Statistics, 1988) health problems than married persons, but that these differences tend to persist for several years after marital breakup (Kitson, 1992). The most compelling findings, however, were those relating to children. A variety of studies reported children living in single-parent families to be at higher risk for an assortment of developmental problems than those residing in two-parent families. Children living with one parent were found to have more difficulty with school, were more sexually active, suffered from higher rates of depression, and were more likely to commit delinquent acts and to abuse substances (Amato & Keith, 1991b; McLanahan & Booth, 1989; McLanahan & Sandefur, 1994). Further, several studies reported that adults who experienced parental divorce as children have poor psychological adjustment, lower socioeconomic attainment, and greater marital instability than adults reared in an intact family (Amato & Keith, 1991a). Thus there is evidence that parental divorce is associated with reduced social and psychological adjustment among both children and adult children of divorce.

Publication of these findings dampened the optimism that had existed among social scientists regarding the structural transformation of the family in America. In 1987, Norval Glenn, then editor of the *Journal of Family Issues,* invited 18 prominent family scholars to assess the current state of the family in this country. Most scholars expressed apprehension over recent changes. They were concerned about the effect of these changes on the welfare of children.

Reports that members of single-parent families are at greater risk for problems than those of two-parent families have done more than stifle the sanguine attitude about divorce that pervaded the social scientific community during the 1970s. This body of evidence has been a cause of significant polarization and acrimony within the social scientific community. The divisiveness that has been generated by this research is exemplified by the responses to Amato and Keith's (1993a) recent article on children's adjustment to divorce and to Popenoe's (1993) article on changes in the family.

In light of findings linking single-parent families to developmental risk, some social scientists have come to view recent transformations in the American family with great alarm and have taken the position that this revolution in family structure is a major determinant of the social problems facing the United States (Popenoe, 1993; Whitehead, 1993). They contend that researchers have been slow to recognize the social implications of these changes and that more attention needs to be devoted to this issue.

On the other side, some maintain that social scientists have placed too much emphasis on family structure (Allen, 1993; Demo, 1993; Stacey, 1990, 1993). They argue that differences in developmental outcomes between single- and two-parent families are small and that researchers should abandon their obsession with comparing people living in different family forms and instead turn their attention to factors that affect people's psychological well-being regardless of family structure (e.g., conflict, poverty). This group includes some feminists who fear that negative evaluations of recent family trends serve as fuel for conservative political forces that threaten to undermine improvements in the status of women (Allen, 1993; Stacey, 1993). These theorists point to people on the political right who not only assert that the primary cause of society's problems is the breakdown of family values but also believe that the family can be repaired only by a return to traditional gender roles. From this point of view, social scientists should discontinue research focusing on the developmental risks associated with single-parent families because the findings from such studies may be used to subordinate women.

We take a middle position. It is certainly true that differences in outcomes between children of divorce and those raised in intact families are modest and the effects of divorce may be becoming weaker

(Amato & Keith, 1991a, 1991b). It is also true that there is great variability in outcomes among children of divorce and that the majority of these children show no lasting negative effects (Emery, 1988). And, it should be noted that there is great variability of outcomes for children raised in two-parent families, with a significant proportion of these children developing problems as well. Thus, the difference in outcomes for children in single- and two-parent families is one of central tendency rather than dispersion (Amato & Keith, 1993b). Although the distributions for children for the two types of families overlap, the mean level of problem behaviors is greater in single-parent than in two-parent samples.

It does not follow, however, that because the distributions for problem behaviors for children for the two types of families overlap and the differences between the means are modest that there is little reason for further research on the relationship between family structure and personal well-being. Although most children of divorce do not show lasting ill effects, research suggests that these individuals are approximately twice as likely to develop serious problems as persons raised in an intact family (McLanahan & Sandefur, 1994). The doubling of a hazard is certainly considered to be a significant elevation in risk among public health researchers. Dietary cholesterol, Type A personality, and hypertension, for example, are considered important risk factors for coronary heart disease although they do not double a person's chances of developing this illness. Thus, in epidemiological terms, parental divorce represents a significant risk factor for child developmental problems. The danger that it poses may be less than that of other factors, such as poverty or abuse. The fact remains, however, that children of divorce are at significantly greater risk for problem outcomes than those raised in intact families. This persistent finding suggests the need for research on the mechanisms that account for this increased jeopardy.

Although we consider study of the relationship between family structure and child outcomes to be an important social scientific endeavor, we admit to ambivalent feelings about such research. A recent article by Whitehead (1993) identifies many of our concerns: First, most parents who divorce are quite concerned about the welfare of their children and their decision to divorce is a wrenching, last resort. It seems cruel to conduct research that reminds them of the problems their children may suffer as a result of family breakup.

Second, such research can be misinterpreted as an attack on single women who are struggling to do the best they can. Third, sociological studies have demonstrated that changes in the American family are linked to broad social forces and it is unlikely that they will be reversed (Kain, 1990; Skolnick, 1991). One might question the point of research on the consequences of variations in family structure when the new family forms are now an inevitable feature of our society. Finally, the findings from such research are often used by political groups opposed to our commitment to diversity and gender equality.

Although these issues are important, social science is concerned with describing and explaining empirical reality. Hence it is essential that we as scientists do our best to avoid distorting or denying facts because of personal values or ideology. Such a commitment is not only in the best interests of science, it is also the approach that is most likely to benefit society. Research has clearly established a link between childhood exposure to parental divorce and an elevated risk for developmental problems. This information by itself is not very helpful to policymakers. Rather, there is a need for research that goes beyond documenting differences by family structure to identifying the circumstances and social processes that account for the higher rate of negative outcomes for children in disrupted versus intact families (Amato, 1993).

One might argue that such research is especially important for women. As Glenn (1993) recently observed,

> If some recent family changes are having negative consequences for the quality of life and for the socialization of children, denial of this reality will not help feminists bring about the kind of society for which they strive, especially if, as much evidence suggests, negative consequences of recent family change have fallen disproportionately on women and especially children, almost half of whom are the women of the future. (p. 543)

Indeed, studies indicate that daughters in single-parent families are more likely than sons to experience certain types of long-term problems (e.g., educational disadvantage, early parental responsibilities; Amato & Keith, 1991b). Thus it would seem to be in the best interests of women that research be devoted to understanding the processes that account for differences in rates of negative developmental outcomes between disrupted and intact families. Such information is a requisite if we are to design social policies that reduce or eliminate the elevated risk associated with life in single-parent families. This book is an attempt to add to the stock of such knowledge.

Explaining Family Structure Differences

STRESS AND QUALITY OF PARENTING

I have noted that a variety of studies have investigated the relationship between family structure and child welfare and that overall the evidence indicates that children in single-parent families are at greater risk for both conduct problems and emotional difficulties than those living in intact families. Two general hypotheses are frequently offered as explanations for these associations between family disruption and child maladjustment. The first suggests that the low income of single-parent families accounts for negative developmental outcomes (Demo & Acock, 1988; Krein & Beller, 1988; Michael & Tuma, 1985). The second contends that single parents engage in less effective parenting and that this discrepancy in parenting practices explains differences in developmental outcomes between single- and two-parent families (Dornbusch et al., 1985; Hogan & Kitagawa, 1985; Matsueda & Heimer, 1987; McLanahan & Booth, 1989). Although these two explanations are sometimes treated as competing hypotheses, our study tests a model that combines these two ideas. This model builds on research findings obtained by our research team over the past several years.

Some years ago, one of us (Elder) used data collected from California families during the Great Depression to show that parental behavior largely mediates the effect of family economic hardship on child outcomes (Elder, 1974; Elder, Liker, & Cross, 1984; Elder, Van Nguyen, & Caspi, 1985). In recent years, we have used data collected from families living in the Midwest to corroborate and elaborate on this finding. Our results indicate that family economic pressure and other aversive events increase psychological distress, and that such distress has a disruptive effect on parenting practices (Simons, Beaman, Conger, & Chao, 1993; Simons, Lorenz, Conger, & Wu, 1992;

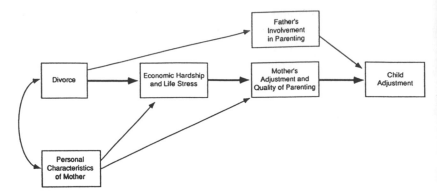

Figure 1.1. A General Model of the Effect of Divorce on Child Adjustment

Simons, Lorenz, Wu, & Conger, 1993). Disrupted parenting, in turn, increases the probability that children will develop behavioral or emotional problems (Conger, Conger, Elder, Lorenz, Simons, & Whitbeck, 1992, 1993). Thus, our findings suggest that adult exposure to aversive events often indirectly affects the adjustment of children. This indirect influence is produced through a ripple effect whereby stressors experienced by parents tend to intrude on their psychological well-being and parenting practices, with reductions in quality of parenting leading to negative developmental outcomes for children.

The vast majority of single parents are women, who typically experience a dramatic reduction in income with the transition to unmarried status (Arendell, 1986). Furthermore, research indicates that single adults display higher rates of psychological disorder than married persons (Kitson & Morgan, 1990; Raschke, 1987) and that single parents tend to make fewer demands on children and use less effective disciplinary strategies than married parents (Hetherington, 1989; McLanahan & Booth, 1989). Integrating these results with our findings regarding the indirect effect of family economic pressure on child outcomes suggests one avenue by which divorce influences the well-being of family members. This avenue is depicted in Figure 1.1.

Figure 1.1 shows an arrow from divorce to level of maternal stress. Our study emphasizes two types of stress: economic pressure and negative life events. Divorced mothers and their children are likely to experience greater economic pressure and higher rates of stressful life changes than intact families. The economic pressure results from the loss of the absent father's earnings (Gongla & Thompson, 1987). On average, families experience a 30% to 50% reduction in income following divorce (Arendell, 1986; Cherlin, 1992). This economic pressure, as well as the new living situation faced by the single mother and her children, increases the probability of stressful life events, for example, change in residence or mother begins to work outside of the home. Marital disruption is a role transition that tends to trigger a number of associated life changes (Chiriboga, Catron, & Associates, 1991). Indeed, one recent study found that several years after divorce, single parents continue to report more negative life changes than married persons (Kitson, 1992).

Figure 1.1 also indicates that level of stress (degree of economic pressure and number of negative events) influences women's adjustment. The model identifies two components of adjustment: psychological well-being and quality of parenting. The elevated rates of psychological distress and inept parenting that studies have found among single mothers is posited to be a function, at least in part, of the financial hardship and negative life events common to single-parent families. Finally, the model depicts an association between mother's adjustment and adjustment of the child. This relationship is consonant with the large body of research linking the emotional state and parenting practices of parents to developmental outcomes for children (Maccoby, 1992; Maccoby & Martin, 1983). Our general model suggests that the relationship between divorce and child adjustment is explained in large part by the level of stress experienced by the mother and her adaptation to this stress.

Our model presents a clear set of hypotheses regarding the manner in which economic pressure contributes to family structure differences in child outcomes. Several authors have argued that the prevalence of poverty and economic distress may explain negative developmental outcomes among children in single-parent families. For example, Demo and Acock (1988), in their review of research concerning the effect of divorce on children, state that "effects that appear to be caused by divorce may actually be the result of inadequate income— the loss of the father being relatively less critical than the loss of his financial contribution" (p. 640). We agree with this contention and go a step further by positing the avenue whereby economic hardship achieves its affect: Family financial pressure influences children indirectly through its disruptive effect on the mood and parenting practices of the mother.

Much of the research on family structure and child adjustment has failed to consider the effect of family financial hardship. When researchers include economic factors in their analyses, they usually do so by controlling for current family income. Unfortunately, merely controlling for family income is not a very effective strategy for testing the idea that financial difficulties following marital disruption explain family structure differences in child adjustment (McLanahan & Sandefur, 1994). In most studies, controlling for family income substantially reduces the relationship between family structure and child outcomes (McLanahan & Booth, 1989), but it is difficult to know how this effect is to be interpreted.

The problem is that couples of low social status are more likely to divorce (i.e., low income is both a precursor as well as a consequence of marital disruption; McLanahan & Sandefur, 1994). Thus in most samples, differences in income between single- and two-parent families probably existed prior to marital breakup. To the extent that this is true, a reduction in the relationship between family structure and child adjustment after controlling for family income may indicate either that children are negatively affected by decreases in family finances following divorce or that the correlation between family structure and child development is spurious due to the association of both variables with social class. We were able to avoid this confound in our study because our single-parent families had predivorce levels of income and education comparable to our two-parent families. Our sample allowed us to rule out predivorce differences in social class or income as an explanation for the family structure differences in child adjustment that exist in our data.

Furthermore, to examine better the consequences of limited economic resources following divorce, we focus on family structure differences in economic pressure rather than simply income. Families suffer economic pressure to the extent that they (a) cannot meet material needs, (b) often fall behind in paying debts, and (c) have had to cut back on everyday expenses in an attempt to live within available means (Conger, Ge, Elder, Lorenz, & Simons, 1994). Economic pressure should not be thought of as a subjective perception of family finances that is less "real" or "objective" than the construct family income. Economic pressures such as cutting back on expenditures and having difficulty paying bills are real, everyday experiences, not simply subjective impressions of reality.

Economic pressure is determined by a family's level of income relative to its financial needs and obligations. Such a variable captures the financial strain experienced by divorced women better than the variable family income. Disrupted marriages usually produce a single-parent family with a significantly reduced income (Arendell, 1986; Cherlin, 1992). This decreased income results in economic pressure to meet the family's financial needs. Income may decrease by 30% to 50% but costs such as taxes, insurance, medical bills, house payments, automobile maintenance, and the like often remain the same. Predivorce obligations and commitments dictate, at least in part, the financial demands that a divorced mother faces.

Evidence indicates that economic pressure, rather than low income per se, has a disruptive influence on individuals and families (Conger et al., 1990; Conger, Ge, et al., 1994; Elder, 1974; Kessler, Turner, & House, 1988). Low income is stressful to the extent that it creates demands for painful behavioral adjustments, such as cutting back on expenditures. When income is low, parents with high financial demands (e.g., medical costs, automobile repairs) need to make more difficult economic adjustments than those without such demands. Thus, although people with lower income will, in general, experience greater economic pressure than those with higher income, the psychological effect of level of income will vary depending on financial obligations and requirements. The economic pressure construct takes these financial demands into account in a manner that the variable family income does not. For these reasons, we view economic pressure as a better indicator of the economic difficulties faced by single-parent families than level of income. Our general model suggests that the negative influence that economic pressure has on maternal adjustment and parental functioning accounts for much of the relationship between family structure and child outcomes.

ANTISOCIAL CHARACTERISTICS

The sequence of relationships discussed, up to this point, portrays a traditional *stress perspective* on the problems often associated with single-parent families. Stress explanations maintain that aversive events and circumstances brought about by family disruption account for the higher rates of maladjustment in single-parent households. An alternative view is provided by the *selection perspective,* which asserts that some people have characteristics or traits that place them at risk for marital discord and divorce, as well as for other difficulties in functioning (Bachrach, 1975; Halem, 1980, Kitson & Morgan, 1990). In addition to increasing the probability of marital breakup, these vulnerabilities are seen as impeding adjustment following divorce (Kitson, 1992). The strain perspective argues that stress associated with single-parent status intrudes on emotional well-being and quality of parenting, whereas the selection argument suggests that problematic characteristics of the individual account for the finding that marital status is related to stressful life events, negative psychological well-being, and caliber of parenting. Patterson and his associates (Capaldi & Patterson, 1991; Patterson & Dishion, 1988), for example, provide evidence that antisocial parents are at high risk for marital disruptions, social disadvantage, and inept parenting practices.

Although often presented as competing hypotheses, the strain and selection perspectives might best be considered complimentary perspectives. There is empirical support for both views, and hence any comprehensive account of the factors that account for the higher rate of problems in single-parent families relative to two-parent households must incorporate elements from both frameworks. I have already noted the manner in which the general model presented in Figure 1.1 includes a stress explanation. In addition, the model shows family structure to be correlated with mothers' personal characteristics, which in turn are depicted as causally related to their level of stress and parental functioning. This set of relationships represents the selection explanation for the relationship between family structure and personal well-being.

We are particularly concerned with involvement in antisocial behavior, often considered to be an ongoing trait or behavioral predisposition. A trait consists of a pattern of behavior that is exhibited across time and settings (Allport, 1937). Antisocial behavior involves actions deemed to be risky, inappropriate, shortsighted, or insensitive by the majority of people in society. Individuals display an antisocial behavior trait to the extent that they engage in delinquent behavior during adolescence and continue as adults to participate in deviant actions such as interpersonal violence, substance use, sexual promiscuity, minor violations of the law, and the like. Our model posits that the higher levels of economic pressure, negative events, depression, and inept parenting among single compared to married women is at least partially explained by the fact that the social category of single parents has a larger proportion of individuals with antisocial dispositions.

Note that Figure 1.1 includes a two-headed arrow between divorce and personal characteristics. The selection perspective suggests that personal characteristics are a cause of marital disruption. It also seems likely that divorce enhances or amplifies personal dispositions. Thus, although antisocial tendencies increase the probability of marital discord and divorce, antisocial behavior may also be a consequence of marital disruption. The stress of divorce may promote substance abuse or temper outbursts, and social life as a newly single adult may involve heavy drinking, late-night parties, and the like. Based on recent research showing that social deviance is relatively stable across the life course (Gottfredson & Hirschi, 1990), we assume that the primary causal flow is from antisocial tendencies to divorce (i.e., a selection effect). Nonetheless, we use a two-headed arrow to link the two constructs because marital disruption probably also fosters antisocial behavior among persons with such inclinations.

Most studies of family structure and adjustment emphasize some type of stress framework and ignore the extent to which a selection perspective might account for findings. Our model includes elements of the selection as well as the stress explanation. The arrows in Figure 1.1 linking divorce, stress, emotional well-being, and parenting are in bold as a way of indicating that we believe that the stress perspective is the primary determinant of family structure differences in family member adjustment. Nevertheless, our model suggests that both stress and selection processes exert an influence; in the chapters that follow, we have tried to identify the relative power of each explanation.

FATHERS AND CHILD ADJUSTMENT

Recent reviews of research on divorce and child outcomes conclude that the emotional well-being and parenting practices of the custodial parent—usually the mother—are fundamental determinants of child adjustment (Amato, 1993; Cherlin, 1992). We agree with this view; that is why the arrows in Figure 1.1 connecting family structure, maternal adjustment, and child problems are in bold. Although our model identifies maternal functioning as the primary cause of child adjustment, it also recognizes the influence exerted by fathers.

Although the idea that child adjustment to divorce is facilitated by involvement by nonresidential fathers is intuitively appealing, social scientists have noted that there is actually little empirical evidence for the claim; most studies find that frequency of visitation by nonresidential fathers is unrelated to child adjustment (Amato, 1993; Emery, 1988; Furstenberg & Cherlin, 1991). We believe that such a finding has little relevance to the issue of whether the parenting provided by nonresidential fathers is consequential for child development. There is little reason to expect that simply having contact with the nonresidential father significantly influences a child's development. We believe that the quality, rather than simply the quantity, of interaction with this parent is the key to understanding father's effect on child adjustment.

Past research suggests that nonresidential fathers often behave toward their children more as an adult friend or relative than as a parent (Arendell, 1986; Furstenberg & Nord, 1985; Hetherington, Cox, & Cox, 1976). Much of the time with their children is spent joking and roughhousing, watching TV, attending movies, going out to eat, and the like. Fathers who limit their involvement to such activities would not be expected to exert any more influence on the developmental outcomes of their children than that exercised by other friendly adults (e.g., uncles, grandparents, mom's boyfriend). If a nonresidential father is to influence his child's psychosocial development, he must be more than a friend and entertainer. He must behave as a parent. Past research has shown that effective parenting involves activities such as providing encouragement and emotional support, establishing and explaining standards for conduct, and administering consistent discipline (Maccoby & Martin, 1983). Fathers do not need to live with their child to engage in these behaviors. Our research indicates that adolescents are less likely to display adjustment problems when their nonresidential fathers engage in these parenting behaviors (Simons, Whitbeck, Beaman, & Conger, 1994). The effect was particularly strong for boys' conduct problems.

Past research indicates that fathers in intact families also show low involvement in parenting (Parke & Sterns, 1993). Interaction between fathers and their children in intact families, like that in divorced families, tends to be focused around play and mutual entertainment (Parke & Sterns, 1993). Regardless of whether they live in the home, fathers are less likely than mothers to engage in parenting activities that have been shown to be crucial for the positive psychosocial development of children (e.g., setting standards, providing encouragement and emotional support, administering consistent discipline). Although the frequency of these parenting behaviors is low regardless of family structure, fathers in intact families are undoubtedly more likely to engage in these activities than nonresidential fathers.

Paternal involvement in parenting is critical for divorced families because, as noted earlier, studies show that many divorced mothers evidence a decline in quality of parenting. Single mothers tend to make fewer demands on children and use less effective disciplinary strategies than those who are married (Hetherington, 1989; McLanahan & Booth, 1988). Thus it is essential that fathers behave as parents following marital disruption so that they can counteract any decline in quality of parenting by the mother. Involvement by fathers is probably crucial in preventing conduct problems, especially among boys (Simons, Whitbeck, et al., 1994).

DISTRESSED MARRIAGES AND CHILD MALADJUSTMENT

People often assert that divorce is preferable to exposing children to recurrent marital strife. They argue that divorce is certainly no more injurious to children than persistent quarreling between parents. This is undoubtedly the case when marital conflict stems from alcohol or drug abuse or involves physical violence. In such instances, marital separation might be expected to reduce the child's risk for emotional or behavioral problems. In most cases, however, marital conflict, even during the months preceding marital breakup, is much less intrusive than parental divorce. Often the couple's predivorce interaction consists of a cold war, with little overt conflict (Gottman, 1994). And although marital discord may be very disturbing to the adults involved, we expect that children are fairly resilient to parental conflict to the extent that it does not involve threats of violence, does not disrupt family routine, and does not intrude on the parent-child relationship. Thus the important issue, as we see it, is the level of marital conflict. McLanahan and Sandefur (1994) suggest that children living in violent or abusive families are likely to be better off when their parents divorce. They go on to note, however, that

> if both parents are reasonable people and care about the child, and if conflict arises because one (or both) of the parents is bored with the marriage or falls in love with someone else, the answer to the question "What is best for the child?" is less clear. From the child's point of view, these two types of conflict (abuse versus weak commitment) are very different matters. In the latter case, the child would probably be better off if the parents resolved their differences and the family remained together, even if the long-term relationship between the parents was less than perfect. (p. 31)

Several studies have reported findings consistent with this idea. Wallerstein and Kelley (1980) found that children of divorce were usually well aware of the long history of discord between their parents and knew that their parents were not happily married. Still, few of them greeted the divorce with relief, and most were surprised and upset by the news that their parents were separating. Evidence from various longitudinal studies shows that following divorce, children manifest significantly more conduct problems, academic difficulties, and psychological distress than they did prior to divorce (Cherlin et al., 1991; McLanahan & Sandefur, 1994). This indicates that the problems that children demonstrate following divorce are not merely a product of predivorce conflict between the parents. Children undoubtedly perceive persistent parental discord as frustrating and annoying, but in most cases its effect on the child's emotional and behavioral functioning appears to be much less than that of divorce (Cherlin, 1992; Furstenberg & Cherlin, 1991).

Divorce is a relief for most adults, however. Studies show that the vast majority of divorced adults report that their lives would be worse if they had remained married to their former spouse (Hetherington, Cox, & Cox, 1982). Albeit, whereas marital breakup often entails few costs for fathers, mothers with custody of children encounter a number of new strains and difficulties. Thus, although a woman may be glad to be out of a distressing marriage, she often has to pay a substantial price for her freedom. Consequently, we expect that divorced mothers are more apt to show adjustment problems, such as depression or disrupted parenting, than those who are in a distressed marriage.

Men are less likely than women to experience serious economic pressures following marital breakup (Cherlin, 1992). In addition, they rarely face the burden of child rearing, as mothers usually receive custody of the children (Raschke, 1987). Although fathers generally encounter less stressful living circumstances than mothers following divorce, marital disruption has a major effect on their functioning as parents. Generally, men substantially reduce involvement with their children following divorce (Furstenberg & Cherlin, 1991). This negative effect of marital breakup on quality of fathers' parenting is likely to be much greater than that of marital discord.

In summary, we expect that in most cases divorce exerts a more negative influence than marital distress on the quality of parenting by fathers and mothers and on the emotional and behavioral functioning of children. This hypothesis is tested throughout this book. We presume that family structure is more strongly associated with ineffective parenting than is marital distress. And, children in divorced families are expected to exhibit significantly more problems than those living in an intact family with a distressed marriage.

Plan of the Book

The various chapters of this book are designed to elaborate on and test specific hypotheses suggested by the general model presented in Figure 1.1. All the analyses are based on a sample created by pooling the families from two related studies. The 407 intact families that constitute the sample for the Iowa Youth and Families Project (IYFP) were combined with the 207 divorced families that constitute the sample for the Iowa Single Parent Project (ISPP). The authors of the following chapters represent the investigators and staff for these two projects. Details regarding sample selection and data collection procedures for the IYFP and ISPP are provided in Chapter 2.

Although the general model of divorce and adjustment presented in Figure 1.1 may appear rather simple, it actually implies a number of hypotheses. Consequently, a test of the model requires that it be broken down into its various components and examined in a series of steps. This is the focus of the following chapters. For the most part, each chapter elaborates and tests some portion of the general model. The chapters in Part I are concerned with differences between divorced and married parents regarding exposure to stress, access to social support, and personal characteristics. The analyses include factors such as economic pressure, work stress, social support, and antisocial behavior trait. Part II is concerned with the effect of these stressors and personal characteristics on the psychological well-being of parents and the interaction that takes place within families. The chapters consider the extent to which divorced and intact families differ in terms of parental adjustment, parenting practices, and sibling relationships. Part III concentrates on family structure differences in child adjustment. Delinquency, premarital sex, academic performance, and psychological well-being are the outcomes considered.

The chapters are arranged so as to provide a systematic examination of the processes suggested by our general model. In most cases, the chapters build on each other. The family structure differences in stress identified in Part I, for example, are used as explanatory variables in Part II to account for dissimilarities in parental adjustment and family interaction. The differences in family interaction discussed in Part II are used in many of the chapters in Part III to explain disparities between the two types of families with regard to child outcomes. The overall purpose of the book is to provide a systematic account of the processes by which differences between divorced and intact families in terms of stress and personal characteristics produce discrepancies in child outcomes by reducing parental adjustment and disrupting parenting practices.

2

The Sample, Data Collection Procedures, and Measures

RONALD L. SIMONS

S tudies of single-parent families are roughly of two types (Demo & Acock, 1988; Raschke, 1987). First, there are national surveys. Although these studies are based on large random samples, they either fail to include many theoretically relevant variables, as the data are usually collected for some purpose other than investigating family processes, or they utilize very abbreviated measures for constructs. Alternatively, studies are organized around the objective of providing an in-depth analysis of single-parent families. Although such inquiries usually include measures of a wide range of family constructs, they tend to be based on small, convenient samples and frequently do not employ comparison groups (Wallerstein & Kelly, 1980). We have tried to avoid these problems in the present inquiry.

The analyses reported throughout this book are based on a sample created by pooling data collected from families in two related studies. Data collected during spring 1991 from families in the Iowa Youth and Families Project (IYFP) were combined with data collected during this same time period from families in the Iowa Single-Parent Project (ISPP). The IYFP is a panel study beginning in 1989 of 451 families, all containing two parents, a target adolescent, and a second sibling within 4 years of age of the target child. By the third wave of the panel

(1991), the period used in the present analyses, 407 families remained in the study.

The sample was recruited through the cohort of all 7th grade students, male and female, who were enrolled in public or private schools during winter and spring 1989 in eight counties in North Central Iowa. The study site was selected because it is fairly representative of the state as a whole with regard to a number of characteristics (e.g., income, size of communities). Seventy-seven percent of the eligible families agreed to participate in the study. Additional details regarding the sample are presented in Conger et al. (1992).

Prior to collecting wave 3 data from the IYFP sample, funding was obtained to launch the ISPP. The ISPP is a panel study of 207 mother-headed households containing target adolescents of approximately the same age as those in the IYFP sample. The sample was generated through lists of students provided by schools. The lists identified the name of each student's parent. Telephone calls were made to residences where the parent's name suggested the parent was female.

Mothers were screened according to the criteria that they had divorced within the past 2 years, that their former spouse is the biological parent of the target child, and that the target child had a sibling within 3 years of his or her age. These are rather stringent criteria and only about 15% of the women telephoned met all these requirements. To obtain a pool of households large enough to produce a sample of approximately 200 single-parent families, the study site had to be expanded to include counties beyond the eight used to generate the IYFP sample. An attempt was made, however, to exclude counties that differed in potentially important ways from the IYFP study area. For example, the larger urban areas of Des Moines and Davenport and the university communities of Ames and Iowa City were not included.

Of the divorced women who met the study criteria, 99% agreed to participate. Out of the 210 women recruited, only 3 later refused to be involved. This high response rate appeared to be a function of two factors: the women's need for the $175 compensation fee and their desire to facilitate research concerned with the difficulties experienced by single mothers. Indeed, several single mothers called our research center and asked to be included in our research project even though

TABLE 2.1 Comparison of the Two-Parent and Single-Parent Families on Selected Characteristics

	Two-Parent Families		Single-Parent Families	
	X	S.D.	X	S.D.
Mother's education	13.38	1.68	13.36	1.94
Mother's age	39.80	3.97	38.33	3.84
Number of children	3.06	1.16	3.05	1.15
Age of target child	14.61	.55	14.33	.67
Percentage of targets female	52.80	—	52.60	—
Percentage of mothers employed	82.60	—	80.30	—
Hours worked per week	31.43	16.10	32.48	16.76
Current income	$39,116	$24,361	$24,281	$22,037
Estimate of predivorce income	—	—	$35,478	$33,973

they did not meet our study criteria. Thus, whereas most studies must use persuasive appeals to recruit subjects, the ISPP was unique in that we had to turn away families who pleaded to be included. We believe this speaks to the desperate circumstances faced by many divorced women living in small communities.

A little less than one third of the families in the IYFP sample lived on farms, whereas none of the ISPP single-parent families lived on farms. In an effort to maximize the comparability of the samples, the farmers in the IYFP sample were deleted. This left a pooled sample of 534 families: 328 two-parent families and 206 single-parent families.

As demonstrated by the comparisons presented in Table 2.1, the two sets of families were quite similar regarding several important characteristics. First, the women in the ISPP sample did not differ from those in the IYFP sample in terms of educational attainment. Mean education was 13.36 years for single mothers and 13.40 for married mothers. These figures parallel those for the state as a whole; Iowa has a very low drop-out rate, especially for females, and a majority of young people seek additional education following high school graduation. The two groups of women were also of roughly the same age. On average the single women were 38.3 years old and the married women were 39.8 years old.

Approximately the same proportion of divorced and married women were employed outside the home. As shown in Table 2.1, the percentage was 82.6 for married mothers and 80.3 for divorced. On average, the two groups of women worked about the same number of hours per week. The number of hours per week spent working outside the home averaged about 31.5 for the married women and 32.5 for the divorced women.

Table 2.1 shows that the gender and age of the target children did not differ by family structure. Roughly 53% of the target children in both the single- and two-parent families were female. Mean age was 14.3 years for children living with a single parent and 14.6 years for those living with two parents.

As expected, the single-parent families reported lower average incomes than married families. Table 2.1 shows that the single-parent families reported an average income of $26,074, whereas the figure for two-parent families was $39,116. The correlation between family structure (coded two-parent = 1, single-parent = 2) and family income was −.31 ($p \leq .01$). Unfortunately, it was not clear whether this family structure difference in income existed prior to divorce or was a consequence of the rather dramatic decline in income that women often experience following marital breakup. In an effort to address this issue, we asked the divorced women to indicate how much their monthly family income had changed from the amount they had available prior to marital breakup. Response categories for the question ranged from 1 (increased more than 20%) to 9 (decreased more than 50%). A rough measure of predivorce income was established for each of the single-parent families by correcting their current income for the proportion of income lost (or gained) following divorce. This adjustment undoubtedly underestimated predivorce income for the single-parent families because the response categories for the income change question only went as far as a 50% reduction. Many of the families may have experienced a decline of 60% or more but only had their income adjusted upward by 50%.

As shown in Table 2.1, our estimation procedure suggests that the single-parent families had an average income of $35,478 prior to divorce. Although this figure is approximately $3,500 less than the average income of the two-parent families, this difference is not statistically significant. After adjusting the incomes of the single-parent families, the correlation between family structure and income is only −.06 ($p = .28$). Thus, our crude approach to estimating predivorce income suggests that, prior to marital breakup, the divorced families in our sample did not differ significantly in earnings from the married.

Analysis did indicate, however, that on average the divorced families lived in slightly larger communities than the married. Thus community size was included as a control variable in the analyses reported in the following chapters. In no instance did controlling for size of community influence the magnitude of the associations between theoretical constructs.

It should be noted that one of the limitations of the IYFP and ISPP samples is that all the families were white and lived in relatively small communities. Although there is no apparent reason to assume that the processes investigated in this study are specific to families with these characteristics, there is a need to replicate the models presented in the subsequent chapters using a more ethnically and geographically diverse sample.

Methods and Procedures

Similar methods and procedures were employed in collecting data from the IYFP and ISPP families. Each family was visited twice at home. During the first visit, each family member completed a set of questionnaires focusing on family processes, individual family member characteristics, and economic circumstances. On average, it took approximately 2 hours to complete the first visit. Between the first and second visits, family members completed questionnaires left with them by the first interviewer. These questionnaires dealt with information concerning the parents' parents; beliefs about parenting, work, and earnings; and plans for the future. Each family member was instructed to place his or her completed questionnaire in an envelope, seal it, and give it to the interviewer at the time of the second visit.

During the second visit, which normally occurred within 2 weeks of the first, the family was videotaped while engaging in several different structured interaction tasks. The visit began by having each individual complete a short questionnaire designed to identify issues of concern that led to disagreements within the family (e.g., chores, recreation, money). The family members were then gathered around a table and given a set of cards to read and consider. They were asked to discuss among themselves each of the items listed on the cards and to continue talking until the interviewer returned. The items on the cards concerned family issues such as discipline and chores and the children's friends and school performance. The second task focused on family problem solving and was 15 minutes in length. The family was asked to discuss and try to resolve the issues and disagreements that they had cited in the questionnaires they had completed earlier in the visit.

The third task involved only the children and was 15 minutes in length. The youth were given a set of cards listing questions related to the way they got along, the manner in which their parents treated them, their friends, and their future plans. The IYFP families participated in a fourth task involving the married couple that lasted for 30 minutes. Spouses were asked to discuss issues related to aspects of their relationship, areas of agreement and disagreement (e.g., parenting, finances), and their plans for the future. This task was omitted for the single-parent families.

The family's interaction was videotaped. Interviewers explained each task and then left the room while the family members discussed the issues raised by the task cards. When family members were not involved in a videotaped interaction task, each family member completed an additional questionnaire asking about significant life events, attitudes toward sexuality, and personal characteristics. The second visit lasted approximately 2 hours.

The videotapes were coded by project observers using the Iowa Family Interaction Rating Scales (Melby et al., 1989). These scales focus on the quality of behavior exchanges between family members. The project observers were staff members who had received several weeks of training on rating family interactions and specialized in coding one of the four interaction tasks. Before observing tapes, coders had to rate precoded interaction tasks independently and achieve at least 90% agreement with that standard. For purposes of assessing interobserver reliability, 25% of the tasks were randomly selected to be independently observed and rated by a second observer.

Measures

The IYFP and ISPP used similar measures of constructs in addition to similar methods and procedures. Both studies emphasized a multiple measure, multiple informant approach to measurement in an effort to increase validity and reduce the problem of shared method variance (Bank, Dishion, Skinner, & Patterson, 1989; Patterson, 1986b). Family survey research usually uses reports from a single source as a measure for all study constructs. For instance, mothers are often asked to report on their level of stress, their parenting, and their child's problem behavior. Such an approach is problematic in that the mother's mood or other personal characteristics may color her perceptions of these various phenomena. When correlations are found, it may merely reflect a tendency to view items and events from a common frame of reference. Depressed persons, for example, tend to perceive themselves, their environment, and other people in negative, pessimistic terms (Abramson, Seligman, & Teasdale, 1978); spouses who are dissatisfied with their marital relationship are more inclined to see their partner's moment-by-moment behaviors and intentions as negative than either the partner or a trained observer is (Gottman, 1979). The implication of these findings is that when one family member reports his or her perceptions of another's behavior or attitudes (e.g., hostile acts or intentions), as well as his or her own personal characteristics (e.g., feelings about the quality of the relationship), the correlation between the two is likely to be upwardly biased. By incorporating more than one informant in the measurement process, one can attenuate the magnitude of this shared method bias (Bank et al., 1989).

Another advantage of using multiple informants is that no single perspective on family processes gives a comprehensive view of what actually occurs in the family. Olson (1977) suggests that one remedy for this problem is to ascertain reports both from insiders (family members) and outsiders (trained observers), a strategy used in both the IYFP and the ISSP. As noted, individual family members are often poor observers of their own and one another's behavior (Furman, Jones, Buhrmester, & Alder, 1989), yet they have the greatest opportunity to observe one another in myriad contexts. Trained observers, on the other hand, have only limited access to a family's time together but can assess family interactional patterns using a well-defined coding system and a broader view of normative behavior from having applied that system to numerous families.

Based on these considerations, we assume that the best strategy for obtaining a comprehensive view of a particular family process is to combine various sources of information whenever possible. Hence the following chapters often use multiple indicators to build measures of constructs. Several observational ratings, self-report scales, and child report indexes are used, for example, as indicators for the construct mother's inept parenting.

Following is a description of the measures we used for the various constructs included in the analyses reported in the following chapters. The measures are grouped according to the major elements of the theoretical model presented in Chapter 1.

STRESS AND PERSONAL
CHARACTERISTICS OF THE MOTHER

Antisocial Behavior Trait

Three mother report measures were used as indicators of antisocial behavior trait. The first instrument consisted of a list of 14 delinquent acts involving items such as shoplifting, skipping school, drinking alcohol, and fighting. Respondents were asked to indicate which of the acts they had engaged in prior to age 15 (0 = no, 1 = yes). Cronbach's alpha for this instrument was .68.

The second measure consisted of a deviant behavior checklist that asked respondents how often (0 = never, 4 = 4 or more times) during the past 12 months they had engaged in each of five deviant acts. The acts focused on fighting, traffic violations, lying, gambling, and having been arrested.

The third indicator consisted of 14 items concerned with substance use. The respondents were asked to report how often during the last 12 months (1 = never, 4 = often) they had engaged in the behavior or experienced the phenomena described in each question. The items involved incidents such as getting drunk, getting in trouble at work because of alcohol, and using illicit drugs. Most of the items concerned alcohol use. Cronbach's alpha for the scale was .86.

Attends PTA

Adolescents were asked to respond to the statement "My mom and/or dad often go to things like parent/teacher conferences, school events, PTA meetings, or other things at my school." The response format ranged from 1 (strongly disagree) to 5 (strongly agree).

Church Attendance

Mothers reported how often they attend church or religious services. Responses ranged from 1 (never) to 5 (more than once a week).

Depression

The construct depression was measured by 13 items from the depression symptomology subscale of the SCL-90-R (Derogatis, 1983). Respondents were asked how much, on a 5-point scale from not at all (1) to a little bit (2) to extremely (5), in the past week they were bothered by symptoms of depressed mood, such as crying easily, feelings of being trapped or caught, blaming themselves for things, feeling lonely, feeling blue, feeling worthless, and feeling hopeless about the future. Physical symptoms of depression included feeling low in energy or slowed down and feeling everything is an effort. The reliabilities were 0.92 for both single and married women.

Divorced

All the women in the IYFP sample were married to and living with their husbands at the time of data collection, whereas all those in the ISPP had obtained a legal divorce from their former spouse within the last 3 years. Women in the IYFP sample received a score of 0 on this variable, whereas those in the ISPP sample were given a score of 1.

Economic Pressure

Three indicators were used to measure economic pressure (Conger et al., 1992; Simons, Whitbeck, Beaman, & Conger, 1994). The first consisted of two items that assessed the degree to which the mothers felt they could not make ends meet. The items asked about difficulty paying bills each month (1 = no difficulty at all; 5 = a great deal of difficulty) and whether there was money leftover at the end of the month (1 = more than enough money left over; 4 = not enough to make ends meet). The two items correlated .62.

The mothers also responded to seven items that asked if they agreed or disagreed on a 5-point scale that their family had the money needed for a home, clothing, household items, a car, food, medical care, and recreational activities. The items were summed to form a material needs indicator of economic pressure. Cronbach's alpha was .89.

The final indicator, economic adjustments, focused on changes made in response to financial difficulties. The women noted (1 = yes, 0 = no) whether their family had used any of 17 possible strategies in an attempt to cope with financial difficulties during the past year. The strategies included behaviors such as cashing in life insurance, changing residence, eliminating medical insurance, borrowing money, and selling property. The alpha coefficient for this scale was .79.

Interest in Education

Two items were used as indicators for this construct. The target adolescent reported how often he or she and the mother "talk about what's going on at school" and "discuss what you want to do in the future." The response format for both items ranged from 1 (never) to 4 (often). Responses to the two items were summed to form a 2-item scale.

Negative Life Events

Respondents were asked to indicate which of 49 negative events they had experienced during the previous 12 months. The events included incidents such as being laid off or fired, changing residence, experiencing the death of a friend or an unwanted pregnancy, getting robbed, revocation of a driver's license, and having an automobile accident. Cronbach's alpha for the measure was .73.

Organizational Membership

Mothers listed their club and organizational memberships. An organizational score was obtained by counting the number of memberships listed.

Perceived Social Support

Three of the four dimensions of social support were measured using items from Cohen and Hoberman's (1983) Interpersonal Support Evaluation Checklist (ISEL). Based on a factor analysis of the pretest data from the IYFP, 12 items were selected from among 40 to reflect the dimensions of appraisal, belonging, and tangible support. All the items had a response framework from definitely true (1) to definitely false (5), with positively worded items reverse coded so that higher scores reflect higher levels of support. Each subscale was formed by summing the responses to the items.

Appraisal support represents the extent to which the respondents feel they have someone with whom they can talk about their problems. The four appraisal items asked respondents whether they had people other than immediate family members who "I trust to help solve my problems," "can give me an objective view of how I'm handling my problems," "I can turn to for advice about handling problems with my family," and "I could turn to for advice about making career plans or about changing my job." Using internal consistency as a measure of reliability, Cronbach's alpha was 0.83 for both married and single women.

The sense that a woman belonged to a group of friends was assessed by summing the responses to four items: "I feel like I'm always included by my circle of friends"; "If I wanted to go on a trip for a day, I would have a hard time finding someone to go with me other than my children"; "If I wanted to have lunch with a friend, I could easily find someone to join me"; and "No one I know would throw a birthday party for me." The four items had a reliability of 0.74 for married women and 0.70 for single women.

Tangible support reflects the extent to which the respondents felt they had someone who could help them out by providing specific resources. For example, one item was "If I need an emergency loan of $100, there is someone (friend, neighbor, other relative, or acquaintance) I could get it from." Other items asked about the extent to which the women had someone "who would put me up" if "I needed a place to stay for a week because of an emergency," who would "help me with my daily chores" in case of illness, who would "lend me their car for a few hours." Tangible support had reliability of 0.83 and 0.78 for married and single women, respectively.

Finally, two additional items, "My friends really care about me" and "My friends appreciate me," were added to the three ISEL dimensions to form a closeness subscale. A global measure of social support was created by summing the items from the various subscales. Cronbach's alpha for this measure was above .90 for both married and divorced women.

Predivorce Income

Husbands and wives in the intact families and mothers in the divorced families were asked to report their average monthly income. The divorced women were also asked to report how much this differed from the amount they had available prior to marital separation. Response categories for the question ranged from 1 (increased more than 20%) to 9 (decreased more than 50%). Answers to this item were used to adjust the divorced family's monthly income either up or down. This procedure provided a rough estimate of family income in divorced families prior to marital breakup.

Population Size

Each mother was asked to report the name of the community in which she currently lived. The population size for the community was then determined using data from the 1990 U.S. census.

Residential Moves

Mothers reported how many times their family had moved during the previous 12 months.

Sexual Permissiveness

This construct was assessed by a 3-item scale. Mothers were asked how wrong they thought it was for someone their adolescent child's age to (1) make out, (2) have sexual intercourse, and (3) have a child. Response categories ranged from 1 (very wrong) to 4 (not at all wrong). Cronbach's alpha for the measure was .53 for mothers in two-parent families and .60 for divorced mothers' reports.

Work Stress

The following procedure was used to form a work-related stress scale. First, mothers responded to the following two statements:

There is a lot of stress and tension in my job.
I have to work too many hours on this job.

The response format for the items ranged from 1 (strongly disagree) to 5 (strongly agree). The responses to these items were summed and standardized. Second, a series of questions was used to determine the total number of hours worked at various jobs during the preceding year. This number was also standardized and the two sets of standardized scores were then summed. The result was a score that gave equal weight to objective assessments of the number of hours worked and subjective perceptions of job-related stress.

FAMILY PROCESSES

Father's Inept Parenting

Quality of parenting by fathers was measured by a 14-item scale developed by Simons, Whitbeck, Beaman, et al. (1994). The items represented actions that parents might continue to perform even though they no longer live in the same residence as the child. The instrument asked adolescents to report how much they agree (1 = strongly disagree, 5 = strongly agree) that their father engaged in each of 14 parenting practices. To make the instrument consistent with the measures of mother's parenting, the items were coded so that high scores indicated inept parenting. Cronbach's alpha for the instrument was above .90 for both boys and girls. Following is a list of the items included in the scale:

1. How often does your dad talk with you about what is going on in your life?
2. When your dad tells you to stop doing something and you don't stop, how often does he punish you?
3. How often does your dad punish you for something at one time and then at other times not punish you for the same thing? (reverse coded)

4. When your dad is punishing you, how much does the kind of punishment depend on his mood? (reverse coded)

5. How often does your dad disagree with your mom about how or when to punish you? (reverse coded)

6. How often do the same problems seem to come up again and again with your dad and never seem to get resolved? (reverse coded)

7. When you and your dad have a problem, how often can the two of you figure out how to deal with it?

8. How often do you talk to your dad about things that bother you?

9. How often does your dad ask what you think before deciding on family matters that involve you?

10. How often does your dad give you reasons for his decisions?

11. How often does your dad ask you what you think before making a decision that involves you?

12. When you don't understand why your dad makes a rule for you to follow, how often does he explain the reason?

13. How often does your dad discipline you by reasoning, explaining, or talking to you?

14. When you do something your dad likes or approves of, how often does he let you know he is pleased about it?

It was important that our measure of father's parenting focus on actions that can be performed by fathers regardless of whether they share a residence with the child. A measure that failed to do this would be biased against nonresidential fathers and very highly correlated with family structure. The present scale avoids this problem. A father does not need to live with the child to perform the activities cited in the scale items, and fathers do not necessarily manifest these behaviors simply by virtue of sharing a residence with the child.

Hostility Between Siblings

Hostile adolescent behaviors were assessed by three different sources: target child report, sibling report, and observer report. The target child reported how often his or her sibling in the study behaved in an angry or hostile fashion during the previous month (1 = never behaved that way, 7 = always behaved that way). The 12 items included behaviors such as gets angry, fights and argues, shout or yells, and hits, pushes, or shoves. The sibling reported on the same items, which were summed to create an index of target child hostility. Internal consistency for the target child report and sibling report was .86 and .84, respectively.

In addition, each child reported on his or her own hostile behaviors toward the sibling in the study. Five items, a subset of those used in the report of the other's behavior, were used to report on one's own behavior. Internal consistency was .75 for target report of own behavior toward sibling and .74 for sibling report of own behavior toward target. Two composite indicators were created from these four indexes, one representing target hostile behavior toward sibling (target report of sibling behavior plus sibling report of own behavior, standardized, then summed, $r = .68$) and the other representing sibling behavior toward target ($r = .58$).

Hostile behaviors between the siblings during three different interaction tasks were rated by observers on three dimensions: hostility, antisocial behaviors, and angry coercive behaviors. Ratings for each child were summed across task 1 (family discussion), task 2 (problem solving), and task 3 (sibling discussion) to create a composite rating of hostile interactions (alpha = .84) between the two siblings in the study. Each task was rated by an independent observer.

Marital Happiness

An 8-item marital happiness scale was used to assess the extent to which the parents in the intact families were satisfied with their relationships. Both mothers and fathers answered the following four questions:

How well do you and your husband (wife) get along compared to most married couples? (1 = a lot worse, 5 = a lot better)

Overall how happy or satisfied are you with your marriage? (1 = extremely unhappy, 5 = extremely happy)

Which best describes your husband's (wife's) degree of happiness with your marital relationship? (1 = extremely unhappy, 5 = extremely happy)

All in all, how satisfied are you with your marriage? (1 = not at all satisfied, 5 = completely satisfied)

Husband and wife responses were summed to form a marital happiness score for each family. Cronbach's alpha for the instrument was .86.

Mother's Inept Parenting

Past research has established that competent parents are warm and supportive, monitor their child's behavior, are consistent in enforcing rules, and eschew harsh punishments (Maccoby, 1992; Maccoby & Martin, 1983). Our construct inept parenting focused on the obverse of these components of effective parenting. Thus our indicators of inept parenting assessed the extent to which the mother showed hostility, low monitoring, inconsistent discipline, and harsh punishments. Measures for these four dimensions of parental behavior were formed by aggregating mother self-reports, adolescent reports, and observer ratings of the videotaped family interaction tasks.

Family member reports about family processes are apt to be biased by the emotional state, attributional style, or personality of the respondent (Baucom, Sayers, & Duhe, 1989; Lorenz, Conger, Simons, Whitbeck, & Elder, 1991). Simply substituting observational ratings for family member reports is not a wholly satisfying solution. Olson (1977) suggests that one remedy is to use reports from both insiders (the parent and child) and outsiders (trained observers) in constructing measures, the strategy used in constructing the measure of inept discipline the present study. Family members are often poor observers of one another's behavior (Furman et al., 1989), and yet they have the greatest opportunity to observe one another in myriad contexts. Trained observers, on the other hand, have only limited access to a family's time together but can assess family interactional patterns using a well-defined coding system and a broader view of normative behavior from having applied that system to numerous families. Pooling the two types of information should enable a more valid assessment of parental behavior than by using either of the two sources of data alone.

Cronbach's alpha for the several child and mother report scales were generally above .80. On average, the correlation between child and mother reports, or between either child or mother report and the observational ratings, was .25 to .35., and the intraclass correlations used to measure intercoder reliability averaged .60. These levels are within the range of acceptable values and suggest the presence of basic agreement between coders (Bakeman & Adamson, 1984; Hartmann, 1977) and between family member reports (Schwarz, Barton-Henry, & Pruzinsky, 1985). Although the measures are briefly described below, a more detailed description of the instruments and the factor analytic procedures used to generate them is presented in McGruder, Lorenz, Hoyt, Ge, and Montague (1992).

Mothers used a 4-item scale to report on the extent to which they used harsh disciplinary practices (e.g., "When punishing your 9th grader, how often do you hit him/her with a belt, paddle, or something else?"). Response format for this instrument ranged from 1 (never) to 5 (always). Adolescents used the same four items to report on their mothers' harsh discipline. Observational coders rated the harsh discipline of mothers toward their children based on family interaction and content of discussion in task 1 of the videotaped interaction. The mother reports, child reports, and observational ratings were standardized and summed to form a measure of harsh discipline.

Mothers reported on their monitoring using a 4-item scale (e.g., "How often do you know who your 9th grader is with when he/she is away from home?"). The response format ranged from 1 (never) to 5 (always). The adolescents reported on their mothers using the same items. The observational rating of monitoring was based on the interaction and content of the discussion in task 1. The mother reports, child reports, and observational ratings were reverse coded, standardized, and then summed to form a measure of low monitoring.

Mothers were asked to rate their consistency of discipline using a 4-item scale (e.g., "How often do you punish your 9th grader for something at one time and then at other times not punish him/her for the same thing?"). The response format ranged from 1 (never) to 5 (always). Adolescents rated their mothers' consistency using the same items. The observational ratings of inconsistent discipline were based on family interaction and content of discussion in videotaped task 1. The mother reports, child reports, and observational ratings were standardized and summed to form a measure of inconsistent discipline.

Finally, mothers reported on their hostility toward their child using a 5-item scale. Each mother was asked to think about times during the past month when she had spent time talking with her adolescent and to report how often (1 = never, 7 = always) she had gotten angry, argued, criticized, shouted or yelled, or pushed or shoved the child. Adolescents rated their mothers' hostility using a longer 12-item version of this scale. In addition to the items completed by the mothers, the adolescent scale contained items concerned with being threatened, blamed, nagged, sworn at, made to feel guilty, or ignored by the mother. The observational ratings of mothers' hostility toward the adolescent were based on family interaction in videotaped tasks 1 and 2. The mother reports, child reports, and observational ratings were standardized and summed to form a measure of mothers' hostility.

Warmth and Support Between Siblings

This concept was included to investigate possible buffering effects that a warm, supportive sibling relationship might provide for a young adolescent (i.e., the compensatory model). As with the sibling hostility construct, this construct was estimated using three different sources of information: 9th grade target child report, sibling report, and observer report of sibling interactions. The first measure consisted of 9 items reported by the target child about his or her sibling's behavior during the previous month (1 = never, 7 = always behaved that way). Items included behaviors such as listens carefully to your point of view, acts loving and affectionate, and lets you know he or she appreciates you and your ideas (alpha = .90). These same items were answered by the sibling about the target child's behaviors (alpha = .88). As with the hostility construct, each child reported on his or her own behavior toward the other child. These scales were standardized and summed to create an indicator of target child warm and supportive behaviors toward the sibling (self-report and sibling report, $r = .68$). The second indicator represented target report and self-report of the sibling behaviors toward the target child ($r = .62$). Consistent with the hostile behaviors construct, the third indicator of warmth and support between the two siblings was based on observer ratings of four behavioral dimensions such as warmth, prosocial exchanges, and listener responsiveness. Ratings for each child were summed across all three tasks to create a composite rating of warmth and support between the two siblings in the study (alpha = .79).

CHILD OUTCOMES

Academic Performance

This construct was measured with information provided by the mother and the target. Both reported (1) the target's closest current grade point average, (2) whether or not "he or she got a D, an F, or an Unsatisfactory in any class on the last grade report," and (3) how well the target "keeps up with classes." In addition, mothers were asked to rate the target child's performance in school on a range from far below average to superior.

Affiliation With Deviant Peers

Adolescents reported about the deviant behavior of their friends using a 6-item scale. The scale asked them to indicate how much they thought various statements described their "closest friends." The statements involved acts such as breaking the law, fighting with parents, being arrested by the police, and getting bad grades. The response format for each item ranged from 1 (strongly disagree) to 5 (strongly agree). Cronbach's alpha was above .80 for both boys and girls.

Delinquent Behavior

A delinquency inventory adapted from the National Youth Survey (Elliott, Huizinga, & Ageton, 1985; Elliott, Huizinga, & Menard, 1989) was used to assess adolescent antisocial behavior. Respondents were asked to indicate how often (0 = never, 5 = 5 or more times) during the preceding year they had engaged in each of 28 delinquent activities. The acts varied from relatively minor offenses such as using alcohol to more serious offenses such as attacking someone with a weapon or stealing something worth more than $25.

We had several reasons for using self-reports rather than parent reports to measure delinquency. First, much delinquent behavior is clandestine and does not come to the attention of parents. Second, the meta-analysis reported by Amato and Keith (1991b) indicates that the association between family structure and child conduct problems is stronger when child self-reports or observer ratings are used to assess the child's behavior than when mother reports are used. Finally, several studies have shown that a mother's emotional state influences the extent to which she perceives her child as difficult and antisocial (Brody & Forehand, 1988). Together, these findings suggest that mothers may be unreliable reporters of their children's conduct problems.

Depression

Because the properties of depressed mood are quite similar for adults and adolescents (Compas, Ey, & Grant, 1993), the scale used to measure adolescent depressed mood included the same set of items that were used to assess parent depression, except that the item concerning loss of interest in sex was omitted for the youth in the study. The resulting 12-item measure of depression has been shown to have good psychometric properties when used with older children and adolescents (Ge, Lorenz, Conger, Elder, & Simons, 1994).

Early Sexual Intercourse

Adolescents were asked whether they had experienced sexual intercourse during the past year. Individuals who had had sex prior to the past year were excluded from the analysis. Thus our measure assessed whether the subject had become sexually active during the year prior to data collection.

Mastery

Adolescents' perceptions of mastery were assessed by the 10-item Mastery Scale developed by Pearlin, Lieberman, Menaghan, and Mullan (1981). Cronbach's alpha was approximately .75 for adolescents in both single- and two-parent families.

Analysis

The following chapters involve partitioning and testing elements of the general model presented in Chapter 1 (see Figure 1.1). In most cases, a chapter starts by documenting a bivariate relationship between family structure and some variable. Then, based on ideas presented in our general model, various constructs are introduced as potential mediators of this association. To the extent that a factor mediates the relationship between family structure and some variable, it is seen as "explaining" the association between the two constructs. Variables treated as outcomes in a particular chapter are often employed as explanatory factors in subsequent chapters. Thus the chapters build on each other and provide an interrelated set of arguments concerning the processes that account for differences between single- and two-parent families.

Most of the chapters test a hypothesized model using latent-variable structural equation modeling (SEM). This analytic procedure has a number of advantages over an ordinary-least-square approach to path analysis (see Bollen, 1989). First, multiple measures of constructs are treated as separate indicators (whereas regression procedures require that multiple measures be combined into a single composite scale). Indeed, SEM begins with confirmatory factor analysis to establish that the assumed measurement model fits the data for the sample. Second, it corrects the paths between constructs for attenuation due to measurement error. Third, it allows for correlated residuals. Finally, the model comparison option enables one to examine the extent to which relationships between variables differ for two or more groups. This procedure allows one to test for moderator effects and to explore differences between single- and two-parent families in associations between constructs.

Although the following chapters present results consistent with various hypothesized causal sequences, it is important to remember that the logic of multivariate analysis is being applied to cross-sectional data. Therefore, although causal assumptions are made in the path analytic procedures used to perform the analyses, the reader is reminded that the relationships found represent covariations between variables. Although cross-sectional data can verify that a relationship exists between two constructs, it cannot establish the causal priority that exists between them. This caveat should be kept in mind as the various findings are discussed.

PART II

MATERNAL STRESS
AND
PSYCHOLOGICAL WELL-BEING

3

Family Structure Differences in Stress and Behavioral Predispositions

RONALD L. SIMONS

CHRISTINE JOHNSON

FREDERICK O. LORENZ

The model presented in Chapter 1 posits that differences between intact and divorced families in terms of stress and personal characteristics produce discrepancies in child outcomes by reducing parental adjustment and disrupting parenting practices. This book represents an attempt to provide a systematic test of the various elements of this contention. This chapter examines the effect of divorce on a mother's level of stress and access to social support. We begin by reviewing past research on the relationship between family structure, social support, and three types of stress: economic pressure, negative life events, and work-related tensions. This is followed by a brief consideration of selection factors (e.g., antisocial tendencies) and potential confounds (e.g., pre-divorce income) that might account for these relationships. We develop a set of hypotheses based on this discussion and use structural equation modeling to test these predictions.

Economic Hardship

Beyond differences in number of parents, perhaps the most striking dissimilarity between single- and two-parent families is level of income and economic disadvantage. Most single-parent families are the result of marital disruption (Gongla & Thompson, 1987). A dramatic drop in income is a predictable consequence of marital disruption given the loss of the absent spouse's (father's) earnings. On average, families experience a 30% to 50% reduction in income following divorce (Arendell, 1986; Cherlin, 1992). Such a drop in income meets the definition of economic hardship used by Elder (1974; Elder, Van Nguyen, & Caspi, 1985) in his classic studies of the effect of the Great Depression on family processes and child development.

Hoffman and Duncan (1985, 1988), using data from the Panel Study of Income Dynamics (PSID), found that middle-class women suffer the largest declines in income. Many of them had worked as homemakers prior to divorce and had to depend on meager child support payments and whatever low-paying jobs they could find following marital breakup. Almost one third of the women who had above-average incomes prior to divorce experienced a decline of more than half in their standard of living during the year following separation.

Family structure differences in income are particularly pronounced when one considers the proportion of families living below the poverty threshold set by the U.S. Census Bureau. In 1992, this threshold was $14,812 for a family of four and $11,973 for a single mother and two children (U.S. Bureau of Census, 1993). Using the PSID data set, McLanahan and Sandefur (1994) found that 26.5% of single-parent families are poor; only 5.3% of two-parent families are poor. Thus the risk of being poor is several times higher for single- compared to two-parent households.

To better examine the consequences of limited financial resources following divorce, we focus on family structure differences in economic pressure rather than in family income. Families suffer economic pressure to the extent that they (a) cannot meet material needs, (b) often fall behind in paying debts, and (c) have had to cut back on everyday expenses in an attempt to live within available means (Conger et al., 1994). Economic pressure should not be thought of as a subjective perception of family finances that is less "real" or "objective" than the construct family income. Economic pressures such as cutting back on expenditures and having difficulty paying bills are real, everyday experiences, not simply subjective impressions of reality.

Economic pressure is determined by a family's level of income relative to its financial needs and obligations. Such a variable better captures the financial strain experienced by divorced women than the variable family income. As noted, disrupted marriages usually produce a single-parent family with a significantly reduced income. This decreased income results in economic pressure. Although income may decrease by 30% to 50%, costs such as taxes, insurance, medical bills, house payments, automobile maintenance, and the like often remain the same. Predivorce obligations and commitments dictate, at least in part, the financial demands that a divorced mother faces following divorce.

Furthermore, past studies indicate that it is economic pressure, rather than low income per se, that has a disruptive influence on individuals and families (Conger et al., 1990; Conger et al., 1994; Elder, 1974; Kessler, Turner, & House, 1988). Low income is stressful to the extent that it creates demands for painful behavioral adjustments, such as cutting back on expenditures. When income is low, parents with high financial demands (e.g., medical costs, automobile repairs) need to make more difficult economic adjustments than those without such demands. Thus, although people with a lower income in general experience greater economic pressure than those with a higher income, the psychological effect of level of income varies depending on financial obligations and requirements. The economic pressure construct takes these financial demands into account in a manner that the variable family income does not. For these reasons, we view economic pressure as a better indicator of the economic difficulties faced by single-parent families than level of income.

In our Iowa sample, family structure correlates .31 with family income and .38 with economic pressure; there is a .32 correlation between family income and economic pressure. For the sake of parsimony, family income is not included in the structural equation models presented in this and the following chapters. It should be noted, however, that this variable was not related to any of the parent or child measures once economic pressure was taken into account. In every case, the effect of family income was indirect through economic pressure.

Negative Life Events

Life changes are often stressful. Hundreds of studies conducted in a variety of countries have reported a relationship between events involving changes in one's everyday life and psychological distress (Mirowsky & Ross, 1989). During the 1960s and early 1970s, researchers believed that all major changes, whether positive or negative, were distressing because they disrupted personal habits and required mental and physical energy to adapt. Research since then has established unequivocally that undesirable events—not desirable ones—cause distress.

Dohrenwend, Krasnoff, Askenasy, and Dohrenwend (1978) observe that certain events tend to produce a wave of life changes. Chiriboga, Catron, and Associates (1991) and Kitson (1992) argue that this is the case for marital disruption. They note that economic pressure, as well as the new living situation faced by the single parent and her children, increases the probability of ensuing stressful life events, for example, change in residence or mother begins to work outside of the home. Thus marital disruption is a role transition that usually triggers a number of associated life changes. Although divorce is usually thought of as an event, it is probably more appropriate to view it as the catalyst for a series of negative life changes. This suggests that divorced persons are more likely to report having recently experienced negative life changes than married persons. Consonant with this hypothesis, Kitson (1992) found that 4 years following divorce, single parents continue to report more negative life changes than married persons.

Work-Related Stress

Single parents are more likely than married persons to experience economic pressure and negative life events. Although these two stressors are viewed as explaining differences in adjustment between divorced and married women, we believe that work-related stress may also contribute to the higher levels of distress suffered by divorced mothers. There are several reasons for expecting that working single mothers experience more job-related stress than working married mothers: Divorced mothers are likely to work more hours because they desperately need the income; they are apt to take on more than one job in an effort to meet financial obligations; they often balance the demands of a job with the pressures of pursuing additional education; they are under pressure to be a successful employee to obtain promotions, raises, and additional hours; and they are apt to experience great conflict between the requirements of work and family responsibilities. As a consequence, divorced women might be expected to report higher levels of tension and frustration relating to work than married women.

Although we anticipated a relationship between family structure and work-related stress, we expected the association to be modest. Married women are also likely to experience many of the job-related stressors identified (e.g., conflict between work and family responsibilities). Thus, work-related stress was not expected to show the strong associations with family structure that are posited for economic pressure and negative life events. The latter two stressors are viewed as the fundamental determinants of family structure differences in distress. Work-related stress, however, is seen as making a significant, albeit secondary, contribution to divorced women's higher levels of distress.

Antisocial Behavior Trait

Divorced parents are more likely to experience economic pressure, negative life events, and job-related stress than married persons. Our discussion up to this point has assumed that these family structure differences are a consequence of marital disruption and the shift to single-parent status. It may be, however, that the high levels of stress experienced by divorced parents are at least partially explained by contrasts in personal characteristics. As noted in Chapter 1, this view is often labeled *the selection perspective* on family structure differences.

The selection perspective asserts that some people possess characteristics or traits that place them at risk for marital discord and divorce, as well as for other difficulties in functioning (Bachrach, 1975; Halem, 1980, Kitson & Morgan, 1990). In addition to increasing the probability of marital breakup, these vulnerabilities may impede adjustment following divorce (Kitson, 1992). Whereas we have emphasized the way marital disruption and single-parent status increase exposure to stress, the selection argument suggests that problematic personal characteristics may account for the link between marital status and the experience of stressors such as economic pressure, negative events, and work stress.

To test the selection perspective, one must first identify personal attributes that might be expected to increase an individual's risk for marital disruption and stressors such as economic difficulties and negative events. Presumably these characteristics would involve psychopathology or abnormalities in psychological and interpersonal functioning. Depression is often mentioned in discussions of the selection perspective. However, although a predivorce history of depression is apt to affect a person's adjustment following marital breakup (Kitson, 1992), there is little reason to believe that depression is a major contributor to divorce. Consistent with this idea, Menaghan (1985) found that persons who subsequently divorce are not more psychologically distressed than other married individuals prior to marital disruption. Furthermore, just as there is little reason to assume that depression leads to divorce, it seems unlikely that depression is a major cause of financial hardship and negative life events. Hence, we consider it unlikely that depression operates as a significant selection factor.

Rather, based on prior research, we believe that antisocial behavior trait is the personal characteristic that shows the most promise as an explanation for family structure differences in stress. A trait consists of a pattern of behavior that is exhibited across time and settings (Allport, 1937; Patterson, Reid, & Dishion, 1992). Antisocial behavior involves actions deemed risky, inappropriate, shortsighted, or insensitive by the majority of people in society. Antisocial actions suggest a behavior trait to the extent that they are persistent and represent a wide range of deviant behaviors. Thus, individuals display an antisocial trait to the extent that they engaged in delinquent behavior during late childhood and early adolescence and continue as adults to participate in deviant actions such as interpersonal violence, substance abuse, sexual promiscuity, traffic violations, and the like (Simons, Johnson, Beaman, & Conger, 1993).

Our use of the term *antisocial trait* should not be confused with the psychiatric diagnosis of *antisocial personality*. This psychiatric label treats deviant actions as dichotomous and requires that the behaviors meet strict diagnostic criteria to be classified as indicating an antisocial personality (American Psychiatric Association, 1987). In contrast, we use the term *antisocial trait* to denote a continuous variable. People differ regarding the extent to which they manifest this trait; only a small percentage of the persons who engage persistently in antisocial behavior would qualify for a diagnosis of antisocial personality.

There is evidence that persons with antisocial tendencies are at risk for divorce. Lahey et al. (1988) report a higher incidence of antisocial trait among single mothers in their clinical sample than among mothers from intact families. Capaldi and Patterson (1991) found that women high on the antisocial trait had more marital transitions than those low on this pattern of behavior. Findings from a recent study by Kitson (1992) indicate that divorced persons are more likely than married ones to have had trouble with relatives, to have lost their driver's license, to have appeared in court for a matter unrelated to divorce, to have been detained in jail, and to have been the subject of a lawsuit.

Furthermore, antisocial persons are apt to be irresponsible about work commitments, financial obligations, and interpersonal agreements. As a consequence, they might be expected to experience more negative events (e.g., loss of job, foreclosure on loans, change in residence) and greater financial hardship than their more conventional counterparts. Consistent with this view, Simons, Beaman, et al. (1993) found a relationship between adult antisocial behavior and financial problems. Both Simons, Beaman, et al. (1993) and Patterson and Capaldi (1991) report an association between parental antisocial behavior and the experience of negative life events; Caspi, Elder, and Bem (1987) found that men who were ill-tempered as children manifest erratic work histories as adults and achieve less occupational success than their fathers.

These findings suggest that antisocial individuals are at risk for both divorce and life stress. To the extent that this is the case, part of the association between family structure and stress may be a function of this personal characteristic. The argument that the personal characteristic antisocial behavior trait explains part of the relationship between family structure and stress should not be interpreted as suggesting that most divorced persons engage in antisocial behavior.

The proportion antisocial is likely to be small for both divorced and married persons. Such individuals are likely to be overrepresented among the divorced, however, and this segment of the divorced population, rather than divorced persons in general, may largely account for the high rates of stress compared to married individuals.

Access to Social Support

Social support consists of help or assistance received from others that promotes emotional well-being and facilitates the performance of social roles. This assistance may take the form of instrumental aid, information, or emotional sustenance (Cohen & Wills, 1985; House, 1981). It is often asserted that marital breakup undermines people's relationships with others, thereby diminishing the amount of social support that is available to them (Rands, 1988; Raschke, 1987). This reduced access to supportive social relationships is seen as an important determinant of the emotional distress and disrupted parenting manifested by divorced persons (Gongla & Thompson, 1987).

We are skeptical of the argument that family structure differences in access to social support are a significant determinant of the adjustment of divorced persons. This is not because we question the contribution of social support to people's emotional and social well-being. There is much evidence to suggest that supportive relationships reduce distress and facilitate coping (House, Umberson, & Landis, 1988). We expect that perceived social support is strongly related to adjustment for both married and divorced women. A detailed examination of the relationship between social support and emotional and physical well-being is provided in Chapter 4.

We doubt that social support can explain family structure differences in parental adjustment because we suspect that there is little or no association between marital status and the availability of social support. Of course, by definition, divorced persons lack access to one important source of social support: a marital partner. There is little reason to presume, however, that divorced women have less access than married women to supportive relationships with friends and family. Although relationships with some relatives (e.g., in-laws) may become strained during the divorce process, in general the evidence suggests that single parents tend to maintain or strengthen social ties with blood relatives following marital breakup (Gongla & Thompson, 1987).

Some studies report a decline in the size of friendship networks following divorce (Gongla & Thompson, 1987; Rands, 1988). In large part, this is a matter of dropping relationships in which social ties were between couples rather than individuals or reducing interaction with persons identified as more the former spouse's friend. Although such changes decrease the size of the divorced person's friendship network, it is not clear that this diminution involves a reduction in social support. Although the lost friendships may once have served as a source of recreational enjoyment, it is unlikely that they involved the emotional depth characteristic of socially supportive relationships. Most people probably perceive only a few of the people in their social network as viable sources of instrumental assistance or emotional support. We expect that divorced and married persons have approximately equal access to such individuals. Kitson (1992) reports that divorced persons actually spend more time visiting friends than married persons.

Predivorce Income as a Potential Confound

Studies have shown that low-income couples are more likely to divorce than economically advantaged couples (Cherlin, 1992; McLanahan & Sandefur, 1994). Thus, low income is both a precursor and a consequence of marital disruption. Furthermore, past research indicates that poor persons experience higher levels of negative life events and are more apt to engage in antisocial behavior than persons of middle and upper income (Mirowsky & Ross, 1989; Sampson & Lauritsen, 1994). Given this pattern of findings, there is the possibility that associations found between family structure and antisocial behavior, on the one hand, and economic strain and negative life events, on the other, are spurious due to correlations of these variables with family income. It is imperative that an investigation of the effect of family structure and antisocial behavior trait on level of stress take into account predivorce family income. We do this in the subsequent analyses.

Hypotheses to Be Tested

The various research findings and arguments that have been discussed suggest two sets of hypotheses. The first set involves the bivariate associations anticipated between constructs. We expect that women who are divorced report more involvement in antisocial behavior than those who are married and that both being divorced and a history of antisocial behavior are related to an increased probability of economic pressure, negative events, and work stress. We do not expect a relationship between family structure and perceived access to social support.

A second set of hypotheses relates to the multivariate relationships expected between the constructs. Controlling for predivorce income, we expect that both family structure and antisocial behavior trait will be significantly related to the three types of stress. Such a finding would indicate that the high levels of economic hardship, negative events, and work stress experienced by divorced women are not merely a function of predivorce income but are a consequence of circumstances associated with being a single parent and of personal characteristics overrepresented among divorced persons. In other words, we expect to find support for both the stress and selection perspectives.

Results

The measures for the various constructs used in our analyses are described in Chapter 2. Table 3.1 presents the means and standard deviations for the various indicators of stress and antisocial trait, by marital status. The results are largely as expected. First, divorced women were significantly more likely than their married counterparts to report work-related stress. The standardized scores on the work stress measure for divorced women averaged 0.59, compared with −0.09 for married women. Second, the divorced women had higher mean scores than the married on the three indicators of economic pressure. The means were 23.2 versus 18.4 for financial strain, .79 versus −.48 for felt constraints, and 7.30 versus 4.76 for number of adjustments they had to make. Frequency distributions were com-

TABLE 3.1 Means (with standard deviations) for the Stress, Antisocial, and
Social Support Scales

	Married	*Divorced*
Work Stress	−0.09	0.59*
	(1.46)	(1.52)
Economic Pressure		
Financial strain	18.4	23.2*
	(5.58)	(5.89)
Felt constraints	−0.48	0.79*
	(2.48)	(2.42)
Adjustments	4.76	7.30*
	(3.77)	(3.43)
Negative Events	3.48	5.72*
	(2.86)	(3.72)
Antisocial Trait		
Substance use	11.6	12.3*
	(1.90)	(2.25)
Delinquent as a child	0.40	0.68*
	(0.90)	(1.29)
Deviant behavior last year	0.81	1.16*
	(1.36)	(1.72)
Social Support		
Appraisal	13.3	14.3*
	(2.50)	(1.89)
Belonging	13.3	13.6
	(2.18)	(1.93)
Closeness	6.78	7.11*
	(0.98)	(0.98)
Tangible	14.1	14.5
	(2.11)	(1.79)

*Difference significant at .05 level.

puted for the items in the three economic pressure scales. In general,
divorced mothers were more than twice as likely to concur with these
items as those who were married. A majority of the divorced women
responded affirmatively to most of the items in the economic pressure
scales.

Table 3.2 reports the percentages for items from the adjustments
and strain scales. The table shows, for example, that 71% of the
divorced mothers reported changing food shopping and eating habits
to save money, whereas this was true for 46% of the married women.
Sixty-nine percent of the divorced women but only 37% of the

TABLE 3.2 Family Structure Differences in Response to Economic Adjustment and Strain Items

	Married	*Divorced*
Adjustment Items		
Used savings for daily living expenses	46%	64%
Changed food shopping and eating habits	45	71
Borrowed money to help pay bills	25	41
Reduced household utility use	34	65
Reduced driving car to save money	25	45
Fell behind in paying bills	33	48
Postponed major household purchases	48	70
Cut back on social activities and entertainment	53	79
Postponed vacation plans	30	53
Reduced charitable contributions	30	56
Economic Strain Items		
Difficulty paying bills	37	69
Not enough money for food	7	25
Not enough money for clothing	18	55
Not enough money for car	24	57
Not enough money for furniture	25	57
Not enough money for medical care	15	37

NOTE: All differences significant at .05 level.

married women indicated that they had difficulty paying their bills. Similar differences are evident for the other items.

Table 3.1 shows that the divorced women also reported significantly more negative life events during the past 12 months than their married counterparts. The average score was 5.72 for the divorced and 3.48 for the married. Item analysis showed that, regardless of family structure, only a small number of individuals encountered any particular event. For many events, however, the proportion of the divorced who experienced the incident was several times higher than that of the married. Table 3.3 shows the differences for a few of the items on the life event scale. It shows, for example, that 30% of the divorced women changed residences within the last year, whereas this was the case for only 6% of the married women. Compared with married women, the divorced were more likely to have a close friend move away (20% vs. 9%), to break relations with a close friend (28% vs. 13%), and to have a close friend with marital or family problems (54% vs. 31%). Ten percent of the divorced women had a new person

TABLE 3.3 Family Structure Differences for Selected Life Events

	Married	Divorced
Have close friend move away	9%	20%
Have close friend with marital or family problem	31	54
Break relations with a close friend	13	28
Have a new person move into household	5	10
Get involved in lawsuit or court case	6	24
Have an unwanted pregnancy	0	2
Have stillbirth or miscarriage	0	3
Child got involved with alcohol	8	15
Physically attacked or sexually assaulted	1	8
Have auto accident with injury to someone	1	5
Robbed	0	4
Move to a different home	6	30
Suffered injury or property damage	2	7
Have to leave home because of hazard	1	5

NOTE: All differences significant at .05 level.

move into the household, whereas this was true for only 5% of the married women. Eight percent of the divorced women but less than 1% of the married women indicated that they had been beaten up, physically attacked, or sexually assaulted. Four percent of the divorced women had been robbed in the preceding year and 5% had suffered an automobile accident. The corresponding figures for the married women were 0% and 1%. Thus, the divorced women were several times more likely than those who were married to have experienced many of the stressful events on our checklist.

Table 3.1 shows that the divorced women scored significantly higher on the three measures of antisocial trait than the married women. Mean scores for both groups were low compared with the possible range, but the scores for divorced women were higher than those for their married counterparts in substance use, deviant behavior in the past 12 months, and delinquent behavior before the age of 14.

Frequencies were run separately for divorced and married women for each item in the measure of antisocial behavior. Although only a minority of individuals in either group showed involvement in antisocial behavior, the divorced women were two to three times more likely than the married to have engaged in such activities. These analyses show, for example, that 14% of the divorced women and 7% of the married women stated that they shoplifted on two or more occasions prior to age 14. Five percent of the divorced women indicated that their use of alcohol sometimes interfered with chores or work, whereas only 1% of the married women reported that this was the case. The percentages were 19% versus 9% for having received a traffic ticket during the past year, 14% versus 4% for having gotten into a fight that came to hitting during the past year, and 3% versus 0% for having been arrested in the past year.

Table 3.1 indicates that only with respect to perceptions of support do divorced and married women appear similar. The means for belonging and tangible support are not significantly different; the divorced women's reports of appraisal support (14.3) and closeness to another (7.11) were actually significantly higher than those for the married women (13.3 and 6.78, respectively).

Analysis showed good convergent and discriminate validity for the various indicators of latent constructs. Table 3.4 presents the bivariate associations between constructs obtained using LISREL VII. Chapter 2 notes that there was no correlation between family structure and level of education in our sample. Table 3.4 shows that this is the case for predivorce income as well. The coefficient is −.062 and does not approach significance. Thus, in the present study, family structure is unrelated to predivorce socioeconomic status. Prior to marital breakup, the married and divorced women in our sample did not differ in terms of either education or family income. Unfortunately, this was not the case for size of city of residence. Table 3.4 reports a correlation of .441 between divorce and population size. Thus, the divorced women in our sample tended to reside in larger communities than the married.

As anticipated, divorced status is correlated with antisocial trait (.249) and both divorced and antisocial trait show significant associations with the stressors of economic pressure (.380 and .377, respectively) and negative events (.327 and .403, respectively). There is a modest but significant relationship of .157 between divorced status and work stress. There is also a significant correlation between divorced status and social support (.160). The direction of this coefficient indicates that the divorced women in our sample reported greater perceived access to social support than those who were married.

Having established that the divorced women in our sample reported more economic pressure, negative events, work stress, and social

TABLE 3.4 Bivariate Correlations Between Constructs

	1	2	3	4	5	6	7	8
1. Divorced	—							
2. Antisocial trait	.249*	—						
3. Economic pressure	.380*	.377*	—					
4. Negative events	.327*	.403*	.518*	—				
5. Work stress	.157*	.060	.105	.002	—			
6. Social support	.160*	−.064	−.119	−.037	−.028	—		
7. Predivorce income	−.062	−.042	−.209*	−.057	.053	−.002	—	
8. Population size	.441*	.167*	.205*	.160*	.079	.054	.041	—

*$p \le .05$

support than those who were married, we turned to an investigation of the extent to which differences in personal or socioeconomic characteristics account for these findings. Structural equation modeling (SEM) was used to perform this analysis. The endogenous variables for the SEM consisted of economic pressure, work stress, negative events, and social support. Four exogenous constructs were included in the model. They were divorced, antisocial trait, and two control variables: population size and predivorce income. Education was not included as a control because prior analysis had shown that it was not related to family structure or the other exogenous or endogenous variables in our model.

We began the SEM analysis by running the fully recursive model. This resulted in many paths that were near zero and had very low t values. In an effort to obtain a more parsimonious model, paths with a t of 1.0 or below were deleted and the model was reestimated. This model trimming had no appreciable effect on the magnitude or the significance level of any of the remaining paths. The difference in χ^2 between the reduced and the fully recursive model did not even approach statistical significance. The reduced model is depicted in Figure 3.1. Both the Goodness of Fit Index and the ratio of χ^2 to the number of degrees of freedom suggest that the model provides a reasonable fit to the data.

Figure 3.1 shows that antisocial trait has an effect on economic pressure, but that divorced status also continues to exert an influence. Indeed, the coefficients for the two constructs are of almost identical magnitude (.30 and .29, respectively). Similarly, both antisocial trait

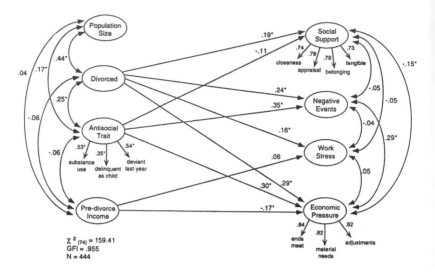

Figure 3.1. A Test of Various Explanations for the Link Between Family Structure and Stress

and divorced status show significant associations with negative events. The path coefficients are .35 and .24, respectively. There are modest but significant paths from divorce to both work stress and social support, whereas antisocial trait is not significantly related to either of these constructs. The sign of the coefficient from divorce to social support is positive, indicating a slight tendency for divorced women to perceive greater access to social support than those who are married.

Predivorce income shows a significant association with economic pressure; it is not related to divorced status. Conversely, population size is significantly related to divorced status but fails to show a significant association with any of the stress constructs. Thus, in the present sample, the relationship between family structure and stress is not a spurious correlation due to socioeconomic or geographic differences between the divorced and married families. Controlling for the latter two variables has no effect on the association between divorced status and the stress constructs.

Thus, the results provide support for both the stress and selection perspectives on divorce. Consonant with the selection perspective, the high rate of economic pressure and stressful events suffered by divorced compared to married women is partly explained by the fact that persons with antisocial tendencies are overrepresented among the divorced. Financial difficulties and negative events continue to be more prevalent among the divorced, however, after taking into account differences in personal characteristics. This finding provides support for the stress perspective.

To estimate the relative importance of the two perspectives, we calculated the proportion of the association between divorced status and economic pressure and negative events that is indirect through antisocial trait. The indirect effect on economic pressure was .075. The indirect effect on negative events was .087. Therefore, antisocial trait accounts for a little under 20% of the relationship between divorced and economic pressure (.075 is 19.7% of .380) and approximately 27% of the association between divorced and negative events (.087 is 26.6% of .327). This indicates that the stress perspective explains 75% to 80% of the relationship between family structure and stressful outcomes.

Discussion

Several studies (see Kitson & Morgan, 1990) report that divorced persons are more likely to experience economic problems and negative life events than those who are married. This finding is usually construed as an indication that financial difficulties and stressful life changes are part of the sequelae of divorce, especially for women. Although this interpretation is widely accepted, other plausible explanations need to be considered.

First, the relationship between divorce and diverse types of stress may be a spurious finding resulting from socioeconomic confounds. There is evidence that persons of low social status are more likely to divorce (White, 1990) and are more apt to experience economic strain and stressful events (Mirowsky & Ross, 1989). Hence, it is imperative that predivorce socioeconomic status be taken into account when investigating the link between divorce and various stressors. Many past studies have failed to incorporate such controls. In the present study, the divorced and the married did not differ with regard to education or family income prior to divorce. This may be because there was little socioeconomic variability in the study sample. Most of the respondents were working-class women living in small, rural communities. Regardless of the cause, these predivorce similarities preclude socioeconomic confounds as an explanation for our finding that financial problems and negative events are more prevalent among divorced than married women.

The selection perspective provides another explanation for the correlation between family structure and life stress. As noted earlier in the chapter, this perspective asserts that some people possess characteristics or traits that place them at risk for marital discord and divorce, as well as for other difficulties in functioning (Bachrach, 1975; Halem, 1980; Kitson & Morgan, 1990). Whereas most researchers emphasize the way marital disruption increases exposure to stress, the selection argument suggests that problematic personal characteristics may account for the link between martial status and the experience of stressors such as economic pressure and negative events.

To research the selection perspective, one must first identify personal attributes that might be expected to increase an individual's risk for marital disruption, economic difficulties, and negative events. Depression is often mentioned in discussions of the selection perspective, but there is little reason to assume that depression leads to divorce, and depression is not likely a major cause of financial hardship and negative life events. Although we viewed depression as having little promise as a selection factor, another deviant psychological characteristic—involvement in antisocial behavior—appeared to offer significant possibilities.

Past studies have shown that single mothers have a higher incidence of antisocial behavior than mothers from intact families (Capaldi & Patterson, 1991; Kitson, 1992; Lahey et al., 1988) and that individuals with a history of antisocial behavior are at risk for financial problems and negative life events (Caspi et al., 1987; Patterson & Capaldi, 1991; Simons, Beaman, et al., 1993). These findings suggest to us that antisocial individuals are at risk for both divorce and life stress and that an antisocial trait might explain part of the association between divorce and both financial difficulties and stressful events. Our results are consistent with this idea. Antisocial trait is more common among divorced than married women and the trait is strongly related to economic pressure and negative events.

These findings should not be interpreted as suggesting that most divorced persons have antisocial tendencies. The percentage who engaged in antisocial behavior was small for both divorced and married women. Such individuals are overrepresented among the divorced, however, and they display a high prevalence of financial difficulties and stressful events.

Although antisocial tendencies account for part of the relationship between family structure and stressful outcomes, the divorced continue to show higher levels than the married of economic hardship and negative events even after controlling for the effect of this behavior trait. Our analyses indicate that the variable antisocial trait accounts for a fifth of the relationship between family structure and economic pressure and for a fourth of the association between family structure and negative events. Thus, although our results indicate that selection factors are important, the stress perspective appears to explain the majority of the covariation between family structure and stressful outcomes. Furthermore, family structure is related to work stress but antisocial trait is not. Consonant with the stress perspective, financial difficulties, stressful life changes, and work stress seem to be a part of the sequelae of divorce for many individuals.

Contrary to the assertions of many, we found no support for the idea that social support is less available to the divorced than to the married. It is certainly true that individuals who are divorced lack access to one potentially powerful source of support: a marital partner. Our findings, however, provide no evidence to suggest that divorced people have less access to supportive relationships with friends and relatives than married persons. Indeed, we found that the divorced women report slightly greater perceived access to social support than married women. We do not think it likely that this association means that divorced persons have more access to social support than those who are married. Rather, the divorced are probably more aware than the married of the support available in their social networks because distressing circumstances have caused them to solicit help and advice from others. This greater awareness may explain the higher levels of access to social support reported by the divorced. Regardless of whether this is true, however, our results provide no corroboration of the contention that the divorced have less access to social support from friends and relatives.

Although married persons may have larger social networks than divorced persons, very few of these relationships serve as important sources of social support. Most people perceive only a small number of the people within their social network as viable sources of instrumental assistance or emotional sustenance. We presume that divorced and married persons have approximately equal access to such individuals. Although people experience a decline in the size of their friendship network following marital breakup, we expect that this is largely a matter of dropping relationships where social ties were between couples rather than individuals or of reducing interaction with persons identified as more the former spouse's friend. Although such changes may decrease the size of the divorced person's friendship network, probably few of the lost relationships involved close, supportive exchanges. Furthermore, a person is apt to establish close ties with one or two single persons following marital breakup; these new friendships substitute for the small number of supportive relationships that were lost.

Although divorced and married persons may have roughly equal access to social support from friends and relatives (excluding a spouse), social support may be more critical for the divorced. Given the stressful circumstances of divorced people, access to social support may be more strongly related to adjustment for the divorced than the married. The next chapter considers such issues. It explores the extent to which financial difficulties, negative events, and work stress mediate the relationship between divorce and psychological well-being. It then examines the degree to which access to social support moderates the effect of these variables.

4

Family Structure and Mother's Depression

FREDERICK O. LORENZ

RONALD L. SIMONS

WEI CHAO

A variety of studies have reported that divorced women are more likely to be depressed than those who are married (see Kitson & Morgan, 1990; Raschke, 1987). As noted in Chapter 1, there are two fundamental arguments regarding the link between marital breakup and adult emotional well-being (Turner, Wheaton, & Lloyd, 1995). The first, the social causation perspective, attributes decrements in psychological well-being to the stress associated with inequality and social stratification (Mirowsky & Ross, 1989; Turner et al., 1995). Thus the relationship between divorce and depression is seen as a consequence of the economic strain and negative life changes that often follow marital disruption. The second view, the selection perspective, contends that individual characteristics account for the link between marital status and well-being; that is, some women exhibit higher levels of antisocial behavior and are consequently destined for greater social disadvantage. These women are both more likely to experience marital disruption and more likely to demonstrate a variety of behavioral and psychological problems.

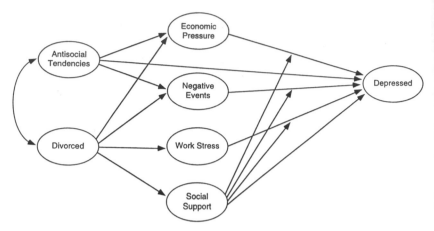

Figure 4.1. Model Depicting the Mediating Effects of the Stress Constructs and the Mediating and Moderating Effects of Social Support

This chapter tests a model that combines these two explanations. Chapter 3 shows that divorced women experience more economic pressure, work stress, and negative life events than married women. Furthermore, women with antisocial tendencies were found to be overrepresented among the divorced. We use these findings to explain the relationship between divorce and psychological distress. Specifically, we test the hypothesis that the association between marital disruption and depression is explained by the high level of stress and the overrepresentation of antisocial persons among the divorced.

Theoretical Model

The model in Figure 4.1 summarizes our arguments regarding the link between divorce and psychological distress. For our purposes, the outcome *psychological distress* refers to depressive symptoms rather than diagnosed psychiatric disorder. Even though depressive symptoms do not necessarily imply clinically significant levels of distress, they are an important outcome because "misery is still miserable" and the "maps of emotional high and low zones reveal a great deal about the nature of life in different social circumstances" (Mirowsky & Ross, 1989, p. 24).

We begin with the simple hypothesis that divorced women are at higher risk for depressive symptoms than those who are married. As noted above, this association has been supported by prior studies (see Kitson & Morgan, 1990). Menaghan and Lieberman (1986), for example, used prospective panel data to demonstrate that divorced men and women are more depressed 4 years after their divorce than they were before, even after controlling for social status. These data provide no support for the contention that the divorced had high levels of depression prior to marital breakup or that elevated levels of depression are due to bad marriages.

Our model suggests that the relationship between marital breakup and depression is explained, at least in part, by the high level of economic pressure, negative life events, and work stress experienced by the divorced. Results presented in Chapter 3 indicate that divorced families experience more economic pressure than intact families. Financial difficulties threaten a family's ability to meet its basic needs. They foster feelings of frustration, anger, and demoralization (Conger et al., 1992; Elder, 1974). Past studies have found a relationship between economic pressure and depression among both married (Lorenz, Conger, & Montague, 1993) and divorced women (Simons, Beaman, et al., 1993). We expect that the association between family structure and psychological distress is partly explained by the fact that divorced families tend to experience greater economic pressure than married families.

Despite growing criticism of the stress-distress research tradition (Anshensel, Rutter, & Lachenbruch, 1991; Pearlin, 1989), strong evidence shows that negative life events are an important cause of psychological distress (Coyne & Downey, 1991; Kessler, Price, & Wortman, 1985; Turner et al., 1995). Negative life events, especially uncontrollable events, leave people feeling helpless and powerless and at the mercy of their environment; this feeling of loss of control or being out of control provokes psychological distress (Mirowsky & Ross, 1989). We expect that the high number of negative life events experienced by the divorced contributes to family structure differences in depression.

Although people, whether single or married, are likely to experience negative events as distressing, the social and economic realities of being a single mother may exacerbate the effects of stressful events

(Pearlin, 1989). Limited economic resources and the physical and emotional demands of adjusting to a new living situation might be expected to increase a single mother's psychological vulnerability to negative life events. In addition to testing the hypothesis that negative events mediate the relationship between family structure and depression, we will examine the extent to which the association between negative events and depression is stronger for divorced than for married women.

Chapter 3 also reports that divorced women are more likely than those living in intact families to experience work-related stress. Compared to married women, divorced women are more apt to report that they work too many hours and that they experience a lot of stress or tension related to their jobs. Divorced mothers probably work more hours than married mothers because they need the income. They may take on more than one job in an effort to meet financial obligations. They probably experience more work-related tension than married women because of conflicts between work and family responsibilities and because they are under financial pressure to obtain promotions, raises, and additional hours. Past research indicates that, regardless of whether mothers are married or single, time pressures and work hours are associated with greater anxiety and distress (Menaghan, 1991). We hypothesize that the higher levels of work-related stress experienced by divorced women explains part of the association between family structure and depression.

To this point, our discussion has reflected the stress or social causation explanation for the higher prevalence of depression among divorced women. We expect that selection processes also play a role in accounting for family structure differences in depression. Results reported in Chapter 3 suggest that persons with antisocial tendencies are overrepresented among the divorced. Figure 4.1 indicates that this finding accounts for part of the association between marital status and depression. The figure depicts a direct association between antisocial trait and depression. This relationship is expected because some forms of antisocial behavior (e.g., substance abuse) may be related to a depressed, irritable emotional state.

In addition, however, Figure 4.1 indicates that antisocial tendencies indirectly influence the probability of depression by increasing stress. Antisocial persons are likely irresponsible about work commitments, financial obligations, and interpersonal agreements. As a consequence, they are likely to experience more negative life events (e.g., job loss, change in residence) and greater financial hardship than their more conventional counterparts (Simons, Beaman, et al., 1993). Consistent with this view, Patterson and Capaldi (1991) found an association between parental antisocial behavior and number of stressful events, whereas Caspi et al. (1987) report that men who were ill-tempered as children manifest erratic work histories as adults and achieve less occupational success than their fathers. Thus, in part, a propensity for antisocial behavior elevates risk for depression by increasing economic pressure and number of negative events.

Finally, in addition to considering the effect of stress and antisocial tendencies, our model suggests that access to social support influences psychological distress. Social support refers to close relationships that provide one with a sense of belonging, a source of assistance, and a sounding board for trying out ideas and discussing problems. A spouse is often an important source of such support (Coyne & Downey, 1991; Fincham & Bradbury, 1990; Lin, Dean, & Ensel, 1986; Reis, 1990). By definition, the divorced in our sample did not have access to a supportive spouse. Findings reported in Chapter 3, however, indicate that divorced women are slightly more likely than married women to have supportive relationships with a friend or relative. In this chapter, we are concerned with the extent to which supportive relationships (with someone other than a spouse) influence risk for depression.

The association between social support and distress, one of the most extensively studied in the stress-distress tradition (Cohen & Wills, 1985; Coyne & Downey, 1991; Hobfoll & Stokes, 1988; Kessler et al., 1985), generally acknowledges two dimensions of social support. The structural dimension of having a network of friends has been associated with reduced levels of distress. People who are integrated into a social network are, almost by definition, less isolated. Large social networks provide regular positive experiences and a set of stable, socially rewarded roles in the community. These experiences and roles, in turn, produce positive affect and well-being and a sense of stability and predictability (Cohen & Wills, 1985). These characteristics of support have been linked to positive psychological well-being. We expect women with less well-developed networks of friends to have higher levels of depression regardless of whether they are divorced or married.

Whereas structural support emphasizes the characteristics of the social network, functional support refers to the specific kinds of relationships and acts of help available from friends (Cohen & Wills, 1985; Hobfoll & Stokes, 1988). Important dimensions of functional support include a sense of belonging, the availability of tangible resources in time of need, and having a person whom one can confide in and receive feedback from about problems (Cohen & Hoberman, 1983). Functional support is often measured using subjective evaluations of the individual receiving the support. Subjective functional support has been shown to provide a buffer against the adverse effects of negative events and aversive situations (Cohen & Wills, 1985; Hobfoll & Stokes, 1988).

Evidence for a buffering effect is present whenever the relationship between some risk factor and psychological distress is smaller for persons with supportive ties to others than for those who lack such relationships (Cohen & Wills, 1985). We test for a buffering effect in our analysis. To the extent that a buffering effect is present, the effect of economic pressure, work stress, negative life events, and antisocial trait on depression is lower for women who perceive high availability of social support than for those who perceive little access to such help and assistance.

Results

The measures used for the constructs included in the analyses presented here are described in Chapter 2. The range of scores on the depressive symptoms index is nearly identical for both divorced and married women, with scores on the SCL-90 ranging from a minimum of 13 for both groups to a high of 56 for the divorced women and 57 for the married women. The distributions, however, are significantly different. The average depression score was 22.9 for the divorced women and 19.7 for the married, whereas the median was 21 for the divorced and 17 for the married. Twenty-eight percent of the divorced women had scores above 26, a level at which respondents averaged at least a little bit of each symptom, compared with only 11% for the married women. Furthermore, as Table 4.1 indicates, divorced women scored higher than their married counterparts on all the symptoms in

TABLE 4.1 Means (with standard deviations) for Depressive Symptoms

Depressive Symptom	Married	Divorced	t-Value
Loss of sexual interest or pleasure	1.75 (1.01)	1.42 (0.96)	1.46
Feeling low in energy or slowed down	2.12 (1.00)	2.30 (1.06)	1.83
Thoughts of ending your life	1.04 (0.25)	1.07 (0.37)	1.32
Crying easily	1.51 (0.91)	1.68 (0.94)	1.47
Feelings of being trapped or caught	1.35 (0.82)	1.58 (0.91)	2.83
Blaming yourself for things	1.45 (0.74)	1.82 (0.97)	4.58
Feeling lonely	1.42 (0.82)	2.17 (1.13)	8.36
Feeling blue	1.62 (0.93)	2.16 (1.03)	5.77
Worrying too much about things	2.05 (1.07)	2.55 (1.16)	4.75
Feeling no interest in things	1.34 (0.75)	1.52 (0.89)	2.29
Feeling helpless about the future	1.36 (0.72)	1.67 (0.94)	3.94
Feeling everything is an effort	1.40 (0.72)	1.57 (0.79)	2.36
Feelings of worthlessness	1.26 (0.72)	1.48 (0.81)	3.04
Overall Mean	19.70 (7.71)	22.90 (8.34)	3.08

the depression index, with the difference being statistically significant for 9 of the 13 items. Compared with married women, divorced women scored especially high on "blaming yourself for things," "feeling lonely," "feeling blue," "worrying too much about things," and "feeling helpless about the future."

SEARCHING FOR MEDIATORS

Having established that there is a relationship between family structure and depression, we tested the extent to which this association is explained by our social causation and selection variables. Structural equation modeling (SEM) was used to perform these analyses. We began by fitting a measurement model to the data. Overall, the model fit the data reasonably well [$\chi^2(67) = 154.6$]. The loadings for the four indicators of social support ranged from .73 to .79, whereas the loadings for the indicators of antisocial trait averaged around .50.

Table 4.2 presents the bivariate correlations between the various constructs. It shows that there is a .20 correlation between divorce and depression. Divorce is also significantly related to the potential mediating variables: antisocial trait, economic pressure, work stress, and negative events. Each of these potentially mediating constructs, in turn, shows a significant association with depression.

TABLE 4.2 Correlations Between Constructs

	1	2	3	4	5	6
1. Economic pressure						
2. Work stress	0.11					
3. Negative life events	0.52*	−.00				
4. Social support	−.12	−.03	−.04			
5. Depression	0.42*	0.14*	0.38*	−.20*		
6. Divorced	0.38*	0.16*	0.32*	0.16*	0.20*	
7. Antisocial trait	0.43*	0.06	0.47*	−.04	0.45*	0.30*

*$p \le .05$

TABLE 4.3 The Standardized Coefficients (with t-values) Linking Depression to Family Structure, Antisocial Trait, and the Mediating Variables

Variables	Response Variables				
	Economic Pressure	Work Stress	Negative Events	Social Support	Depression
Divorce	0.272	0.159	0.202	0.190	0.003
	($t = 4.95$)	(3.15)	(3.89)	(3.31)	(0.06)
Antisocial trait	0.353	0.009	0.405	−.095	0.295
	($t = 3.80$)	(0.13)	(4.35)	(−0.16)	(3.13)
Economic pressure					0.186
					(3.01)
Work stress					0.101
					(2.37)
Negative life events					0.141
					(2.43)
Social support					−.157
					(−3.28)
R^2	26%	3%	25%	3%	31%

Table 4.3 presents the results of using SEM to test for mediating effects. The table shows that economic pressure is predicted by both divorce (.272) and antisocial trait (.353). The same is true for negative events, where the path coefficients are .202 and .405 for divorce and antisocial trait, respectively. Work stress and social support, on the other hand, are only predicted by divorce. The path coefficients are .159 and .190, respectively. The fifth column shows that depression is significantly related to antisocial trait (.295), economic pressure

TABLE 4.4 Comparison of Standardized Regression Coefficients (with t-values) Linking Depression to Stressors and Social Support for Married and Divorced Women

	Married	Divorced
Antisocial trait	0.16	0.13
	(2.83)	(2.40)
Economic pressure	0.19	0.20
	(3.12)	(2.75)
Work stress	0.11	0.13
	(1.89)	(2.03)
Negative events	0.17	0.25
	(2.90)	(3.27)
Social support	–.15	–.20
	(–2.67)	(–2.98)
R^2	20%	28%

(.186), work stress (.101), negative events (.141), and social support (–.157). There is no significant relationship between divorce and depression once the effect of these variables is taken into account.

The pattern of findings presented in Table 4.3 suggests that the effect of marital disruption on risk for depression is indirect through a number of factors. Divorced women are more likely than those who are married to display antisocial behavior and to experience economic pressure, work stress, and negative life events; each of these factors is associated with depression. The only beacon in favor of divorced women is their perception of social support. Divorced women perceive slightly higher access to social support than married women, and perceived social support is negatively related to depression. The combined effects of family structure, the negative implications of antisocial behavior, the three types of stressors, and social support explain 31% of the variance in depressive symptoms.

IS THERE EVIDENCE OF MODERATOR EFFECTS?

We examined hypotheses about moderator effects; overall, they were not supported. First, we addressed the issue of whether the relationships between depressive symptoms and stressors and social support are the same for divorced and married women. The results, summarized in Table 4.4, show some differences between the two

TABLE 4.5 Comparison of Standardized Regression Coefficients (with t-values) Linking Depression to Family Structure, Antisocial Trait, and Stressors for Women With High ($N = 221$) and Low ($N = 239$) Perceived Social Support

	Perceived Social Support	
Outcome/Predictor Variables	High	Low
Eq 1: Economic pressure		
Family structure	0.215 ($t = 2.41$)	0.327 ($t = 4.40$)
Antisocial trait	0.370 ($t = 2.34$)	0.363 ($t = 3.13$)
R^2	24%	30%
Eq 2: Work stress		
Family structure	0.218 ($t = 2.79$)	0.105 ($t = 1.47$)
Antisocial trait	−.004 ($t = -.04$)	0.027 ($t = 0.28$)
R^2	5%	2%
Eq 3: Negative events		
Family structure	0.143 ($t = 1.57$)	0.236 ($t = 3.42$)
Antisocial trait	0.529 ($t = 2.91$)	0.321 ($t = 3.00$)
R^2	36%	30%
Eq 4: Depression		
Family structure	−0.690 ($t = -.98$)	0.051 ($t = 0.75$)
Antisocial trait	0.120 ($t = 0.79$)	0.408 ($t = 3.26$)*
Economic pressure	0.276 ($t = 3.24$)	0.105 ($t = 1.12$)
Work stress	0.131 ($t = 2.07$)	0.084 ($t = 1.38$)
Negative events	0.149 ($t = 1.50$)	0.189 ($t = 2.45$)
R^2	21%	37%

groups, but the strength of the relationships is not so large as to be significantly different. For example, the effects of negative events on depression are relatively stronger for divorced women (.25; $t = 3.27$) compared with married women (.17; $t = 2.90$), but this difference is not statistically significant. Overall, the results of these comparisons suggest that the strength of the relationships linking antisocial trait, economic pressure, work stress, negative events, and social support to depression are essentially the same for both divorced and married women.

Second, we compared the relationships between family structure, antisocial tendencies, stressors, and depressive symptoms for women who reported being high and low on perceived social support. The results of this analysis are presented in Table 4.5. Again, there were differences in the two groups but for the most part the differences were not significant. For example, the relationship between divorce and economic pressure was stronger for those low in perceived social support (.327) than for those high in support (.215), suggesting that feelings of financial strain are intensified among divorced women when they also feel that support is low. But the change in chi-square that resulted when the two slopes were set equal was not significant $[\chi^2(1) = 0.15;$ ns]. The one exception was for the association between antisocial trait and depression. For that relationship, the standardized slope linking the two was a relatively modest .120 for those high on perceived support but a highly significant .408 among those low on support, and the change in chi-square when the two were set equal was significant $[\chi^2(1) = 9.0]$. This suggests that feelings of depression are higher among respondents who demonstrate antisocial tendencies and feel isolated from others.

Discussion

The empirical generalization that divorced women have higher psychological distress than their married peers has been observed repeatedly in previous research (e.g., Duncan & Hoffman, 1985; Weitzman, 1985). It is reaffirmed by our results. The difference in mean depression scores between married (19.4) and divorced (23.1) women translates into a significant total effect of family structure on psychological distress of .23 ($t = 5.3$).

Ross, Mirowsky and Goldsteen (1990) review various explanations for why divorce increases vulnerability to psychological distress. They conclude that there is little evidence to support the idea that living with someone provides protection against depression; studies have found that unmarried people who live alone are no more distressed than those who live with other adults (e.g., Hughes & Gove, 1981). Ross et al. conclude that the association between family structure and psychological distress is probably explained by economic and other stress factors. Our findings support this contention.

Our results indicate that divorced women are more likely than those who are married to experience economic pressure, work stress, and negative life events. These factors, in turn, are related to increased risk for depression. These findings suggest that marital disruption raises the probability that a person will experience life stress; it is this elevation in stress that accounts in large measure for the high level of psychological distress seen among the divorced. Although the data used in our analysis are cross-sectional, the temporal sequencing inherent in the data collection process adds strength to the argument. Most women in the study were divorced prior to the year in which data on financial pressures and negative events were collected (1991), and our depressive symptom inventory focused on feelings during the month previous to data collection. Thus, the intervening variables covered a period of time preceding the reports of distress but subsequent to divorce.

Although these results are consistent with a social causation model, we also found support for the selection argument. Divorced women are more likely than married women to display antisocial behavior trait. This behavior trait is directly related to risk of depression, plus it exerts an indirect effect by increasing a woman's chances of financial hardship, work stress, and negative life events. Overall, our findings indicate that the association between marital disruption and depression is explained by the high level of stress and the overrepresentation of antisocial persons among the divorced.

We found no support for the idea that high levels of depression among the divorced is explained by family structure differences relating to social support. Although it is often asserted that divorced women have less access to social support than those who are married, we found that the divorced reported higher levels of perceived support from friends and relatives than the married. One might argue, however, that family structure differences in social support involve the consequences of such support rather than its degree of availability. Spousal support, by definition, is not available to the divorced. Thus perceived support from friends and relatives may be more important to the emotional well-being of divorced than married women. To the extent that this is true, the association between perceived support and depression, as well as the buffering effect of social support, should be stronger for the divorced than the married.

We found only limited corroboration of this idea. The relationship between social support and depression is the same regardless of family structure. There were few significant buffering effects for the women in our study whether they were married or divorced. The only evidence for family structure differences in the importance of social support involved the construct antisocial trait. We found that perceived social support moderates the relationship between antisocial trait and depression for divorced women, whereas there is no buffering effect for the married. Overall, however, our results provide little indication that family structure differences involving social support help explain the association between divorce and depression. Our analysis suggests that family structure differences in stress and behavioral predispositions account for the increased risk of depression among the divorced.

PART III

FAMILY INTERACTION

5

Mother's Parenting

RONALD L. SIMONS

CHRISTINE JOHNSON

Findings presented in Chapter 3 indicate that the divorced women in our study were more apt than the married women to demonstrate antisocial tendencies and to experience economic strain, negative life events, and work stress. Chapter 4 shows that these family structure differences result in divorced women suffering more psychological distress than married women. This chapter is concerned with the implications of these various findings for quality of parenting. We develop and test hypotheses regarding the extent to which stress, psychological well-being, and antisocial tendencies explain family structure differences in parenting practices.

Family Structure and Quality of Parenting

Rutter (1985a, 1985b) contends that competent parenting involves the provision of a family environment conducive to children's cognitive, emotional, and social development. Over the years, researchers have identified what are believed to be the fundamental features of such an environment. Studies indicate that effective parents are warm and supportive, set standards, monitor child behavior, are consistent in enforcing rules, and eschew harsh punishments (Amato, 1990; Maccoby, 1992; Maccoby & Martin, 1983). Many studies have linked these parental behaviors to positive child outcomes such as academic achievement and prosocial actions. Conversely, research indicates that children are at risk for conduct problems and psychological distress when their parents fail to engage in these parenting practices (Maccoby, 1992; Maccoby & Martin, 1983).

Findings from several studies indicate that divorced parents are less apt to display these parental behaviors than those who are married. Hetherington et al. (1982), for example, found that divorced mothers show less affection to their children, communicate with them less, punish them more, and are more inconsistent in their use of discipline than married women. Similar results have been reported by other researchers (Amato, 1987; Astone & McLanahan, 1991; Capaldi & Patterson, 1991; Furstenberg & Nord, 1985; McLanahan & Sandefur, 1994; Thomson, McLanahan, & Curtin, 1992). These studies provide compelling evidence that divorced parents tend to make fewer demands on children, engage in less monitoring, and use less effective disciplinary strategies than married parents.

Three types of explanations have been offered for family structure differences in parenting. First, it is often asserted that the presence within the household of a second parent reinforces the authority and influence of the other parent (Dornbusch et al., 1985; Thomson et al., 1992). In the absence of a second parenting figure, single-parent families are seen as tending toward a blurring of generational boundaries and a weakening of parental authority (Knok, 1988). Thus, number of parents in the home is seen as an important structural variable that influences quality of parenting. Second, some have noted that most single parents are women and that women often have not been adequately socialized to play the traditionally male role of disciplinarian. This gender role explanation suggests that family structure is related to level of parental control because most divorced families lack an adult male to enforce discipline. Support for this point of view is provided by the finding that single fathers exercise more control than single mothers (Santrock, Warshak, & Elliott, 1982) and that stepfathers exert more control than their wives (Santrock, Warshak, Lindbergh, & Meadows, 1982). However, whereas males may be more controlling parents than females, this fact cannot explain why divorced mothers engage in less effective discipline than married mothers as the two sets of women should have been exposed to the same gender-biased socialization.

Finally, a few researchers argue that family structure differences in stress and emotional well-being largely account for the disrupted parenting seen in divorced families (Brody & Forehand, 1988; Forgatch, Patterson, & Skinner, 1988; Hetherington et al., 1982; Simons, Beaman, et al., 1993). We favor this explanation. As noted in previous chapters, divorced mothers tend to show poorer psychological adjustment than married mothers. They are more likely to be depressed and to demonstrate antisocial tendencies. We expect that difficulties in adjustment explain the inadequate monitoring and inept discipline often seen in divorced families.

Depression and Parenting

Many studies have reported a relationship between psychological depression and quality of parenting (Conger, McCarthy, Young, Lahey, & Kropp, 1984; Grossman, Eichler, & Winickoff, 1980; Orraschel, Weissman, & Kidd, 1980; Radke-Yarrow, Richters, & Wilson, 1988; Simons, Lorenz, Wu, & Conger, 1993; Weissman & Paykel, 1974). This association is to be expected for several reasons: First, a primary symptom of depression is a diminished interest in activities and situations previously experienced as rewarding (Willner, 1985). Social relationships and events seem to lose their reinforcing value, with the depressed person often becoming cantankerous when he or she is required to participate. Consequently, as persons become depressed, they are likely to adopt a more disinterested, irritable approach to people in general, including their children.

Second, past research indicates that depression is associated with negatively biased scanning of the environment; this perceptual bias tends to foster cynical, pessimistic perceptions of people and events (Abramson et al., 1978; Beck, 1976). As a result, depressed persons are apt to be dissatisfied with social relationships, including relationships with their children. Consistent with this argument, studies have reported that depressed mothers are more apt than nondepressed mothers to perceive their children as difficult (Brody & Forehand, 1988; Christensen, Phillips, Glasgow, & Johnson, 1983; Forehand, Wells, McMahon, Griest, & Rogers, 1982; Griest, Wells, & Forehand, 1979). In several of these studies, assessments of the mother's psychological distress account for more variance in maternal perceptions of child conduct problems than objective evaluations of child behavior (Christensen et al., 1983; Forehand et al., 1982; Griest et al., 1979). One would expect that a mother's negative perceptions of her child's intentions and actions would be a major determinant of her behavior toward the child. Consonant with this assumption, research indicates that dissatisfaction with the child is related to parental hostility, nattering, and harsh discipline (Brody & Forehand, 1988; Simons, Beaman, et al., 1993).

We have shown that depression tends to be associated with inept parenting. Chapter 4 reported that divorced parents are more apt to be depressed than those who are married. Putting these findings together, we expect that much of the relationship between family structure and quality of parenting is mediated by level of depression. Furthermore, we presume that stress relating to economic strain, work, and negative events largely influences parenting practices indirectly through its effect on the parent's emotional state. Such stressors may exert a direct effect on parenting as well. They may cause the parent to be preoccupied and self-absorbed, with this emotional state distracting the parent from the task of parenting. We will examine the extent to which stress both affects quality of parenting directly and exerts an indirect influence by fostering depression.

Antisocial Trait and Parenting

Previous chapters discuss the construct *antisocial trait*. A trait is a generalized disposition to engage in a certain class of behaviors. Persons with antisocial trait participate rather persistently in actions perceived as risky, self-centered, inappropriate, shortsighted, or insensitive by the majority of people in society. Competent parenting, as defined earlier in this chapter, requires sensitivity, patience, self-sacrifice, responsibility, and organization. In many ways, these qualities are the opposite of those that characterize antisocial behavior trait.

Thus it seems likely that individuals with antisocial tendencies lack the motivation or skill necessary for competent parenting. Several studies suggest that this is the case.

Using longitudinal data from the Berkeley Guidance Study, Caspi and Elder (1988) report that antisocial children later become ill-tempered, explosive parents. Laub and Sampson (1988; Sampson & Laub, 1993), using the Gluecks' (Glueck & Glueck, 1968) well-known Boston data set, found that parental antisocial behavior is related to poor disciplinary practices. Patterson and his colleagues at the Oregon Social Learning Center have published several papers showing a relationship between mothers' antisocial tendencies and the quality of their monitoring and discipline (Capaldi & Patterson, 1991; Patterson & Capaldi, 1991; Patterson & Dishion, 1988). Finally, we (Simons, Beaman, et al., 1993; Simons, Wu, Johnson, & Conger, 1995) have found an association between parental antisocial behavior and quality of parenting among rural Midwestern families.

As noted in Chapter 3, a higher proportion of divorced than married women displays antisocial tendencies. This suggests that single parents who manifest this behavior trait, rather than single parents in general, may account for much of the difference between the divorced and married with regard to quality of parenting. If this contention is true, controlling for antisocial trait should reduce or eliminate the relationship between family structure and quality of parenting.

Model to Be Tested

We have posited that the relationship between family structure and quality of parenting is a function of the poorer adjustment of divorced compared to married persons. More specifically, we have hypothesized that high levels of stress, depression, and antisocial tendencies among the divorced explain their greater risk for inept parenting. As noted earlier, other explanations for the relationship between family structure and parenting have also been suggested. Some have argued that divorced families are characterized by less competent parenting than married families because single mothers lack the support of a second parent (Dornbusch et al., 1985; Thomson et al., 1992), whereas others have argued that single mothers are less competent parents because women have not been socialized to exercise control and discipline (Santrock, Warshak, & Elliott, 1982; Santrock, Warshak, Lindbergh, & Meadows, 1982). The test of our parental adjustment hypothesis will necessarily provide a test of these alternative explanations as well. If the relationship between family structure and parenting is eliminated when we control for parental adjustment, the alternative explanations must not be correct. On the other hand, the results would be consistent with these explanations if some or all of the association between family structure and parenting remains after controlling for parental adjustment.

Results

We began our analysis by running frequency distributions for the items in our parenting measures. The frequencies were run separately for the divorced, the happily married, and the unhappily married. Scores on the Marital Happiness Scale were used to identify the latter two groups. Women who scored below the median on the scale were considered to have distressed marriages, whereas those who scored above the median were assumed to have happy marriages. The good news was that only a small proportion of women, regardless of marital status or marital quality, showed evidence of inept parenting. The bad news was that the divorced women scored higher on virtually every item contained in our measures regardless of the source of data (observer rating, child report, or mother self-report). Mothers who were happily married scored the lowest on almost all the inept parenting items. The scores for mothers in distressed marriages were generally in between those for the other two groups.

Examples of this pattern are presented in Table 5.1. The top portion of the table reports the percentage of mothers rated by the observers as showing at least moderate involvement (i.e., they received a score of at least 4 on the 5-point rating scale) in various dysfunctional parenting practices. The table also presents items from the mother and child report measures. The percentages for these items refer to the proportion of mothers who self-reported or were reported by their child as engaging in a particular behavior more than half of the time.

TABLE 5.1 Differences in Parenting Between Divorced Mothers, Mothers in
Distressed Marriages, and Happily Married Mothers

	Divorced Mother	Distressed Marriage	Happy Marriage
Observer Ratings*			
Harsh discipline	4.5%	3.1%	2.6%
Hostility	38.6	25.3	25.3
Coercive	17.8	10.5	10.7
Self-centered/inconsiderate	24.3	14.1	11.4
Low monitoring	35.0	24.0	17.4
Child Report**			
Doesn't monitor curfew	11.4	6.8	6.4
Gives up when punishing	6.7	4.3	1.2
Persistent criticism	16.6	11.7	7.6
Argues with you	22.9	13.6	12.7
Kicks you out of house	19.3	11.7	7.6
Mother Report**			
Doesn't monitor curfew	7.1	3.0	4.4
Gives up when punishing	10.5	5.5	3.8
Persistent criticism	24.5	15.3	11.3
Argues with child	29.3	13.5	10.8
Kicks child out of house	17.1	9.8	3.7

*Percentage receiving a rating of 4 ("moderately characteristic") or higher.
**Percentage reporting the behavior almost always when the mother attempts to parent the child.

With a few exceptions (e.g., hostility, coerciveness, failing to monitor curfew), the percentages for the distressed marriage group are higher than those for the happily married group. In turn, the percentages for the divorced mothers are consistently higher than those for the distressed marriage group.

ANOVA was used to test whether group differences in parenting were statistically significant. Scores obtained from each of the three sources of information (observer, child report, mother report) were standardized and summed to form a composite measure of inept parenting. Scores were standardized prior to summation to give equal weight to each source of information. The means for the divorced, maritally distressed, and happily married were 2.12, .39, and –2.57, respectively. The differences were significant at the .001 level. These findings indicate that women who are in unhappy marriages are more likely to engage in dysfunctional parenting practices than those who are happily married. They also indicate, however, that women who

TABLE 5.2 Bivariate Correlations Between Constructs

	1	2	3	4	5	6	7
1. Divorced	—						
2. Antisocial trait	.292*	—					
3. Depressed	.195*	.455*	—				
4. Work stress	.173	.060	.149*	—			
5. Negative events	.325*	.488*	.388*	.009	—		
6. Economic strain	.367*	.440*	.416*	.104*	.527*	—	
7. Inept parenting	.264*	.431*	.356*	.092	.266*	.383*	—

have recently gone through divorce are at even greater risk for inept parenting than those in an unhappy marriage.

LISREL VII was used to calculate the association between family structure and inept parenting and to assess the extent to which stress and psychological adjustment explain this relationship. Table 5.2 presents the bivariate associations between constructs. The table shows a significant association of .264 between divorce and inept parenting. Inept parenting is also related to the two adjustment constructs. The association is .431 for antisocial trait and .356 for depression. Although work stress is not related to inept parenting, the coefficients are significant for the other two types of stress. The coefficient is .383 for economic strain and .266 for negative events.

Structural equation modeling (SEM) was used to investigate the extent to which psychological adjustment mediates the effect of family structure on parenting. We began with the fully recursive model. This resulted in several paths that were near zero and had very low t-values. In an effort to obtain a more parsimonious model, paths with a t of 1.0 or below were deleted. Furthermore, there was no significant path from either negative events or work stress to inept parenting. The coefficients of .02 and −.06, respectively, had t-values of near zero. The effect of these two variables on parenting was indirect through depression. The SEM presented in the previous chapter showed the effect of negative events and work stress on depression; in an effort to avoid duplication and further parsimony, these constructs were dropped from our model of parental behavior. This model trimming had no appreciable effect on the magnitude or the significance level of any of the remaining paths. The difference in χ^2 between the

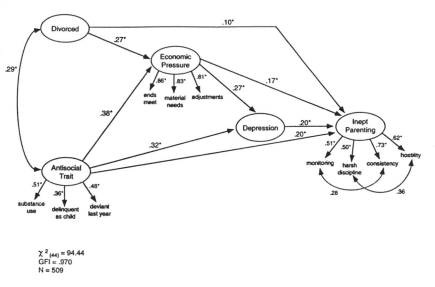

Figure 5.1. Psychological Adjustment as a Mediator of the Relationship Between Family Structure and Quality of Parenting

reduced and the fully recursive model did not approach statistical significance. The reduced model is depicted in Figure 5.1. Both the Goodness of Fit Index and the ratio of χ^2 to the number of degrees of freedom suggest that the model provides a reasonable fit of the data.

Figure 5.1 shows that depression is related to inept parenting. The coefficient is .20. Economic pressure has a direct effect on inept parenting (.17), as well as an indirect effect through depression. Antisocial trait influences inept parenting directly (.20) and indirectly through its effect on economic pressure (.38) and depression (.32). Finally, most of the effect of divorce is indirect through antisocial trait, economic pressure, and depression. Divorce also has a small direct effect (.10), however, that does not go through these variables. Approximately 38% of the relationship between divorce and inept parenting is explained by the direct and indirect effects of antisocial trait. This suggests that the stress perspective explains more of the association between marital disruption and inept parenting than the selection perspective.

It should be noted that the model presented in Figure 5.1 was run separately for mothers of sons and mothers of daughters. The pattern

of coefficients was almost identical for the two models. We also ran
the model separately by family structure. Again, the results were quite
similar across models. Thus we found no evidence that the relationship
between family structure and parenting differs by gender of child or
that the disruptive effect of stress and psychological problems on
parenting varies by family structure.

Discussion

Over the years, social scientists have identified what are believed
to be the characteristics of a competent parent. Research indicates that
competent parents are warm and supportive, set standards, monitor
child behavior, are consistent in enforcing rules, and eschew harsh
punishments (Amato, 1990; Maccoby, 1992; Maccoby & Martin,
1983). Unfortunately, there is rather compelling evidence that divorced parents are less apt to display these parental behaviors than
those who are married. Several studies report that divorced parents
tend to make fewer demands on children, engage in less monitoring,
and use less effective disciplinary strategies than married parents
(Amato, 1987; Astone & McLanahan, 1991; Capaldi & Patterson,
1991; Furstenberg & Nord, 1985; Hetherington et al., 1982; McLanahan & Sandefur, 1994; Thomson et al., 1992). We found this family
structure difference in our data as well. Compared to married women,
the divorced mothers in our sample engaged in less child monitoring,
were less consistent, showed greater hostility, and were more punitive.

Acock and Demo (1994) assert that the majority of mothers, regardless
of marital status, are competent parents. They note that only a minority
of divorced mothers display inadequate discipline and control. Our data
support their contention. Regardless of whether observer ratings, adolescent reports, or mother self-report were used to assess quality of parenting, the data indicate that only about 20% to 25% of the divorced women
were engaging in dysfunctional parenting practices. Taken by itself, this
statistic suggests little reason for alarm, as more than three quarters of
the divorced mothers were doing a good job of parenting their children.
On the other hand, although the percentage of divorced women who
were failing to provide adequate discipline and control was relatively
small, it was about double that of married mothers.

Consistent with prior research (Conger et al., 1992), we found that marital satisfaction is related to quality of parenting among intact families. Mothers in distressed marriages are more likely to engage in inept parenting practices than those in happy marriages. We also found, however, that inept parenting is more prevalent among divorced mothers than among mothers in distressed marriages. This suggests that, in general, divorce increases the probability of inadequate parenting more than marital distress.

We tested the hypothesis that the relationship between divorce and quality of parenting is a function of the stress and poorer adjustment of the divorced compared with the married. Consistent with this idea, much of the association between family structure and parenting practices was mediated by economic pressure and depression. About a third of the relationship was also explained by antisocial tendencies. These findings suggest that the inept parenting sometimes seen among divorced mothers is largely a consequence of the frustration and preoccupation produced by financial difficulties and stressful events and by the negativity and irritability that accompany depression. Secondarily, it is a function of the fact that persons with antisocial tendencies are overrepresented among the divorced, and such individuals tend to lack the motivation and social skills necessary for competent parenting. There is a small but significant association between family structure and parenting after controlling for the strain and selection variables. Some have argued that absence of a second parent within the home tends to produce a blurring of generational boundaries and a weakening of parental authority (Dornbusch et al., 1985; Knok, 1988). The small direct effect between family structure and quality of parenting might be interpreted as evidence for this contention.

McLanahan and Sandefur (1994) note that researchers need to take seriously the possibility that discrepancies in parenting between one-parent and two-parent families may simply reflect parental dispositional differences that existed prior to marital disruption. Although divorced parents may show less parental involvement than married persons, this less effective parenting may have been present prior to marital breakup. Using longitudinal data, McLanahan and Sandefur found that divorce tends to be followed by a decline in quality of parenting. Unfortunately, their report does not indicate whether their data also show predivorce differences in parenting. Our findings suggest that both processes are at work. Single parents with antisocial tendencies account for a significant proportion of the inept parenting seen among the divorced; these persons were quite likely less effective parents prior to marital breakup. On the other hand, financial pressures and emotional distress also contribute to the lower-quality parenting demonstrated by the divorced in our sample. Presumably, these factors are largely responsible for reductions in parental involvement that take place following marital disruption.

Absence of a husband may increase the chances that financial distress and depression will disrupt a mother's parenting. Simons and Johnson (in press) argue that caring spouses (or live-in partners) provide increased encouragement, advice, and assistance with parenting when they perceive their mate to be emotionally upset and that this support reduces the probability that a person's emotional distress will spill over into his or her parenting. Consonant with this idea, some studies have found that spousal support moderates the association between life stress and quality of parenting (Elder et al., 1984; Simons, Lorenz, et al., 1992; Simons, Lorenz, et al., 1993; Simons, Whitbeck, Melby, & Wu, 1994). Thus, at the same time that divorced women are experiencing high levels of stress and turmoil, they lack a household resource that has been shown to reduce the probability that this emotional distress will disrupt their parenting.

It would be nice if nonresidential friends and relatives could substitute for a spouse in providing this buffer for parenting; our data indicate that divorced mothers have as much access to this form of support as married women. Although support from these individuals may moderate the extent to which stressful events result in psychological disorder, there is little reason to believe that such support reduces the probability that stress and emotional turmoil disrupt parenting. A supportive husband may provide encouragement, advice, and assistance with child rearing tasks that directly affect the quality of his wife's parenting. In contrast, friends and relatives are usually not available in the household to help with the everyday duties of parenting and hence they would be expected to exert little or no influence on the quality of a woman's parenting practices (Simons & Johnson, 1995). We have found this to be the case in prior analyses using data from our Iowa Youth and Families Project and Iowa Single

Parent Project families. Support from friends or relatives is not related to quality of parenting, nor does it moderate the effect of emotional distress on parenting for either married (Simons, Lorenz, Wu, & Conger, 1993) or divorced mothers (Simons, Beaman, et al., 1993).

As noted in the introduction to this chapter, parenting practices have been shown to be an important determinant of child developmental outcomes. Thus we would expect the family structure differences in quality of parenting that have been the focus of this chapter to have implications for child adjustment. The chapters in Part III examine the extent to which the greater risk for inept parenting that exists for divorced families explains family structure differences in various types of adolescent problem behaviors.

6

Father's Parenting

RONALD L. SIMONS

JAY BEAMAN

As noted in Chapter 5, there is strong evidence that quality of parenting influences child development. Most of this research has focused on the parenting practices of mothers. There is evidence, however, that quality of parenting by fathers is also related to child developmental outcomes (Lamb & Levine, 1985; Radin & Russell, 1983). Research on fathers indicates that they continue to show low involvement in the parenting activities shown to be consequential for child development. Fathers rarely take responsibility for child management and caretaking. Rather, the time they spend with children tends to involve play and mutual entertainment. This is particularly true for nonresidential fathers (Furstenberg & Cherlin, 1991).

This chapter provides a brief overview of past research on paternal involvement in parenting. Based on this literature, we developed hypotheses regarding differences in parenting between divorced fathers and those living in intact families. We then test these expectations using data from our Iowa families.

94

Father's Parenting in Intact Families

It is generally assumed that fathers have become more involved in the task of child rearing. There is some evidence to support this view. Studies indicate that there has been a substantial rise in the number of fathers who are present during labor and delivery of their child (Lewis, 1986) and there has been a significant increase in the amount of time fathers spend with their children (Caplow & Chadwick, 1979; Daniels & Weingarten, 1983; Vanek, 1981). Studies also report, however, that men continue to be much less involved than their wives in the daily care and supervision of children (Lamb, 1977; Parke, 1981). Once married, couples tend to acknowledge a division of labor whereby the husband is recognized as the expert in certain areas and the wife in others; there is usually strong agreement that parenting is the domain of the wife (LaRossa, 1986; LaRossa & LaRossa, 1981). Husbands continue to see themselves as cast in a supporting role where they play with the child and provide assistance to the primary parent, the mother (LaRossa, 1986; Simons, Beaman, Conger, & Chao, 1992).

Thus, although fathers have become more involved with their children, much of this time is spent joking, roughhousing, or in some other form of play. There has been little change during the past 25 years in the extent to which fathers participate in routine caregiving (Parke & Sterns, 1993). When fathers pick up an infant, it is usually to play with him or her, whereas when the mother picks up a child, it is usually for caretaking purposes (Lamb, 1977). Although historically fathers have been portrayed as performing the role of teacher within the family, studies show that mothers tend to discharge this function (Neville & Parke, 1987; Parke & Bhavnagri, 1989). Furthermore, mothers are much more likely than fathers to provide advice, help with problems, set boundaries, and administer discipline (Parke & Sterns, 1993). Fathers and mothers even differ in terms of the type of play they engage in with the child. Fathers' play is often physical and arousing, whereas mothers' play tends to be verbal and didactic (Parke & Tinsley, 1987).

The bottom line is that fathers are devoting more time to their children, but they have not shown substantial increases in the activities most consequential for children. In Chapter 5, we defined competent parenting as the provision of a family environment conducive to children's cognitive, emotional, and social development. Such an environment requires providing warmth and support, assisting with problems, providing encouragement, setting and explaining standards, monitoring the children, and enforcing discipline. Unfortunately, there is little indication that fathers are making great strides regarding these activities.

Involvement in Parenting by Nonresidential Fathers

Given evidence of a relationship between quality of father's parenting and child adjustment in intact families, social scientists have speculated that low involvement by noncustodial fathers may account, at least in part, for the high prevalence of emotional and behavioral problems among children of divorce. Although the idea that child adjustment is facilitated by involvement with nonresidential fathers is intuitively appealing, there is actually little empirical evidence for the claim (Emery, 1988; Furstenberg & Cherlin, 1991). In a comprehensive review of research regarding this issue, Amato (1993) identified 16 studies that supported the hypothesis that frequency of contact with the noncustodial father is positively related to child adjustment. However, he found an equal number of studies that failed to support the hypothesis. Indeed, seven of the studies in the latter group reported frequency of visitation with the noncustodial father to be negatively related to child adjustment. Thus, overall, the evidence suggests that frequency of visitation by fathers is not related to child adjustment. Recent studies support this conclusion (King, 1994a, 1994b).

Perhaps this finding should have been anticipated; there is little reason to expect that simply having contact with the nonresidential father would significantly affect a child's development. The quality, rather than simply the quantity, of interaction with this parent is the key to understanding his effect on child adjustment. Past research suggests that nonresidential fathers often behave toward their children more as an adult friend or relative than as a parent (Arendell, 1986; Furstenberg & Nord, 1985; Hetherington et al., 1976). Much of the time with their children is spent watching TV, attending movies, going out to eat, and the like. In the previous section, we noted that interactions between fathers and their children in intact families tend to be focused around play. This pattern appears to continue after marital disruption. Although experts often lament the number of divorced fathers who function as "Disneyland dads," in many cases this behavior is probably simply an elaboration of the approach to parenting that the fathers displayed when the marriage was still intact.

If a nonresidential father is to influence his child's psychosocial development, he must be more than an entertainer. He must engage in the behaviors that we have identified as the components of competent parenting, for example, assist with problems, provide encouragement, establish conduct standards, and enforce discipline. Fathers do not need to live with their child to engage in these behaviors. Although studies have failed to find a relationship between contact with nonresidential fathers and child outcomes, an association might be found if the focus was shifted from frequency of visits to quality of parenting.

We tested this idea by forming a scale that assesses the involvement of nonresidential fathers in activities such as emphasizing moral principles, inductive reasoning, reinforcing appropriate behavior, problem solving, and consistent discipline (see Father's Inept Parenting Scale reported in Chapter 2). This measure was inversely related to adolescent conduct problems even after taking into account quality of mother's parenting, parental conflict, and family income (Simons, Whitbeck, Beaman, & Conger, 1994). The effect was particularly strong for boys.

A father does not need to live with his child to engage in such parenting practices, but fathers in intact families are undoubtedly more likely to display these behaviors than nonresidential fathers. This chapter examines the extent to which divorce is associated with changes in the emotional support, guidance, problem solving, and consistent discipline provided by fathers. For a variety of reasons (e.g., geographic distance, limited contact, new love interests), one would expect nonresidential fathers to be less involved in these activities.

Chapter 5 showed that divorce tends to have a disruptive effect on the parenting provided by mothers. We expect that family structure differences in parenting by fathers will contrast in certain respects with those reported for mothers. Although divorced women were about twice as likely as married women to display inept parenting, the vast majority of women, regardless of marital status, showed evidence of competent parenting. We anticipate a somewhat different pattern for fathers. Although nonresidential fathers are expected to show less involvement in parenting than fathers living in intact families, we presume that a low proportion of fathers in either divorced or intact families will show significant involvement in parenting.

Results

The measures for the constructs included in the analyses reported in this section are presented in Chapter 2. We found that divorce is significantly related to father's inept parenting. The Pearson correlation was .42 for boys and .29 for girls. The higher correlation for boys suggests that divorce may disrupt paternal involvement with sons more than daughters. Frequency distributions were run for the various items in the parenting scale to gain further insight into family structure differences in the parenting of fathers. The frequencies were run for divorced, happily married, and unhappily married fathers by gender of child. The results are presented in Table 6.1.

Table 6.1 shows the percentage of fathers from each of the three groups who were reported by their son or daughter as "almost never" engaging in the positive items listed in our parenting measure and as "almost always" engaging the negative items in the scale. The pattern of findings is quite similar for boys and girls. For virtually every item, divorced fathers show the highest percentage and happily married fathers show the lowest. The percentages for fathers in distressed marriages are in between those for the other two groups, although their scores are closer to those of the happily married than to those of the divorced.

Table 6.2 presents the mean scores on the Inept Parenting Scale for the three groups of fathers. The table shows scores of 44.46, 37.03, and 34.08 for the divorced, maritally distressed, and happily married, respectively. Results using ANOVA indicate that the means are significantly different at the .005 level. This finding is consonant with the pattern noted in Table 6.1. The two tables indicate that fathers who are in unhappy marriages are less involved in parenting than those who are happily married, but that fathers who have recently gone through a divorce are even less involved in parenting than those in an

TABLE 6.1 Percentage of Divorced, Unhappily Married, and Happily Married
Fathers Rated as "Almost Never" Engaging in Positive Parenting
and as "Almost Always" Engaging in Negative Parenting

	Divorced		Distressed Marriage		Happy Marriage	
	Boys	Girls	Boys	Girls	Boys	Girls
Positive Parenting						
Discusses events in child's life	52.6%	45.9%	32.5%	47.0%	23.6%	29.9%
Deals with parent-child problems	37.4	42.3	14.9	19.3	0.0	6.8
Provides emotional support	56.5	58.5	30.0	47.0	29.1	39.2
Asks child's opinion	48.5	47.7	20.0	30.1	18.2	24.1
Provides reasons for decisions	41.4	43.2	16.2	21.7	9.7	13.8
Considers child's view	44.5	36.9	17.5	22.9	9.7	12.6
Explains rules	44.5	45.9	20.0	18.1	9.7	10.3
Uses inductive reasoning	47.5	47.7	23.7	22.9	11.1	20.6
Reinforces successes	28.3	28.8	12.5	14.4	1.4	5.7
Negative Parenting						
Fails to follow through	70.7	71.2	38.7	48.2	34.7	41.4
Discipline is inconsistent	29.3	24.3	8.7	5.0	4.2	8.0
Discipline related to mood	41.5	36.9	38.7	32.5	27.7	25.2
Disagrees with mom's parenting	30.3	31.5	12.4	9.6	1.4	3.4
Problems never resolved	29.3	29.7	8.8	9.6	4.2	6.9

unhappy marriage. Thus, although marital distress has a negative
effect on the parenting of fathers, divorce appears to be even more
disruptive of a father's involvement in parenting.

Chapter 5 explores the relationship between family structure and
mother's parenting. Findings reported in that chapter indicate that
divorced women are about twice as likely as married women to engage
in dysfunctional parenting practices. Table 6.1 indicates that a similar
pattern holds for fathers. Although the two- to threefold difference
between fathers in the two family structures is roughly consonant with
the differences reported for mothers in Chapter 5, there is one striking
difference. Although divorced women are about twice as likely as

TABLE 6.2 Mean Scores on the Inept Parenting Scale for the Three Groups
             of Fathers

Divorced	Distressed Marriage	Happy Marriage
44.46	37.03	34.08

married women to display inept parenting, only a small proportion of
the women, regardless of marital status, evidence dysfunctional parenting practices. Table 6.1 indicates that the same is not true for
fathers.

Although Table 6.1 presents strong evidence of family structure
differences, it also shows that a rather high proportion of fathers in
both divorced and intact families are viewed by their adolescents as
not doing a very good job at parenting. Fathers are most involved in
families characterized by a happy marriage. Yet even in these families,
a third of the boys and more than 40% of the girls reported that their
father failed to follow through on threats of punishment. A similar
proportion of boys and girls indicated that their father almost never
talked to them about their problems. A quarter of the boys and 30%
of the girls said their father almost never talked to them about events
and activities taking place in their lives. These findings are consistent
with research suggesting that many American fathers, even when they
are present within the home, continue to be minimally involved in
parenting (Parke & Sterns, 1993).

Discussion

Studies suggest that fathers are devoting more time to their children
but that most father-child interaction is devoted to joking, roughhousing, or some other form of play (Parke & Sterns, 1993). Fathers have
shown little increase in the activities most consequential for child
adjustment. Competent parenting was defined in Chapter 5 as the
provision of a family environment conducive to children's cognitive,
emotional, and social development; such an environment requires
providing warmth and support, assisting with problems, providing
encouragement, setting and explaining standards, monitoring, and

enforcing discipline. Recent research indicates that mothers are still much more involved in these activities than fathers. Results from the present study provide further support for this view.

Findings reported in Chapter 5 indicate that divorced women are at greater risk than married women for dysfunctional parenting practices, but that only a small proportion of mothers, regardless of family structure, show significant involvement in inept parenting practices. The results presented in this chapter suggest a very different situation for fathers. Although divorced fathers show less competent parenting than married fathers, the prevalence of inept parenting is rather high for both groups of men. About a third of the boys and 40% of the girls living in intact families reported that their father never talks with them about problems and does not follow through on threats of punishment. More than half of both males and females from divorced families indicated that their father does not talk with them about problems; 70% reported that he fails to follow through on threats of punishment.

We found that marital satisfaction is related to quality of parenting among intact families. Fathers in distressed marriages are less involved in parenting than those in happy marriages. We also found, however, that dysfunctional parenting is more prevalent, in some instances two or three times as prevalent, among divorced fathers than among fathers in distressed marriages. This suggests that, in general, divorce disrupts a father's involvement in parenting more than marital distress.

In Chapter 5, we noted that custodial mothers often evidence a decline in quality of parenting following divorce. As a result of financial pressures and emotional distress, they tend to make fewer demands on children and to use less effective disciplinary strategies than those who are married. Given this tendency, it may be critical that fathers be involved in parenting following marital disruption so that they can counteract any decline in quality of parenting by the mother. Such involvement is probably most crucial for preventing conduct problems. This hypothesis is explored in subsequent chapters.

Although in general we feel that noncustodial fathers (as well as fathers in intact families) should be encouraged to play a greater role in the parenting of their children, we recognize that there are some instances where this is clearly not in the best interests of the mother or the children. The father may have a history of persistent domestic violence, criminal behavior, or substance abuse. In such cases, the family is likely better off if it has limited contact with the father. Short of a dramatic change in lifestyle, these fathers are likely incapable of behaving as competent parents.

There is also the possibility that high paternal involvement may foster increased conflict between former spouses (Furstenberg, Morgan, & Allison, 1987; Maccoby, Buchanan, Mnookin, & Dornbusch, 1993). Several studies have reported that persistent conflict between parents following divorce is related to depression and anxiety among children (Amato, 1993; Emery, 1988). Thus any benefits that children receive as a result of greater involvement by noncustodial fathers may be negated by the distress produced by enhanced parental conflict. Although this would seem to be a reasonable concern, there has been little investigation of the effect of paternal involvement on parental conflict.

Our own research suggests that nonresidential father involvement in parenting is associated with a reduction in parental conflict over time (Simons, Whitbeck, Beaman, & Conger, 1994). It is our guess that this takes place because most divorced fathers who continue to be involved in parenting try to behave in a manner that complements the parenting efforts of their former spouse. They do so if for no other reason than that they recognize that such an approach to parenting is in the best interests of their children. The majority of divorced fathers engage in little parenting; this is likely to foster feelings of anger and resentment on the part of the custodial mothers who are left with sole responsibility for child rearing. When the noncustodial father shares the parenting duties, the result is likely to be a reduction in maternal resentment and parental conflict.

Although we expect that father involvement in parenting reduces conflict for most divorced couples, there is undoubtedly a small proportion of cases where the father's attempt to function as a parent promotes conflict with his former spouse. For example, an angry father might approach the role of parent with the hidden agenda of undermining the status and authority of the mother. Fathers who behave in this fashion fail to display the parenting behaviors that are beneficial to children and their actions are likely to foster conflict with their former spouse. In such instances, the family may be better off if the noncustodial father is less involved in the role of parent. Thus, although in general we lament the fact that divorced fathers are often uninvolved in the parenting of their children, we realize that there are occasions where the characteristics of the father or the history of the relationship between the parents indicates that low involvement (albeit with stable child support) may be the preferred state of affairs.

7

Sibling Relationships

RAND D. CONGER

KATHERINE J. CONGER

Findings from the last two chapters demonstrate that family structure relates to disruptions in both maternal and paternal behavior. For mothers, family structure affects parenting through its negative influence on family economic conditions and through the mother's depressed mood. A history of antisocial behavior by mothers also increases risk for problems in parenting, both directly and indirectly through economic pressure and psychological distress. Although the analyses for fathers do not examine these mediating processes, they clearly show that divorced fathers demonstrate greater impairments in their interactions with their children than either happily or unhappily married fathers.

This chapter moves from consideration of the parent-child family subsystem to an examination of the influence of divorce on sibling relationships. Our interest in this issue derives from the recent recognition that sibling bonds may play a particularly important role in individual development (Dunn, 1984; Hetherington, 1994). Social and behavioral scientists have devoted increasing attention during the past decade to the multiple influences that siblings may have on one another's lives (e.g., Lamb & Sutton-Smith, 1982; Zukow, 1989).

Evidence from this research suggests that brothers and sisters affect each other's development in several areas, including both the acquisition of important competencies and the exacerbation of significant adjustment problems (Boer & Dunn, 1992). Research also has shown that siblings may play an important part in reducing or intensifying the potentially negative influence of life stresses, such as divorce, on child and adolescent emotional or behavioral problems (Conger, Conger, & Elder, 1994; Jenkins, 1992). With these ideas in mind, we turn to the specific research questions guiding this chapter.

A General Model of Family Structure and Sibling Interactions

The outcome of interest in these analyses concerns the degree to which siblings interact with one another in a hostile and coercive or warm and supportive manner. These dimensions of behavioral exchange appear to have particularly telling consequences for the long-term health of the sibling relationship and for the development of each member of the dyad. For example, Conger and her colleagues (1994) found that hostility and conflict in sibling interactions are associated with both conduct problems and emotional distress in the younger, early adolescent sibling in each pair. More generally, aggressive or hostile interactions between siblings have been found to predict clinical disturbance (externalizing and internalizing problems) and poor peer relations outside the home (Dunn, 1992; Hetherington & Clingempeel, 1992). Warm and supportive behaviors by siblings, on the other hand, appear to have developmental benefits for brothers and sisters. Behaviors of these types are associated with fewer symptoms of emotional distress and seem to protect against the adverse consequences of other life stresses, such as difficulties between parents (Conger, Conger, et al., 1994; Jenkins, 1992).

FAMILY STRUCTURE AND SIBLING RELATIONS

Given these contributions of sibling relationship dynamics to the well-being of children and adolescents, our central question to address here concerns the degree to which disruptions in marriage affect the

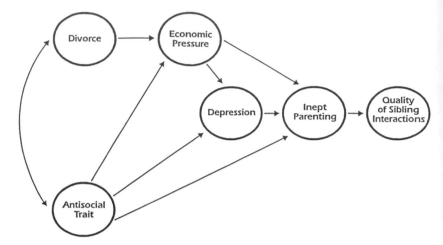

Figure 7.1. The Conceptual Model for the Influence of Family Disruption on Sibling Interactions

level of hostility and coercion or the level of warmth and support in sibling interactions. Although only limited research evidence exists regarding the link between family structure and sibling relationship quality, findings to date suggest that divorce increases negative interactions between brothers and sisters (Hetherington & Clingempeel, 1992). Concurrent with this growth in hostility, siblings in divorced families tend to disengage from one another, producing a loss of warmth and supportiveness. As parent conflict increases to the point of severing marital bonds, children in these disrupted families suffer reductions in the quality of their relationships as well. The research task in the present analyses is to investigate how marital conflict and separation lead to these developmentally compromising problems in sibling interactions.

As shown in Figure 7.1, we propose that the transition from an intact to a single-parent household will affect the quality of sibling interactions primarily through the influence of associated stressors on parenting behavior. The results reported in Chapter 5 demonstrate that marital disruption, combined with adult problem behaviors associated with divorce, leads to increased economic pressure in the family. Economic stress and adult antisocial behaviors, in turn, exacerbate poor parenting practices, both directly and indirectly through parent depressed mood. We hypothesize that decrements in appropriate child-rearing strategies provide the central mechanism through which the stress and adult personality processes associated with the transition in marital status affect the sibling relationship.

The reasoning behind the expected connections among divorce, adult antisocial trait, economic pressure, depression, and inept parenting is reviewed in earlier chapters (see especially Chapter 5) and will not be repeated here. It is important, however, to consider carefully the thesis that parenting practices are the nexus through which these divorce-related processes will affect siblings. We first consider the theoretical rationale for the hypothesis and then review empirical evidence related to the conceptual model.

PARENT-SIBLING COMPENSATION OR CONGRUITY?

In general, two opposing lines of thought have developed regarding the possible influence of disrupted parenting on sibling relationship quality. The first perspective, *the sibling compensation approach,* suggests that siblings may grow closer to one another as an adaptive response to difficulties with parents. The evidence for this view comes primarily from clinical observations that indicate that, when parents are burdened by significant stressors in their lives, they may be overwhelmed by their situation and thus neglectful of their parenting obligations (Bank & Kahn, 1982; Boer, Goedhart, & Treffers, 1992; Bossard & Boll, 1956). According to the compensation perspective, under such conditions siblings may provide one another with the warmth, support, nurturance, and assistance lacking from parents. If this compensatory view is correct, then we should find a positive relationship between inept parenting and warm and supportive sibling interactions in a test of the model presented in Figure 7.1. This perspective would also predict a negative association between inept parenting and hostile and coercive behaviors between siblings.

The *parent-sibling congruity approach* provides a quite different view of the expected relationship between parent-child and sibling relations. From this perspective, the quality of interaction in the sibling relationship should be similar to the quality of interaction in the parent-child relationship (Boer et al., 1992). The theoretical underpinnings of this approach are consistent with predictions from attachment, family systems, and social learning theory (Brody, Stoneman, & McCoy, 1994; Dunn, 1992; Hetherington, 1994; Patterson, 1984). According to attachment theory, children develop internal working models of relationships through interactions with their parents, especially mothers. These models guide their strategies for interacting with other people both within and outside the family. Thus, we would expect that when parents are hostile or withdrawn with their children, siblings in these families would approach their interactions in a similar fashion, consistent with their cognitive maps regarding the nature of interpersonal relationships.

Social learning theory would predict that, through processes of observation and direct training, siblings emulate the behaviors of their parents (Brody et al., 1994; Patterson, 1986b). As with the attachment approach, learning theory proposes that there will be congruity between the actions of parents toward children and brothers and sisters toward one another. Although the proposed causal mechanisms underlying the two perspectives are quite different, the nature of the relationships between interactions in the two family subsystems is quite similar. Family systems theory suggests this same interdependence in linkages between various family subsystems, again proposing congruity in the quality of interactions between parents and children and siblings. The congruity view, then, would predict path coefficients between parenting and sibling interactions (see Figure 7.1) opposite from those predicted by the compensatory approach. That is, if the congruity perspective is correct, inept parenting should be positively related to hostile and coercive sibling interactions and negatively related to sibling warmth and support.

Although there is some empirical support for the compensatory hypothesis (Boer et al., 1992; Dunn, 1992; East & Rook, 1992; Hetherington & Clingempeel, 1992; Stocker, 1994), the preponderance of evidence in the recent literature is most consistent with the congruity approach. For example, Brody et al. (1994) found that relatively more positive and less negative parent-child relationships predict more positive sibling relations across time. They also found that cohesive families with low marital conflict predict greater sibling relationship quality. Similarly, Conger and her associates (1994) found a strong positive association between mother or father hostility toward children and hostile interactions between siblings. In a study that examined not only the quality of parent-child relations but also differential treatment of siblings by parents, Boer et al. (1992) found (a) that positive, supportive parenting was positively related to supportive sibling interactions and negatively related to sibling hostility; (b) no evidence supporting the sibling compensation hypothesis; and (c) no evidence supporting the idea that differential parental treatment of siblings influences the quality of the sibling relationship.

On balance, then, the empirical evidence suggests little support for the compensatory approach to understanding the link between parent-child and sibling interactions. Recent findings indicate a great deal of congruity between the quality of parent-child interactions and sibling relationship dynamics. Based on these results, in the empirical test of the model proposed in Figure 7.1, we expected that inept parenting would be positively related to hostility and coercion in sibling interactions and negatively related to sibling warmth and support for one another. Regarding these predictions, our inept parenting construct includes indicators reflecting a hostile, uncaring, inconsistent, and coercive parenting style (harsh discipline, low consistency in discipline, low monitoring or involvement, and hostile parenting behaviors); thus we would expect congruous interactions between siblings that would be high on hostility and low on warmth and involvement. Although the analyses focus on the role of mothers in these predicted sets of relationships, we also present findings for fathers in relation to the proposed theoretical model. The results for fathers, of course, are limited by the data available for them.

Results

The measures used in the analyses are presented in Chapter 2. The first step in the analyses involved a comparison of sibling interaction quality across the types of families identified earlier (Chapter 5): divorced, distressed, and happily married. If, as the model in Figure 7.1 proposes, family structure is related to the quality of behavioral exchange between siblings, then these basic comparisons should reveal these differences. Specifically, the model hypothesizes that sibling interactions should be qualitatively different in single-parent families

TABLE 7.1 Comparisons of Mean Levels of Sibling Interaction Quality by Family Type

| | Family Type | | | | | | |
| | Divorced | | Distressed Marriage | | Happily Married | | Uni- |
Sibling Interaction Quality	Target Boys	Target Girls	Target Boys	Target Girls	Target Boys	Target Girls	variate F (2,479)
Hostility-Coercion							
1. Target to sib, family report	.52	.41	−.33	−.03	−.24	−.60	12.35***
2. Sib to target, family report	.40	.41	−.20	−.10	−.13	−.60	27.85***
3. Sibling dyad, observer report	47.86	50.57	45.42	48.33	46.46	44.87	2.57$^+$
Warmth-Support							
1. Target to sib, family report	−.67	.13	−.21	−.01	.20	.64	6.85***
2. Sib to target, family report	−.62	.01	−.11	.21	.05	.56	5.58**
3. Sibling dyad, observer report	47.80	51.43	48.83	50.68	48.48	51.81	0.15 (n.s.)

NOTE: Multivariate $F (12,942) = 3.46, p < .001$
$+p < .10$; $*p < .05$; $**p < .01$; $***p < .001$
Because the family report measures are standardized, negative means are possible.

as compared with intact families. The results of the descriptive analyses are reported in Table 7.1. In the table, we consider separately each indicator of hostility and coercion and warmth and support used in later tests of the overall conceptual model. These measures are based on either family member reports (i.e., target and sibling) or on the ratings provided by trained observers. Findings are separated by the gender of the target child in each family. The target children were 9th graders in the intact families and 8th or 9th graders in the single-parent families. By separating the analyses by gender, we assured that at least one male was in every sibling dyad with a target boy and at least one female was in every dyad with a target girl. To the extent that gender tempers the quality of sibling interactions, this difference should be revealed with these subdivisions in the data.

As shown in Table 7.1, the trends in the mean scores for sibling hostility and coercion and warmth and support suggest that brothers and sisters in the divorced families engage in more negative and less positive interactions than those in the other two family types. This interpretation of the pattern in average levels of interaction quality receives initial support from the significant multivariate F test ($p <$ .001) reported in Table 7.1. The results (row 1) show that the target child's mean level of hostility to his or her sibling, as reported by both the target and the sibling, is highest in the divorced families (.52 for boys, .41 for girls), lowest in happily married families when the target child is a girl (–.60), and in between these extremes in the maritally distressed families (–.33 for boys, –.03 for girls). The univariate F test of 12.35 ($p < .001$) attests to the significant differences in this specific set of means. Moreover, the Duncan's Multiple Range Test confirms that the siblings in the divorced families reported a higher mean level of target to sibling hostility than siblings in the other two family types ($p <$ .01). There is no significant difference in these scores for siblings in the distressed compared to the happily married families. Thus, these initial findings are consistent with the model in Figure 7.1 in that family structure accounts for interactional differences in sibling relations.

Results reported in the second row of Table 7.1 tell a very similar story when the focus shifts to brother and sister reports of the sibling's degree of hostile and coercive behavior to the target adolescent. Again, the univariate F test for this set of means is statistically significant and the Multiple Range Test confirms that the difference in scores results from the higher levels of hostility in the divorced families ($p < .01$). There is no significant difference in the average level of negative sibling interaction in the happily married compared to the distressed families. Although the univariate test for observed hostility in the sibling dyads (row 3) is only marginally significant ($p < .10$), the Multiple Range Test again shows that the siblings in divorced families were observed to be more hostile than those in either of the other family types ($p < .05$). Again, there was no significant difference for observed sibling hostility between the happily married and distressed intact families.

The results for the various indicators of hostility and coercion in sibling interaction, then, are consistent with the model in Figure 7.1. That is, boys and girls in divorced families, by every measure, are more hostile toward one another than siblings in intact families, regardless of the degree of happiness or dissatisfaction in marriage. These findings are most consistent for families in which the target child is a girl. For example, the mean scores in row 2 of Table 7.1 show that sibling hostility to girl targets is highest in divorced families (.41), next highest in maritally distressed families (–.10), and lowest in happily married families (–.60). This same pattern obtains for female target adolescents for every measure of hostility and coercion. For families in which the target adolescent is a boy, the means for hostility and coercion are actually slightly higher in the happily married than distressed families, although these differences are not statistically significant. Other analyses show that there are no target gender differences in the overall level of sibling hostility and coercion nor are there any gender × family-type interaction effects.

The last three rows in Table 7.1 contain the mean scores for warm and supportive sibling interactions based on the same reporters as for hostile and coercive behaviors. Again, the trends in the means suggest that siblings in the divorced families differ from those in the intact families. For example, the average score for target boys' positive behaviors to siblings, as reported by target and sibling, was lowest in the divorced families (–.67), next lowest in the maritally distressed group (–.21), and highest for target boys living with parents who were happily married (.20). The univariate F test for this set of means was highly significant ($p < .01$) and the Multiple Range Test confirmed that the divorced group was significantly different from the other two family types ($p < .01$), which were not significantly different from one another. The findings for sibling-to-target warmth and support were essentially the same as those for target to sibling, with the exception that the Multiple Range Test for the difference between the divorced and intact families was significant at the .05 level. Again, the two types of intact families were not significantly different on sibling warmth and support. Finally, the results show that there are no significant differences in observed warmth and support across the three family types. We return to this inconsistency in the findings in the discussion section of the chapter.

To complete the analyses for mean differences in sibling interaction quality, we examined the influence of gender on the degree of supportiveness in sibling relations. An examination of the mean scores in Table 7.1 suggests that sibling dyads containing at least one girl (the target adolescent) are higher in warmth and supportiveness than dyads containing at least one boy. For example, for divorced families, the average score for target-to-sibling supportiveness was –.67 for target boys and .13 for target girls. This pattern repeats itself for all the measures of sibling positive interactions. The univariate F tests for a gender main effect were significant for each measure of warmth and supportiveness, ranging from 10.39, $p < .001$ for family reported sibling behavior to 11.26, $p < .001$ for observed warmth and supportiveness in the sibling dyad. Because there are no significant gender-by-family-type interaction effects, this pattern of gender differences is consistent across family types.

THE MEDIATIONAL MODEL FOR MOTHERS

In the above section, we demonstrate that family structure is related to the quality of sibling interactions. The results are inconsistent with the stress compensation model in that residence in a single-parent family, presumably the more stressful family type for children, leads to less rather than more sibling supportiveness and greater rather than less sibling hostility. In the next series of analyses, we directly tested the association between family structure and family stress and added the parenting measures that allow us to examine the congruity hypothesis. As noted earlier, this hypothesis suggests that stressful family conditions will disrupt effective parenting practices, which, in turn, will have an adverse influence on sibling relations. The interactions between siblings are expected to become less harmonious as a function of the impaired relationship between parents and children.

Because the earlier analyses show a significant association between family structure and siblings' hostility toward one another, if that significant relationship is no longer present when we enter the stress and parenting variables outlined in Figure 7.1 into a structural equation model, we can conclude that this set of variables explains or mediates the tie between family structure and sibling conflict. The findings for the structural equation model using maximum likelihood estimation are reported in Figure 7.2. The conceptual model provided in Figure 7.1 guided the analyses. As expected, both single-parent status and mother's antisocial trait significantly predict economic pressure (the standardized path coefficients are .26 and .38, respectively). The antisocial construct also predicts mother's depressed mood and inept parenting, whereas the influence of single-parent

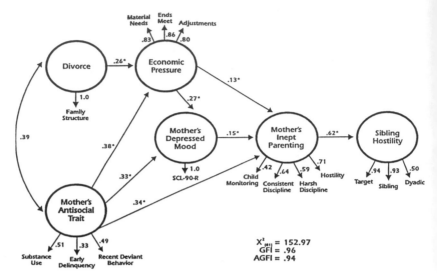

Figure 7.2. The Mediational Model for Mother's Inept Parenting and Sibling Hostility (standardized path coefficients, *$p < .05$)

status is mediated entirely through its association with economic pressure. Separate analyses show that, with economic pressure in the model, being divorced is not significantly related to any of the other endogenous constructs.

Consistent with the conceptual model, there is no direct path from mother's antisocial trait to sibling hostility. Also as expected, economic pressure affects inept parenting both directly and indirectly through mother's depressed mood. Economic pressure, however, does not directly relate to sibling hostility. The final path coefficient of .62 between inept parenting and sibling hostility provides strong support for the congruity and mediational hypotheses. That is, divorced status, family stress, and maternal personality characteristics relate to sibling behavior indirectly through parenting (the mediational hypothesis). Moreover, parenting that is hostile and harsh, as well as inconsistent and uninvolved, is associated with hostile behaviors between siblings (the congruity hypothesis). In addition, all the factor loadings on constructs are statistically significant and there is a

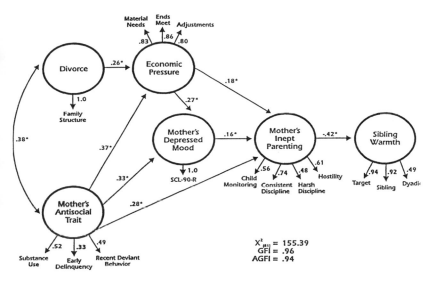

Figure 7.3. The Mediational Model for Mother's Inept Parenting and Sibling Warmth (standardized path coefficients, *$p < .05$)

good match between the data and the conceptual model (the Adjusted Goodness of Fit Index, AGFI, was .94).

The next set of analyses relate to sibling warmth and supportiveness. In this instance, the congruity hypothesis would predict that parenting that is uninvolved and hostile (i.e., specific dimensions of the inept parenting construct) would undermine close relations between siblings. Moreover, the mediational hypothesis would again predict that the influence of prior variables in the model would relate to sibling warmth and supportiveness only through maternal behavior. The findings reported in Figure 7.3 are consistent with the conceptual (mediational) model and with the congruity hypothesis. The results of mother's parenting behavior are consistent with the findings reported in Figure 7.2. In addition, only the parenting variable is directly associated with sibling warmth with a path coefficient of −.42. The results and inferences to be drawn are consistent with those for sibling hostility. As earlier, the data show a good fit with the mediational model (AGFI = .94) and the loadings on all constructs are statistically significant.

THE MEDIATIONAL MODEL FOR FATHERS

Although limitations in the data preclude a complete analysis of the mediational model for fathers, the paths from divorced status through father's parenting to sibling interactions can be evaluated. In considering the findings, one must keep in mind that the measure of parenting is far more limited because, for noncustodial fathers, there are no observational data. Thus, for consistency across fathers from intact and divorced families, we had to rely on target self-report alone for a parenting variable. In addition, the measure had to be restricted to behaviors the father could engage in even if living separate from his children (see Chapter 6 for a description of the dimensions of the measure). Figure 7.4 provides an analysis of the mediational model for fathers.

Panel A in Figure 7.4 provides the results for sibling hostility. Before considering these findings, note that the zero-order regression coefficient between divorced status and sibling hostility is .22 ($p <$ .05). To the extent that this direct path is reduced by the inclusion of father's parenting in the model, one can conclude that father's behavior mediates the relation between family structure and sibling hostility. As shown in panel A, the path coefficient from divorced status to father's inept parenting is .35 and the path coefficient from parenting to sibling hostility is .21. Even with parenting in the model, however, there is still a direct and significant association (.14) between a history of divorce and sibling interactions. The difference between this direct path and the original zero-order relationship (.08) suggests that father's parenting accounts for about 36% of the relationship between divorced status and sibling hostile interactions. We believe this is an extremely conservative finding given the necessary limitations in the parenting measure.

Turning to panel B, the results show that no direct path exists between divorced status and sibling warmth with father's parenting in the structural model. As before, divorce relates to greater inept parenting, which, in turn, is associated with reduced warmth and supportiveness in sibling interactions. Because the zero-order relationship between divorce and sibling warmth is negative and statistically significant (−.13, $p < .05$), we can conclude that the father's parenting explains or mediates the connection between the two. Especially

Panel A: Sibling Hostility

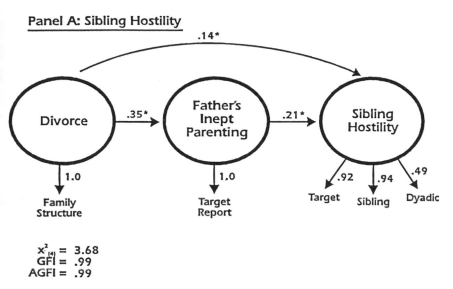

$x^2_{(4)} = 3.68$
GFI = .99
AGFI = .99

Panel B: Sibling Warmth

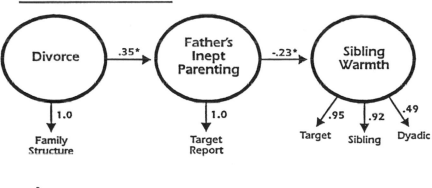

$x^2_{(4)} = 24.25$
GFI = .98
AGFI = .93

Figure 7.4. Family Structure, Father's Inept Parenting, and Sibling Interactions (standardized regression coefficients, $*p < .05$)

important, the results for father's parenting replicate the findings for mothers in that sibling interactions are congruous with paternal behavior. For both the hostility and warmth models in Figure 7.4, the fit indexes suggest a good match between the mediational hypothesis and the data (AGFI = .99 for hostility, .93 for warmth).

Discussion

The theoretical model that guides the present analyses (Figure 7.1) proposes that family structure should affect sibling interactions through a series of intervening processes. Divorced status is predicted to increase risk for economic pressures in single-mother households. These pressures, in turn, are expected to increase mothers' depressive symptoms and to disrupt effective parenting practices. Depressed mood also is predicted to undermine mothers' roles as parents. The final leg in the model proposes that child-rearing practice is the key variable that links family structure to the quality of sibling interactions and relationships.

An important corollary of divorce, mothers' antisocial behavior trait, is the second exogenous variable in the theoretical model. This construct adds an individual differences factor to the social conditions of family structure and economic difficulties. Mothers with a history of antisocial behaviors are predicted to suffer greater economic problems, to demonstrate greater depressed mood, and to be less effective in their child-rearing practices. Again, parenting behaviors are expected to provide the proximal mechanism through which the earlier steps in these mediational processes affect the quality of the sibling relationship.

An especially important issue concerns the direction of the relationship between parenting and sibling interactions. Previous theory and study suggest two opposing points of view. On the one hand, the clinical literature suggests that during stressful times, such as those associated with the transition from an intact to a single-parent family, siblings may come together to shield one another from the decrements in parenting often associated with these types of events. This compensatory perspective, then, would propose that the inept parenting construct in Figure 7.1 should be positively related to warmth and support between siblings and negatively related to hostility and coercion. That is, siblings should become more supportive and less hostile toward one another to compensate for stress-related disruptions in parenting behaviors.

The congruity approach, on the other hand, makes an opposite set of predictions. According to this view, siblings emulate the behaviors of their parents. Thus, if parents demonstrate a hostile, uninvolved style of interaction with their children, as indicated by high scores on the inept parenting construct, then siblings should follow a similar path and be more hostile and less warm toward one another. Because past research provides greater evidence for the congruity perspective, we expected that the results from the present analysis would be consonant with this approach.

The present findings are supportive of the overall mediational model and of the congruity hypothesis regarding the association between parent and sibling behaviors. As a first step in assessing the overall model, we examined mean differences in the quality of sibling interactions using reports by each sibling and by trained observers. These analyses contrast patterns of sibling behaviors for three family types: single-parent, intact but unhappily married, and intact and happily married. Consistent with study hypotheses, there are significant differences in terms of sibling hostility and coercion and warmth and support between single-parent and intact families, but no significant differences between the two types of intact families. Siblings in single-parent families are less supportive and more hostile toward one another.

Thus, when it comes to the influence of marital ties on the quality of sibling relationships, these data suggest that it is the actual disruption of marriage rather than the degree of distress in intact marriages that most adversely affects relations between brothers and sisters. To the extent that divorce represents the extreme of marital distress, the results indicate a threshold effect such that only the highest levels of marital difficulties have a demonstrable, direct influence on sibling interactions. It may well be the case that intact families close to divorce would demonstrate the same problems in parenting and sibling behaviors that we observed here for the divorced families. The data available for this study do not allow such a fine-grained comparison, however.

Interestingly, gender has no affect on the degree of hostility and coercion in behavioral exchanges involving siblings. Nor does gender interact with family structure to influence the level of animosity within these sibling dyads. For warm, supportive behaviors, however, gender plays an important role. Sibling dyads that contained at least one girl demonstrated higher levels of positive social exchange than dyads containing at least one male. Even with these adolescent boys and girls, then, the often-noted tendency of women to demonstrate greater warmth, supportiveness, and nurturance than men in interactions with family members finds support in these results. There is no gender-by-family-type interaction effect for warmth and support, however, suggesting that these gender-linked behaviors are not a response to stressful life circumstances. Rather, they appear to represent a consistent difference between boys, girls, and their siblings.

The findings for mean differences in the quality of sibling interactions as a function of family type and gender are consistent with earlier research (e.g., Hetherington & Clingempeel, 1992). The next step was to examine the mediational pathways through which the transition to divorce affects sibling relations. In general, the findings are consistent with the model outlined in Figure 7.1. Each of the proposed pathways from family status to mother's inept parenting is statistically significant and in the expected direction. Moreover, the final link in the model, from parenting to quality of sibling interaction, is consistent with the congruity hypothesis. That is, parents who are less involved and more harsh with their children have children who are more hostile and less supportive of one another. Also important, there is no direct association between family structure and sibling interactions with the parenting construct in the model, providing strong support for the mediational nature of the proposed theoretical model.

Moreover, mothers who demonstrate a history of greater antisocial behavior experience more economic problems, more depressive symptoms, and greater impairments in parenting. As expected, inept parenting is the final mechanism in the process through which the antisocial trait influences sibling interactions. As is the case for family structure, and as predicted by the theoretical model, there is no direct path from mother's antisocial behavior to the quality of interactions in the sibling dyad; this again provides significant support for the mediational nature of the proposed theoretical model.

As the last step in the analyses, we examined the mediational model for fathers' parenting behaviors. Because of the limitations in data available for noncustodial fathers, this part of the investigation had to deal with an extremely simple model involving only marital status, father's parenting (as reported by the target adolescent), and the quality of behavioral interactions between these boys and girls. Even with these limitations, however, the findings provide preliminary support for the hypothesized model. That is, the relationship between family structure and sibling interactions is entirely mediated by father's parenting for warm and supportive sibling behaviors and substantially mediated for hostile and coercive behaviors. These findings need to be replicated with more complete information on custodial and noncustodial fathers in future studies.

Although consistent with study hypotheses, these findings must be interpreted with some caution. First, the sample itself is limited. The results must be replicated with more diverse samples living in urban as well as rural locations before we can be assured of their generalizability. Second, these findings relate only to a limited number of possible dimensions of sibling relationships. Future research regarding the influence of the divorce process needs to consider specific roles that brothers and sisters play in each other's lives, such as teacher or caretaker, as well as sibling perceptions of their relationship. Such research will demonstrate whether the transition to divorce has a relatively narrow or quite broad effect on sibling relationships. Finally, the test of the compensation and congruity hypotheses performed here relates only to a community sample. Evidence for sibling compensation may more likely be provided in clinical situations involving extremely stressful situations (Dunn, 1992).

PART IV

CHILD OUTCOMES

8

Conduct Problems

RONALD L. SIMONS

WEI CHAO

Numerous studies have examined the relationship between divorce and child adjustment. Although the differences are often not large, this research has established that children from divorced families generally show poorer patterns of adjustment than those from intact families. Divorce has been shown, for example, to place children at greater risk for delinquency and substance use, early sex, pregnancy, school failure and dropout, and emotional problems (Amato & Keith, 1991b; Emery, 1988; Krantz, 1988; McLanahan & Booth, 1989). Furthermore, there is evidence that these difficulties persist into adulthood. Several studies have found that adults who experienced parental divorce as children tend to exhibit lower socioeconomic attainment, greater marital instability, and poorer psychological adjustment than persons who grew up in continuously intact families (Amato & Keith, 1991a; McLanahan & Sandefur, 1994). These findings do not mean, of course, that most children of divorce develop adjustment problems. Indeed, this is clearly not the case. The majority of children in both disrupted and intact families show healthy patterns of development.

Child adjustment problems have low base rates. Although rates vary by type of problem, the prevalence of most difficulties is less than 10%.

Although prevalence is usually relatively low regardless of family structure, it tends to be higher, often two or three times higher, in disrupted than in intact families. For example, the prevalence of a particular child adjustment problem might be 5% for intact families and 15% for divorced families. Although such a finding would indicate that the majority of children in both intact and disrupted families fail to develop the problem, it also suggests that there is a threefold increase in the risk of developing the difficulty among children of divorce. Thus, the finding that the majority of children from disrupted families display normal patterns of development does not negate the contention that family disruption significantly increases a child's risk for psychosocial difficulties.

This chapter, as well as the three that follow it, examine family structure differences in adjustment among the adolescents in our Iowa sample. Findings from previous chapters are used to develop explanations for the higher level of problems for children whose parents are divorced. This chapter focuses on adolescent delinquency. We begin by briefly reviewing past research on the relationship between family structure and child conduct problems. We then develop hypotheses regarding the manner in which parental adjustment and parenting practices explain these family structure differences. Finally, we test these hypotheses using structural equation modeling and multiple regression procedures.

Family Structure and Conduct Problems

Probably the strongest evidence for a link between divorce and child adjustment has been provided by Amato and Keith (1991b). They completed a meta-analysis of 92 studies concerned with the effect of family structure on children. These studies included data on more than 13,000 children. Although the investigation found rather small effects for some outcomes, the average effect size for conduct problems was .23. This indicates that children of divorce score about one quarter of a standard deviation higher on conduct problems than those living in intact families. Most researchers would consider this to be a moderately strong association between family structure and child behavior problems.

Even stronger effect sizes emerged when Amato and Keith (1991b) completed their meta-analysis taking into account gender of child. The average effect size was .40 for samples of boys, .32 for samples of girls, and .18 for mixed samples. Although the difference in effect size between girls and boys was not statistically significant, the effect size for the mixed samples was significantly smaller than those based on same-sex samples. This finding is probably a consequence of the fact that parents of boys are less likely to divorce (Morgan, Lye, & Condran, 1988) and boys are more likely than girls to display behavior problems (Emery, 1988; Simons, Whitbeck, & Wu, 1994). In a random sample of families, such a pattern of associations would operate to suppress the association between family structure and child antisocial behavior. Thus it appears essential that researchers control for gender of child when examining the relationship between family structure and delinquency. When such controls are introduced, there is a rather strong association between family disruption and child conduct problems.

Based on past research showing that males are at greater risk for antisocial behavior than females (Gottfredson & Hirschi, 1990), some have speculated that the association between family structure and conduct problems may be higher for boys than for girls. Amato and Keith (1991b) investigated this possibility in their meta-analysis and failed to find a gender difference. Their results indicate that boys and girls do not differ in terms of the increased risk for conduct problems posed by family disruption. This does not mean that boys and girls in disrupted families show the same prevalence of conduct problems. Boys are more apt to display conduct problems than girls; these gender differences probably exist regardless of family structure. Although boys may show higher rates of misconduct than girls, Amato and Keith's (1991b) findings indicate that the association between family structure and conduct problems, or the difference in the prevalence of misconduct for children in divorced versus intact families, is the same regardless of gender. We will try to replicate this finding in the analyses presented in this chapter.

The Mediating Role of Mother's Parenting

Both control theories (Gottfredson & Hirschi, 1990; Hirschi, 1969) and social learning theories (Elliott, Huizinga, & Menard,

1989; Patterson, 1982; Patterson et al., 1992) posit that quality of parenting has a significant effect on the probability of conduct problems. Although these two theoretical perspectives differ in some important respects, they both assert that inept parenting (i.e., hostility, little monitoring, inconsistent discipline) increases the probability that adolescents will be impulsive, defiant, and risk taking. Such youths find delinquent acts more alluring than youths who have been socialized to possess strong internal controls. Furthermore, poorly socialized adolescents are attracted to peers with the same rebellious characteristics. Such affiliation is particularly apt to take place when parents exercise little supervision or control. Involvement with deviant peers, in turn, leads to amplification of the adolescent's antisocial tendencies, because the deviant peer group serves as a training ground for delinquent and criminal behavior.

In other words, inept parenting is viewed as having both a direct and an indirect effect on adolescent delinquent behavior. It directly contributes to oppositional and defiant tendencies that make delinquent behavior attractive to the child and it allows the youth to drift into association with peers who encourage antisocial behavior. Several cross-sectional and longitudinal studies provide support for this perspective (Elliott et al., 1989; Patterson et al., 1992; Sampson & Laub, 1993; Simons, Johnson, & Conger, 1994; Simons, Wu, et al., 1994). We expect to replicate this pattern of results in this chapter. A significant relationship is expected between quality of mother's parenting and adolescent delinquent behavior. In addition, we expect that mother's parenting affects delinquency indirectly by influencing the adolescent's probability of affiliating with deviant peers.

There is strong evidence that family structure is related to quality of a mother's parenting. The results of several studies (Amato, 1987; Astone & McLanahan, 1991; Capaldi & Patterson, 1991; Furstenberg & Nord, 1985; Hetherington et al., 1982; McLanahan & Sandefur, 1994; Thomson et al., 1992), as well as findings reported in Chapter 5, provide compelling evidence that divorced mothers tend to make fewer demands on children, engage in less monitoring, and use less effective disciplinary strategies than married mothers. As noted in Chapter 5, this difference in quality of supervision and control appears to be a function of the high stress and impaired psychological functioning experienced by many divorced women.

If low monitoring and inconsistent discipline are an important determinant of child conduct problems, and if divorced women are more likely to engage in such parenting than married women, it follows that the relationship between marital disruption and adolescent delinquent behavior may be explained, at least in part, by differences in parenting practices (Brody & Forehand, 1988; Hetherington et al., 1982). This hypothesis is investigated in this chapter. We expect that quality of mother's supervision and control mediates much of the relationship between family structure and adolescent delinquent behavior. Furthermore, we believe it likely that the effect of negative life events and economic pressure on adolescent delinquent behavior is indirect through their disruptive effect on parenting. We view quality of parental involvement as the most fundamental determinant of a child's psychological well-being. Hence, we presume that family financial hardship and stressful life changes only increase an adolescent's probability of conduct problems to the extent that they have a corrosive effect on parental involvement.

Mother's Antisocial Behavior

Chapter 3 presents data that indicate that divorced women are more likely than married women to participate in behaviors considered deviant, risky, or irresponsible by the general population. Although prevalence is low for both groups, the divorced are two to three times more likely than the married to engage in such actions. Chapters 4 and 5 show that these family structure differences in antisocial tendencies help explain the high levels of economic strain, stressful life events, emotional and physical distress, and inept parenting seen among divorced women. In this chapter, we are concerned with the manner in which this overrepresentation of antisocial tendencies among divorced women may contribute to the increased risk for conduct problems seen among children of disrupted families. There are two ways in which this might occur.

First, there may be a modeling effect. Longitudinal studies have found evidence of continuity of antisocial behavior across generations within families (Eron, Huesmann, Dubow, Romanoff, & Yarmel, 1987; Robins, 1966; West & Farrington, 1977). Social scientists often assume that this intergenerational transmission occurs via modeling. Given the multitude of studies showing that children often imitate actions displayed by others (Bandura, 1977, 1986), these researchers argue that children might be expected to adopt antisocial behaviors modeled by their parents.

In contrast, other researchers have argued that child conduct problems have little to do with the behavior modeled by others, including parents (Gottfredson & Hirschi, 1990; Patterson et al., 1992). Patterson et al. (1992), for example, argue that, as a result of observing media depictions, playground events, family interaction, and the like, virtually all children are exposed to models of aggressive, antisocial behavior. Patterson et al. suggest that the central question, therefore, is why some children choose to perform antisocial actions they have seen modeled, whereas others do not. The answer, these researchers assert, relates to quality of parenting. Parents inadvertently foster antisocial behavior to the extent that they are hostile and uninvolved and engage in inconsistent discipline.

Patterson et al. note that antisocial parents are particularly apt to display this inept approach to parenting. Findings consistent with this contention are presented in Chapter 5. Patterson and his colleagues argue that this relationship between parental antisocial tendencies and quality of parenting accounts for the intergenerational transmission of antisocial behavior. Children of antisocial parents develop conduct problems because they are subject to inept parenting practices. Consistent with this idea, two studies report that quality of parenting mediates the relationship between parent and child antisocial behavior (Capaldi & Patterson, 1991; Caspi & Elder, 1988).

In this chapter, we are concerned with identifying the manner in which overrepresentation of antisocial tendencies among divorced parents may contribute to the increased risk for conduct problems seen among children of disrupted families. Toward this end, we will examine the extent to which the effect of mother's antisocial tendencies is indirect through ineffective parenting practices. Patterson's mediation model will be supported if the association between parent and child antisocial behavior is eliminated when quality of parenting is introduced as a control. On the other hand, the findings will support a modeling explanation if a significant relationship remains between mother's antisocial behavior and adolescent delinquency after controlling for quality of mother's parenting.

The effect of the mother's antisocial behavior on adolescent conduct problems may vary by gender of child. Past research has shown that children are more heavily influenced by behavior modeled by persons of their own sex (Bandura, 1977, 1986). This suggests that girls may be more likely than boys to emulate antisocial actions displayed by the mother. Hence, it may be that for boys the effect of mother's antisocial behavior is mediated by quality of parenting, whereas for girls there is a modeling effect in addition to any indirect influence through parenting. This possibility is considered in the analyses presented below.

The Mediating Role of Father's Parenting

Both social scientists and lay people often speculate that low involvement by noncustodial fathers may account, at least in part, for the high prevalence of conduct problems among children of divorce. Although the idea that child adjustment is facilitated by involvement by nonresidential fathers is intuitively appealing, there is actually little empirical evidence for the claim (Emery, 1988; Furstenberg & Cherlin, 1991). In a recent review of research regarding this issue, Amato (1993) identifies 16 studies that support the hypothesis that frequency of contact with the noncustodial father is positively related to child adjustment. An equal number of studies fail to support the hypothesis, however. Indeed, seven of the studies in the latter group find frequency of visitation with the noncustodial father to be negatively related to child adjustment. Thus, overall, the evidence suggests that frequency of visitation by fathers is not related to child adjustment.

Perhaps this finding should have been anticipated; there is little reason to expect that simply having contact with the nonresidential father would significantly affect a child's development. The quality, rather than simply the quantity, of interaction with this parent is likely the key to understanding his affect on child adjustment. Contrary to this idea, several studies that examine closeness of relationship with the father and child outcomes have failed to find significant effects. Furstenberg et al. (1987), for example, found that child reports of closeness to the father, such as reports of frequency of contact, are unrelated to child developmental outcomes.

One might argue, however, that closeness per se is not the important dimension when assessing the quality of the relationship between fathers and their children. Past research suggests that nonresidential fathers often behave toward their children more as an adult friend or relative than as a parent (Arendell, 1986; Furstenberg & Nord, 1985; Hetherington et al., 1976). Much of the time with their children is spent watching TV, attending movies, going out to eat, and the like. Although such interaction is apt to enhance feelings of closeness, there is little reason to believe that it will have a major effect on child adjustment. Fathers who limit their involvement to such activities would not be expected to exert any more influence on the developmental outcomes of their children than that exercised by other friendly adults (e.g., uncles, grandparents, mother's boyfriend). On the other hand, these fathers may affect child adjustment to the extent that they continue to play the role of parent. As noted earlier, single mothers often show deficiencies in the area of monitoring and discipline. Thus, nonresidential fathers might be expected to influence child development to the extent that they provide assistance with child socialization and control.

We tested this idea by forming a scale that assessed the involvement of nonresidential fathers in activities such as emphasizing moral principles, conducting inductive reasoning, reinforcing appropriate behavior, enacting problem solving, and enforcing consistent discipline. This measure was inversely related to adolescent conduct problems even after taking into account quality of mother's parenting, parental conflict, and family income (Simons, Whitbeck, Beaman, et al., 1994). The effect was particularly strong for boys. A father does not need to live with his child to engage in such parenting practices, but fathers in intact families are undoubtedly more likely to display these behaviors than nonresidential fathers. This chapter examines the extent to which the low level of emotional support, guidance, problem solving, and consistent discipline provided by many nonresidential fathers helps explain the high prevalence of conduct problems among children of divorce.

Results

The measures for the constructs used in these analyses are presented in Chapter 2. Although most social scientists acknowledge that paren-

TABLE 8.1 Mean Delinquency Scores for Children of Divorce, Children With Happily Married Parents, and Children With Unhappily Married Parents

	Divorced		Distressed Marriage		Happy Marriage	
	X	N	X	N	X	N
Boys	28.90	99	25.37	80	25.90	71
Girls	26.05	111	24.81	83	24.00	87

Note: For both boys and girls, the mean delinquency score is significantly higher for children from divorced families than for children from intact families.

tal divorce increases a child's chances of developing conduct problems, there is much disagreement regarding the magnitude of this increased risk. Thus, our first concern was with describing the degree to which divorce increases an adolescent's risk for delinquency. We began examination of this issue by comparing the delinquency scores for children from divorced families with those for children from intact families high or low on marital distress. Comparing adolescents from divorced families to adolescents whose parents were either happily or unhappily married allowed us to establish that it is family structure, not simply parental discord, that accounts for any differences obtained. Intact families were identified as high or low on marital distress using the criteria described in Chapter 5. Table 8.1 shows mean delinquency scores for adolescents from the three types of families. The results are presented separately by gender given the consistent evidence from prior research that boys are more likely to engage in delinquent behavior than girls.

Table 8.1 shows that there is no significant difference in average level of delinquency between children whose parents are happily married and those whose parents are unhappily married. On the other hand, the table indicates that parental divorce is associated with increased involvement in delinquent behavior. Children with divorced parents report significantly higher levels of delinquency than children with either happily or unhappily married parents. This is true for both boys and girls.

Although this analysis suggests that marital disharmony has little effect on adolescent conduct problems, group comparisons involving

TABLE 8.2 Prevalence of Delinquency for Adolescents Living in Different Types of Families

Indicators of Delinquency	Divorced		Distressed Marriage		Happy Marriage	
	Boys	Girls	Boys	Girls	Boys	Girls
Ran away from home	3.0%	7.2%	1.1%	1.9%	.0%	1.9%
Drunk in a public place	11.1	14.4	5.5	9.3	4.2	5.3
Shoplifted item worth more than $25	10.1	3.6	3.3	1.9	2.1	.9
Purposely damaged property	34.3	11.7	17.6	7.5	14.7	5.6
Picked up by the police	20.2	9.9	9.9	4.7	9.5	4.7
Gone to court	11.1	5.4	5.5	2.8	1.1	.9
Six or more delinquent acts in the last year	17.2	8.1	4.4	4.7	4.2	1.9

total delinquency scores may underestimate the effect of marital discord because it is related to only certain types of delinquency. And, although divorce is associated with high scores on our delinquency measure, parental breakup may be related to certain forms of delinquency but not others. Therefore, in an effort to obtain a clearer understanding of the effect of marital distress and divorce on conduct problems, we ran frequency distributions by type of family for each of the items in the delinquency scale.

These analyses indicate that marital distress has little effect on the antisocial behavior of boys. For nearly every item on the delinquency scale, boys residing with unhappily married parents had prevalence rates that were identical to, or only slightly higher than, those for boys living with happily married parents. Although this was generally true for girls as well, there were a few acts that girls with unhappily married parents were more likely to have committed than those with happily married parents.

These findings are exemplified in Table 8.2, which reports the prevalence rates for a few of the items on the delinquency instrument. The first two behaviors—"ran away from home" and "drunk in public"—are included in the table because they are the only activities with a higher prevalence rate for girls than boys. "Purposely damaged property" is included as an indicator of involvement in minor forms of misconduct, whereas "picked up by the police" and "gone to court" are included as indicators of involvement in more serious types of antisocial behavior. Finally, we included having committed six or more delinquent acts during the last year as an indicator of persistent conduct problems.

Table 8.2 shows similar percentages for boys regardless of the quality of their parents' marriage. The only exception is having gone to court. Although girls show no difference for running away or having been picked up by the police, those living in an atmosphere of parental dissension are more than twice as likely as those residing in families with happy marriages to have shoplifted, to have gone to court, or to have committed six or more delinquent acts. It should be noted, however, that even when girls with unhappily married parents demonstrate higher involvement in an act than those with happily married parents, their level of participation remains lower than that reported for girls from divorced families. Indeed, for most of the acts considered in these tables, adolescents from divorced families, regardless of gender, show prevalence rates two to three times higher than those for adolescents living with parents high on marital distress.

Table 8.2 indicates, for example, that 10.1% of the boys and 3.6% of the girls from disrupted families had shoplifted an item worth more than $25 during the last year. This was true for only 3.3% of the boys and 1.9% of the girls from families with an unhappy marriage. More than 11% of the boys and 5.4% of the girls from divorced families had gone to court during the previous year, whereas the corresponding figures are 5.5% and 2.8% for boys and girls, respectively, from families with an unhappy marriage.

Family structure differences are particularly strong when one examines persistent delinquency. Table 8.2 shows that 17.2% of the boys and 8.1% of the girls from divorced families had engaged in six or more delinquent acts during the preceding year. This is true for only 4.4% of the boys and 4.7% of the girls living with unhappily married parents. This indicates that family disruption doubles the risk of chronic delinquency for girls and quadruples the risk for boys. Overall, the results reported in Tables 8.1 and 8.2 suggest that parental divorce is a much greater risk factor for delinquent behavior than marital disharmony.

Past research has provided strong evidence for gender differences in delinquent behavior (Gottfredson & Hirschi, 1990). Studies have consistently found that boys are at least twice as likely as girls to be delinquent. This is true for all but two of the items included in our measure. The exceptions consist of the first two acts listed in Table 8.2, having run away from home and having been drunk in a public place. Girls scored higher than boys on these two items regardless of family structure. Our guess is that girls' higher prevalence of running away is a result of their being more predisposed than boys to stay with a friend or relative when they are having difficulties at home. Their higher prevalence for public drunkenness is probably a result of dating older boys who are experimenting with alcohol.

Criminologists have long considered gender to be a major determinant of an individual's probability of antisocial behavior, with boys being much more apt to display such actions than girls (Gottfredson & Hirschi, 1990). Given this widely accepted view, it is interesting to note that the girls in our sample who were from divorced families had similar or even higher prevalence rates for most of the delinquency items than boys from intact families. Table 8.1 shows, for example, that the mean delinquency score for girls with divorced parents was 26.05, whereas the mean score for boys with unhappily married parents was 25.37.

Table 8.2 indicates that 3.6% of the girls from disrupted families and 3.3% of the boys with unhappily married parents had shoplifted an item worth more than $25. The proportion of girls with divorced parents and boys with unhappily married parents who had been picked up by the police or gone to court is almost identical. Girls from divorced families were almost twice as likely as boys with unhappily married parents to have engaged in six or more delinquent acts during the past year. The percentages were 8.1 and 4.4, respectively. Thus it appears that the protection from conduct problems associated with being female is overridden by the effect of parental divorce.

Having established that there is a relationship between parental divorce and adolescent conduct problems, we turned to an examination of the variables that might account for this relationship. Table 8.3 reports the bivariate correlations between the measures used in these analyses. Variables with multiple indicators (e.g., mother's inept parenting) are treated as composites (i.e., the various indicators were standardized and summed to obtain a composite score). Coefficients above the diagonal are for girls, whereas those below the diagonal are

TABLE 8.3 Correlation Matrix for Constructs[a]

	1	2	3	4	5	6	7	8
1. Divorced	—	.30*	.25*	.29	.32*	.46*	.20*	.23*
2. Mother antisocial	.20*	—	.25*	.18*	.41*	.34*	.18*	.12*
3. Mother's parenting	.22*	.23*	—	.38*	.21*	.26*	.28*	.33*
4. Father's parenting	.42*	.17*	.40*	—	.21*	.26*	.21*	.28*
5. Negative events	.43*	.32*	.17*	.21*	—	.56*	.16*	.13*
6. Economic pressure	.29*	.26*	.27*	.26*	.50*	—	.19*	.18*
7. Delinquent behavior	.26*	.14*	.33*	.34*	.07	.18*	—	.55*
8. Deviant peer group	.24*	.21*	.44*	.31*	.12*	.19*	.48*	—

a. Coefficients above the diagonal are for girls (N = 247), whereas those below the diagonal are for boys (N = 216).
*$p \leq .05$

for boys. The table shows that delinquent behavior and deviant peer group are significantly related to divorced families. The correlations with delinquent behavior are .26 for boys and .20 for girls, and the correlations with deviant peer group are .24 and .23 for boys and girls, respectively.

Consistent with the findings reported in Chapters 5 and 6, divorce is related to both mother's inept parenting (.22 for boys and .25 for girls) and father's inept parenting (.42 for boys and .29 for girls). Quality of parenting by both mothers and fathers is significantly related to delinquent behavior and deviant peer group. With one exception, mother antisocial, economic pressure, and negative events also show significant (though small) correlations with delinquent behavior and deviant peer group. The exception is the relationship between negative events and delinquent behavior, where the coefficient fails to achieve statistical significance.

We used structural equation modeling (LISREL VII) to investigate the factors that mediate the relationship between family structure and delinquency. There is the possibility that the mediating processes differ by gender of child. Hence, we ran our models separately for boys and girls. Given the several variables to be included and the reduced sample size resulting from separating the sample by gender of child, there were not sufficient cases to estimate all the parameters associated with a multiple indicator model. To simplify the model, we treated variables with multiple indicators as composites and all con-

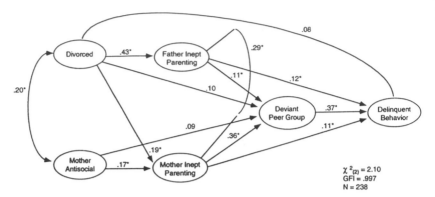

Figure 8.1. Quality of Mother's and Father's Parenting as Mediators of the Relationship Between Family Structure and Conduct Problems (boys' model)

structs as observed (rather than latent) variables in performing the analyses.

The structural equation modeling (SEM) for both boys and girls began with the fully recursive model. This resulted in several path coefficients that were near zero and had very low t-values. In an effort to obtain a more parsimonious model, paths with a t of 1.0 or below were deleted. Furthermore, in both the boys' and the girls' models, there were no significant paths from negative events or economic pressure to either deviant peer group or delinquent behavior. The effect of these two variables on adolescent conduct problems was indirect through mother's inept parenting. The SEM presented in Chapter 5 shows the effect of negative events and economic pressure on mother's inept parenting; in an effort to avoid duplication and further parsimony, these constructs were dropped from our model of adolescent conduct problems. This model trimming (dropping negative events and economic pressure and deleting paths with a t of less than 1) had no appreciable effect on either the magnitude or the significance level of any of the remaining paths. For both boys and girls, the difference in χ^2 between the reduced and the fully recursive model did not approach statistical significance.

The reduced model for boys is depicted in Figure 8.1. Both the Goodness of Fit Index and the ratio of χ^2 to the number of degrees of freedom suggest that the model provides a reasonable fit of data.

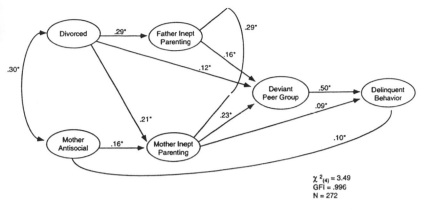

Figure 8.2. Quality of Mother's and Father's Parenting as Mediators of the Relationship Between Family Structure and Conduct Problems (girls' model)

Figure 8.1 shows that the effect of divorce on delinquent behavior is indirect through quality of parenting. There is a significant path from divorce to both father inept parenting and mother inept parenting. The two parenting constructs, in turn, have a direct effect on delinquent behavior, as well as an indirect effect through deviant peer group. The model provides no support for a modeling argument because there is no significant path from mother's antisocial trait to either deviant peer group or delinquent behavior. Rather, the effect of mother's antisocial trait on adolescent antisocial behavior is indirect through its disruptive influence on mother's parenting.

The results for girls are depicted in Figure 8.2. The various indexes indicate that the model fits the data. The pattern of findings is similar to that for boys in that the effect of divorce is indirect through quality of parenting. As is the case for boys, mother's inept parenting has both a direct effect on delinquent behavior as well as an indirect effect through deviant peer group. Unlike boys, however, father's inept parenting does not directly affect delinquent behavior for girls. Rather, its effect is indirect through deviant peer group.

The effect of mother antisocial also differs for girls. Its effect on boys' delinquent behavior is indirect through mother's inept parenting. Figure 8.2 shows that this is true for girls as well. In addition, however, there is a small direct effect from mother antisocial to delinquent behavior. This path is consistent with a modeling argument. It suggests that mothers who engage in antisocial behavior may inadvertently serve as role models for their adolescent daughters. Although the gender differences reflected in the path models are interesting, they must be interpreted with caution. They were not statistically significant when they were tested using the LISREL VII model stacking procedure. Thus they may reflect random error.

The results of the path analysis indicate that parental divorce increases chances of delinquent behavior because it disrupts parenting. Reduced monitoring and discipline allow the adolescent to affiliate with deviant peers and to experiment with deviant behavior. Furthermore, women with antisocial characteristics are overrepresented among the divorced. This behavioral tendency contributes to family structure differences in delinquency because it disrupts the parenting of sons and daughters and serves as a model of antisocial behavior for daughters. For boys, approximately 6% of the relationship between divorce and delinquent behavior is explained by the correlation between divorce and mother antisocial (i.e., 6% of the effect of divorce on delinquency is indirect through its association with mother antisocial). The corresponding figure for girls is approximately 20%.

Having identified the processes that increase the probability of delinquency in divorced families, we completed a series of regression analyses using only the divorced families in hopes of locating social resources that protect adolescents against these risk factors. First, we regressed delinquent behavior on mother antisocial, father's inept parenting, and mother's inept parenting, plus the interaction term formed by multiplying the father's and mother's parenting variables. This analysis was conducted to determine whether high-quality parenting by one parent might protect a child against the deleterious consequences of inept parenting by the other. The interaction term did not approach significance for either boys or girls. The same negative results were obtained when deviant peer group was substituted as a dependent variable.

Similar analyses were performed for two other potential protective factors: church attendance and quality of relationship with grandparents. Church attendance was assessed by child reports of how often they attend religious activities. Responses ranged from 1 (never) to 5 (more than once a week). This variable was unrelated to either delinquent behavior or deviant peer group when the parent constructs were in the model and it did not show a significant interaction with any of the parent variables. Quality of the adolescent's relationship with his or her grandparents, on the other hand, showed an effect for girls.

Four items were combined to assess quality of the adolescent's relationship with his or her grandparents. Adolescents were asked to use a 5-point scale (1 = very poor, 5 = excellent) to describe their current relationship with their maternal grandmother. They also reported how often they had had contact with the grandmother during the past 6 months. Response categories ranged from 1 (no face-to-face contact) to 6 (daily contact). Respondents were asked to complete the same two items for their maternal grandfather. These four items were standardized and summed to form a measure of the quality of the grandparent-grandchild relationship.

This grandparent variable did not have a main effect on either delinquent behavior or deviant peer group. The interaction term between this variable and mother antisocial was significant ($p \leq .05$), however, for the regressions involving girls. The interaction term accounted for an increase in explained variance of 9.1% ($p \leq .001$) in delinquency and 4.0% ($p \leq .05$) for deviant peer group. This interaction indicates that daughters are strongly influenced by their mother's deviant behavior when there is little involvement with grandparents, but that the mother's antisocial characteristics exert little influence when the daughter has a strong relationship with the grandparents. Apparently the grandparent relationship reduces the extent to which the mother is accepted as a role model by her child.

Discussion

The majority of children in our sample, regardless of family structure, showed minimal involvement in delinquent behavior. This might be taken as an indication that family disruption is not an important cause of adolescent behavior problems. This interpretation would be a mistake. Although the base rate for delinquency was low in both divorced and intact families, adolescents from divorced families were two to three times more likely to have engaged in serious delinquency than those from intact families. Family disruption doubled the risk of chronic delinquency for girls and quadrupled the risk for boys.

Parental divorce was a much greater risk factor for delinquent behavior than marital disharmony.

Indeed, girls from divorced families showed more involvement in delinquent behavior than boys from intact families. Social scientists have long considered gender to be a major determinant of an adolescent's probability of antisocial behavior, with boys being much more apt to engage in such actions than girls (Gottfredson & Hirschi, 1990). We found the effect of divorce to be stronger than that of gender. Therefore, although the majority of children from divorced families do not develop behavior problems, our data suggest that parental divorce greatly increases the chances that such difficulties will occur.

We used SEM in an effort to identify the processes by which divorce elevates a child's risk for conduct problems. Our results suggest that divorce increases the probability of delinquent behavior because marital disruption is associated with a decline in parental control. There is a tendency for divorced mothers and fathers to engage in less monitoring and discipline than parents in intact families. This reduced control allows children to affiliate with deviant peers and to experiment with deviant behavior. The effects of family economic pressure and negative events on delinquency are indirect through quality of parenting. Thus it appears that the financial hardship and stressful life events often associated with marital disruption increase the chances of child behavior problems to the extent that they disrupt parenting.

Furthermore, we found that overrepresentation of women with antisocial tendencies among the divorced accounts for a portion of the increased delinquency seen among children from disrupted families. In part, this was a result of the disruptive influence of this characteristic on quality of parenting. In addition, however, we found evidence that mothers who engage in antisocial behavior serve as role models for their adolescent daughters. Girls are more likely to affiliate with deviant peers and to engage in delinquent behavior when their mothers have antisocial tendencies.

We were largely unsuccessful in our efforts to identify social factors that help children of divorce cope with the risks posed by inept parenting or an antisocial custodial parent. We had anticipated that effective parenting by fathers would moderate the effect of antisocial tendencies or inept parenting by mothers. The data provide no support for this idea. There is no significant interaction between quality of father's parenting and the behavior of the mother. The effect of fathers' and mothers' behavior on their adolescent children is additive. Divorced mothers and fathers each make an independent contribution to their child's adjustment, with neither being able to moderate the effect of the other.

We did find evidence of one coping resource, but it only operated for girls. We found a strong statistical interaction between the antisocial behavior of the mother and quality of the grandparent-granddaughter relationship. Girls with antisocial mothers are less likely to affiliate with a deviant peer group or to engage in delinquent behavior if they have strong relationships with their grandparents. Apparently, the grandparent relationship reduces the extent to which the mother is accepted as a role model by her daughter. The finding that grandparents are an important coping resource for girls, but not boys, may be a product of differences between boys and girls in the types of relationships they establish. Past research indicates that, compared to boys, girls establish closer relationships with others and are more inclined to seek help and emotional comfort from adults (Nelson-LeGall, Gumerman, and Scott-Jones, 1983; Simons, Whitbeck, & Wu, 1994; Wolchik, Sandler, & Braver, 1984). Thus, girls may be more likely than boys to be influenced by grandparents to oppose antisocial behavior modeled by the mother.

In conclusion, our findings are consonant with prior studies that report a relationship between family disruption and delinquency. Past research has linked high levels of conduct problems among children of divorce to the life changes, economic pressure, and ineffective parenting that often characterize single-parent families (Cherlin, 1992; Emery, 1988; McLanahan & Sandefur, 1994). Our results suggest that these variables form a causal sequence in which marital disruption fosters stressful events and economic pressure, which in turn foster the inept parenting that promotes delinquent behavior. Prior research also provides evidence that number of adults in the household is related to risk of delinquency. Studies have found that children from disrupted families are less likely to engage in antisocial behavior when another adult, such as a grandparent, lives in the home (Dornbusch et al., 1985). Our findings suggest that adults can exert a positive effect even when they do not live in the home. Nonresidential fathers reduce the risk of delinquency to the extent that they continue to play the role of parent; involved grandparents reduce the chances that girls will emulate antisocial actions displayed by their mothers.

9

Adolescent Sexual Intercourse

LES B. WHITBECK

RONALD L. SIMONS

ELIZABETH GOLDBERG

Past studies have provided strong evidence of a link between family structure and adolescent sexual behavior. Young people who live in single-parent households engage in sexual activity at an earlier age and more frequently than those from two-parent households (Forste & Heaton, 1988; Hogan & Kitagawa, 1985; Miller & Bingham, 1989; Zelnik, Kantner, & Ford, 1981). The effects of family configuration have been found to be stronger for adolescent girls than for boys (Miller & Bingham, 1989) and are persistent when other important predictors such as religiosity, age, race, and social class are controlled (Day, 1992; Miller & Bingham, 1989). Though numerous studies document an association between family structure and adolescent sexuality, we still know very little about the specific mechanisms through which parents' marital status affects the sexual behaviors of adolescents (Brooks-Gunn & Furstenberg, 1989; Hayes, 1987). In this chapter, we examine factors associated with family structure that may mediate the relationship between living in a single-mother household and adolescents' early sexual activity. Behavior modeled by the mother and quality of parenting by both the mother and father are included as potential mediators.

Hypotheses

MOTHER'S PARENTING

As noted in Chapter 5, divorced women tend to experience higher levels of economic pressure, negative events, and emotional distress than women living in intact families; this increased stress has a disruptive effect on quality of parenting. More specifically, divorced mothers tend to exert less monitoring and discipline than mothers who are married. Past studies have shown that lax supervision and inconsistent discipline are associated with negative developmental outcomes and early transition to adult behaviors (Patterson, 1982; Patterson, DeBaryshe, & Ramsey, 1989). Thus, we expected that reduced parental control by divorced mothers increases the chances of adolescent early sex.

A recent study by Newcomer and Udry (1987) finds support for this idea. In one of the few studies actually investigating possible mechanisms associated with family structure, Newcomer and Udry argue that increased sexual activity among adolescent girls in divorced mother-headed households originates from a decline of effective parenting associated with father absence. Their longitudinal data indicate that the long-term effects of living in a single-mother household are more important for adolescent girls than the more acute stress of the parents' marital disruption. The most important mechanism associated with the long-term effects of living in a single-parent household is the decrease in parental control associated with the presence of only one supervising adult.

Past studies have shown that peers influence the chances that an adolescent will participate in deviant behavior, including early coitus (Patterson, 1982; Patterson & Bank, 1987; Whitbeck, Conger, Simons, & Kao, 1993). And, as noted in Chapter 8, diminished parental control increases the prospect that a child will become involved in a deviant peer group. Hence, it may be that a mother's inept parenting elevates an adolescent's risk for early sex by increasing the probability of affiliation with deviant peers. Stated in statistical terms, the effect of the mother's parenting on early sex may be indirect through the child's choice of friends. This hypothesis was tested in our analysis.

MOTHER AS ROLE MODEL

Another often-cited explanation for the relationship between girls' early sexual activity and living in a mother-headed household is that daughters copy the sexual attitudes and behaviors modeled by their mothers (McLanahan & Sandefur, 1994). As single mothers reestablish their social lives, begin dating, and establish new intimate relationships, their sexual attitudes and behaviors may become more apparent to their daughters. Daughters may then adopt such adult behaviors in their own early romantic relationships. Thornton and Camburn (1987) found that in the process of adjusting to single life, divorced mothers develop less restrictive attitudes toward sexual behaviors than women who remain in intact marriages. Similarly, daughters perceive their divorced mothers to be more sexually permissive than daughters in intact families, and, in turn, are more sexually active themselves. Inazu and Fox (1980) also found that daughters of single mothers who have cohabited are more likely to be sexually active. Mothers' cohabitation interacts with supervision in that the mothers who have been in cohabiting relationships during their daughters' lifetimes are less likely to wait up for their daughters than mothers who have not cohabited.

Whitbeck, Simons, and Kao (1994) found evidence of a modeling effect for both daughters and sons of divorced mothers. Mothers' dating influences daughters' sexual behaviors indirectly through attitudes about sexuality. The sexual behaviors of sons, however, are directly influenced by mother's dating. Whitbeck and colleagues suggest that divorced mothers and their adolescent offspring are experiencing similar developmental processes that involve learning and making decisions about dating behaviors and sexual norms. This makes mothers' dating behaviors particularly salient for their adolescent children.

Based on the findings of Thornton and Camburn (1987), we expected divorced women to have more permissive sexual attitudes than women from intact families and we expected a positive association between mother's attitudes and adolescent's early coitus. Mother's attitudes of sexual permissiveness communicate acceptance of such behaviors to the adolescent, who may adopt similar attitudes or perceive the behavior as acceptable. In turn, the degree to which the adolescent perceives such behaviors as acceptable increases the likelihood that he or she will engage in such behaviors.

Because early sexuality is commonly viewed as part of a pervasive adolescent deviance syndrome (Donovan & Jessor, 1985; Rowe, Rodgers, & Meseck-Bushey, 1989), it is possible that mothers contribute to adolescent sex through a more general modeling effect. Mothers who engage in antisocial behavior may promote the impression on the part of their adolescent children that deviant behavior of all sorts, including sexual intercourse, is socially acceptable. As described in Chapter 3, persons with antisocial tendencies tend to be overrepresented among the divorced. Thus, part of the relationship between family structure and adolescent early sex may be explained by the fact that divorced mothers are more likely to model antisocial behavior than mothers living in intact families.

FATHER'S PARENTING

Chapter 5 shows that divorced fathers are less involved in parenting than fathers in intact families, and Chapter 8 presents findings suggesting that this difference in parenting explains, in least in part, why parental divorce increases the probability that an adolescent will affiliate with deviant peers and engage in delinquent behavior. We did not expect to find this mediating effect for early sex. Chapter 5 reports evidence that fathers, regardless of family structure, are much less involved in parenting than mothers. We suspect that this is particularly true regarding discussions of sex. Whereas mothers may sometimes talk about such matters with their adolescent children, we presume that the vast majority of fathers avoid participating in such discussions. Thus, although fathers in intact families may be more involved in parenting than nonresidential fathers, we expect that they exert little influence in the area of sexual attitudes and behaviors. Rather, their influence on sexual behavior is likely to be indirect through their child's friendship choices. Chapter 8 shows that adolescents are less likely to become involved in a deviant peer group if their father exercises discipline and control. By reducing the probability of association with deviant peers, a father indirectly lowers his children's chances of early sexual intercourse.

Although it is unlikely that parental involvement by residential fathers deters a child from developing permissive sexual attitudes, involvement in parenting by nonresidential fathers is even less apt to deter adolescent early sex. Divorced fathers are likely to hold relatively liberal attitudes regarding sex outside of marriage (Reiss & Lee, 1988) and they model these attitudes to the extent that they participate in dating relationships that appear to include sex. Furthermore, we assume that nonresidential fathers are even less apt than fathers in intact families to discuss sexual issues with their children. Therefore, the effect of parenting by nonresidential fathers, like that of residential fathers, is likely to be indirect through its effect on the adolescent's friendship choices.

We used stepwise logistic regression to investigate our hypotheses regarding the factors that mediate the association between marital disruption and early sexual activity among adolescents. The sample used for this analysis differed slightly from that used in the other chapters in this book. Some of the sexually active adolescents living in divorced families likely had experienced intercourse before their parents' divorce. In those instances, factors associated with a change in family structure could not be an explanation for early sex. To eliminate this confound, adolescents who had experienced sexual intercourse prior to the year preceding data collection were excluded from the analysis for this chapter. This left 499 boys and girls. We used logistic regression to assess the extent to which family structure, quality of parenting, and mother's sexual attitudes and antisocial behavior predicted which of these individuals became sexually active during the year preceding data collection.

Results

The measures used in the analyses are described in Chapter 2. Of the 499 adolescents included our analysis, 55 (30 boys and 25 girls) reported that during the preceding year they had experienced sexual intercourse for the first time. Table 9.1 presents the bivariate associations between the constructs used in the analyses for this chapter. Age

TABLE 9.1 Bivariate Correlations (boys above diagonal, girls below diagonal)

	1	2	3	4	5	6	7	X	S.D.
1. Adolescent sexual intercourse	—	.23**	.24**	.18**	.09	.06	.33**	.13	.33
2. Family structure	.14*	—	.23**	.40**	.14*	.19**	.12	.60	.49
3. Mother's inept parenting	.17**	.26**	—	.40**	.04	.24**	.41**	.34	2.95
4. Father's inept parenting	.19**	.31**	.37**	—	-.05	.16*	.15*	38.78	12.56
5. Mother's anti-social trait	.17**	.19**	.06	.15*	—	.24**	.02	-.03	2.06
6. Mother's sexually permissive attitudes	.19**	.30**	.25**	.17**	.18**	—	.12	4.20	1.34
7. Affiliation with deviant peers	.28**	.16**	.41**	.23**	.07	.19**		1.31	1.32
X	.10	.59	-.28	38.96	.12	4.07	4.14		
S.D.	.29	.49	3.13	12.65	2.07	1.31	1.31		

$*p < .05; **p < .01.$

is included as a variable given variations in the timing of puberty development. The table shows that adolescent sexual intercourse is significantly associated with all the explanatory variables for girls, and all but mother's antisocial trait and mother's sexually permissive attitudes for boys. Family structure is positively associated with mother's and father's inept parenting for both sons (mothers $r = .23$; fathers $r = .40$) and daughters (mothers $r = .26$; fathers $r = .31$) and with mother's antisocial trait (sons, $r = .14$; daughters, $r = .19$). Family structure also is associated with mother's sexually permissive attitudes (girls $r = .30$; boys $r = .19$) and affiliation with deviant peers for girls ($r = .16$). As a way of comparing the effect of parental divorce to that of parents' marital distress, the zero-order relationship between parents' marital quality and early sexual intercourse was calculated for the intact families. Marital quality was assessed using the Marital Happiness Scale described in Chapter 5. Marital quality is not significantly related to early coitus for either boys or girls. Comparing these negative findings to the significant effects for family structure reported in Table 9.1, it appears that, for the adolescents in our sample, marital disruption was a better predictor of early sex than marital distress.

We ran separate stepwise logistic regression models for boys and girls as a way of identifying the variables that mediate the effect of family structure on adolescent early sex. Table 9.2 presents the results for girls; Table 9.3 presents those for boys. Family structure was entered into the model first, followed by each of the potentially mediating variables and the multiplicative interaction of these variables with family structure. If the interaction term was nonsignificant, it was dropped from subsequent runs to reduce multicollinearity in the model. The final model was made up only of main effects and those interaction variables that remained significant through the stepwise procedure. Age was controlled for both the boys and girls, but had no significant effect. Hence it was dropped from the models.

For the girls' models, family structure initially had a strong effect ($\beta = .92$). Family structure no longer had an effect once father's and mother's inept parenting were included in the model. Mother's inept parenting remained statistically significant until the last variable, affiliation with deviant peers, was added to the model. The interaction between mother's inept parenting and family structure was initially significant, but became nonsignificant when father's inept parenting was stepped into the model. Neither father's inept parenting nor the interaction term was statistically significant; the interaction was dropped from subsequent runs. Mother's sexually permissive attitudes remained significant through the final model ($\beta = .31$), suggesting a modeling effect. The multiplicative interaction for mother's sexually permissive attitudes and family structure was nonsignificant. The effect of mother's antisocial trait was nonsignificant, as was the interaction between mother's antisocial trait and family structure. By far the strongest effect on adolescent sexual intercourse for girls was affiliation with deviant peers ($\beta = .53$). Interaction with family structure was nonsignificant. Only mother's sexually permissive attitudes and affiliation with deviant peers remained significant in the final model.

The multiplicative odds reported in Table 9.2 indicate that girls in single-parent families are 2.5 times more likely to become sexually active than girls in intact families, prior to controlling for the mediating variables. The odds reduce to just 1.16 in the final model. In the final model, mother's sexually permissive attitudes (1.37) slightly increase the probability of early coitus among adolescent girls, but

TABLE 9.2 Logistic Regressions and Multiplicative Odds for Adolescent Girls

Measures										Final
Family structure	.92**	.66	.92*	.79	-.12	37	2.10	.24	.18	.14
Mother's inept parenting		.16**	.33***	.29**	.14*	15**	.14*	.13*	.14*	.05
Interaction with family structure			-.26*	-.24						
Father's inept parenting				.02	.01	02	.02	.02	.02	.02
Interaction with family structure					.02					
Mother's sexually permissive attitudes						32**	.55**	.29**	.30**	.31**
Interaction with family structure							-.37			
Mother's antisocial trait								.14	.05	.13
Interaction with family structure									.12	
Target affiliation with deviant peers										.53***
Multiplicative Odds Measures										
Family structure	2.51	1.93	2.52	2.21	.89	1.45	8.14	1.27	1.20	1.16
Mother's inept parenting		1.17	1.39	1.34	1.16	1.17	1.15	1.14	1.15	1.06
Interaction with family structure			.77	.79						
Father's inept parenting				1.02	1.01	1.02	1.02	1.02	1.02	1.02
Interaction with family structure					1.02					
Mother's sexually permissive attitudes						1.38	1.73	1.34	1.35	1.37
Interaction with family structure							.69			
Mother's antisocial trait								1.15	1.05	1.14
Interaction with family structure									1.13	
Target affiliation with deviant peers										1.71

$*p < .10; **p < .05; ***p < .01; ****p < .001.$

151

TABLE 9.3 Logistic Regressions and Multiplicative Odds for Adolescent Boys

Measures										Final
Family structure	1.44****	1.23***	.80	.71	−.19	.60	1.80	.62	.56	.36
Mother's inept parenting		.20***	.01	−.01	.02	−.01	−.01	−.01	−.04	−.10
Interaction with family structure			.34**	.34**	.31*	.35**	.35**	.36**	.41**	.39**
Father's inept parenting				.01	−.01	.01	.01	.01	.02	.02
Interaction with family structure					.03					
Mother's sexually permissive attitudes						.18	.35	.22	.24	.28
Interaction with family structure							−.26			
Mother's antisocial trait								−.08	.15	.14
Interaction with family structure									−.33*	−.33*
Target affiliation with deviant peers										.53***
Multiplicative Odds **Measures**										
Family structure	4.22	3.42	2.23	2.04	.83	1.83	6.06	1.86	1.74	1.43
Mother's inept parenting		1.23	1.01	.99	1.02	.99	.99	.99	.96	.91
Interaction with family structure			1.40	1.41	1.36	1.42	1.41	1.43	1.51	1.48
Father's inept parenting				1.01	.99	1.01	1.01	1.01	1.02	1.02
Interaction with family structure					1.03					
Mother's sexually permissive attitudes						1.20	1.42	1.24	1.28	1.32
Interaction with family structure							.77			
Mother's antisocial trait								.93	1.16	1.15
Interaction with family structure									.72	.72
Target affiliation with deviant peers										1.70

*p < .10; **p < .05; ***p < .01; ****p < .001.

affiliation with deviant peers has the strongest effect. It increases the likelihood of early intercourse 1.71 times.

Chapter 8 shows that quality of both father's and mother's parenting are predictors of affiliation with deviant peers. Table 9.1 shows that these parenting variables are also related to involvement in early sex. The regression analysis reported in Table 9.2 shows, however, that parenting variables are not related to adolescent sexual intercourse when affiliation with deviant peers is in the model. This suggests that the parenting practices of mothers and fathers affect a daughter's sexual behavior indirectly through their effect on her friendship choices. Overall, the results suggest that girls from divorced families are more likely than those from intact families to engage in early sex because their mothers model sexually permissive attitudes and because their mothers and fathers fail to display the monitoring and supervision necessary to deter affiliation with deviant peers.

Table 9.3 presents the regression models for boys. The table suggests some interesting gender differences in the determinants of early sexual activity. When the multiplicative interaction between family structure and mother's inept parenting was added to the regression model, the main effect of mother's parenting was completely lost. The interaction term remained significant through to the final model. A plot of the means (high mother's inept parenting = 75th percentile and above; low mother's inept parenting = 25th percentile and below) indicates that inept parenting has little effect on early coitus for boys in intact families, but strong effects for boys in single-mother families (see Figure 9.1). Father's inept parenting has no effect when mother's parenting is controlled. Its effect is limited to an indirect effect through affiliation with deviant peers.

There were no modeling effects of mother's sexually permissive attitudes for young men; however, the interaction between family structure and mother's antisocial trait was negatively related to early sexual intercourse ($\beta = -.33$; $p \leq .10$). The means for this interaction were plotted (high mother's antisocial behaviors = 75th percentile and above; low mother's antisocial behaviors = 25th percentile and below) to determine the nature of the interaction. As Figure 9.2 indicates, the interaction suggests a weak positive effect for mother's antisocial behaviors in two-parent families and almost no effect for boys in single-mother households. As with adolescent girls, affiliation

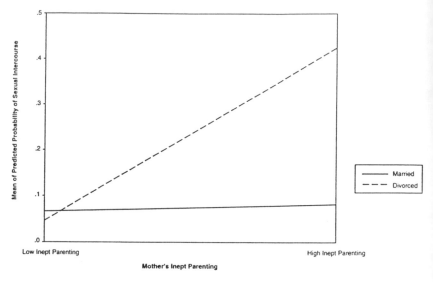

Figure 9.1. Interaction of Family Structure and Mother's Inept Parenting (boys)

with deviant peers is strongly associated with sexual intercourse for boys ($\beta = .53$).

The multiplicative odds (Table 9.3) indicate that for boys residing in a single-mother family, the likelihood of early sex increases 4.22 times. When other predictors of early coitus are controlled, the multiplicative odds drop to 1.43. Inept parenting by the single mother (the interaction term) increases the likelihood of early intercourse for boys in single-mother households 1.48 times. Mother's antisocial behaviors interact with family structure so that the net effect is to increase the odds of early sex for boys in intact families slightly. As is the case with adolescent girls, affiliation with deviant peers increases the odds of early coitus 1.70 times.

Discussion and Conclusions

We used logistic regression to test hypotheses regarding the factors that mediate the relationship between family structure and early sexual intercourse among adolescents. Theoretically important mechanisms

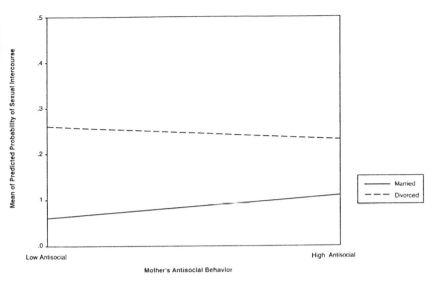

Figure 9.2. Interaction of Family Structure and Mother's Antisocial Trait (boys)

such as inept parenting and the modeling of single mother's attitudes about sexuality were introduced into the regression model in a stepwise fashion to determine their effects on early adolescent intercourse and the extent to which they mediated the zero-order effects of marital disruption. The results indicate that the effects of family structure, although initially quite strong, are diminished when other predictors of early adolescent sexual activity are included in the model.

There is evidence of a modeling effect for girls because mother's sexually permissive attitudes are related to early sex. This is congruent with other research that reports that mothers' sexual attitudes affect their daughters' sexual attitudes and behaviors (Thornton & Camburn, 1987; Whitbeck et al., 1994). For boys, mother's inept parenting interacts with family structure so that boys in single-mother households are more strongly affected by mother's inept parenting than boys in two-parent households. There also is an interaction between family structure and mother's antisocial trait, suggesting that a mother's deviant behavior promotes early sex in two-parent households but has no effect in single-mother families.

Affiliation with deviant peers strongly predicts early intercourse for both boys and girls. This finding is consistent with previous research on early sexuality (Rowe, Rodgers, & Meseck-Bushey, 1989). Findings from this chapter, as well as those reported in the previous chapter, indicate that inept parenting by mother or father is related to an increased risk of involvement with deviant peers. Thus, quality of parenting by mother and father appears to decrease the chances of early sex indirectly by reducing the probability that adolescent children will associate with deviant peers.

We found support for both the inept parenting and modeling explanations for the effects of parents' marital status on adolescent sexuality. When measures of inept parenting and mother's permissive sexual attitudes were introduced into the regression model, the main effects of family structure were largely eliminated. These results suggest that contextual characteristics of single-parent families are largely responsible for the consistent differences found in early sexual experimentation between children from two-parent and single-mother households. More specifically, our findings indicate that parental divorce increases the odds of early sex through the following mechanisms: Divorced mothers are more likely to possess permissive sexual attitudes than those who are married and divorced mothers and fathers are less apt than married parents to engage in parenting behaviors that discourage affiliation with deviant peers.

These findings suggest that experiencing adolescence in a single-mother household presents a distinctive context for sexual development that influences adolescents' sexual decisions. For the divorced mother, the pressures of heading a household alone may erode her ability to parent effectively. Simultaneously, her attempts to reestablish intimate relationships may provide models for her daughter's own early sexual experimentation. For the adolescent, the mother's sexual attitudes and behaviors may be more apparent and powerful in the context of single-mother households. At the same time, diminished parental time and monitoring may offer greater independence to associate with nonconventional friends who experiment with other adult behaviors (Rowe et al., 1989; Whitbeck et al., 1993).

10

Adolescent Depressed Mood

RAND D. CONGER

WEI CHAO

The findings reported in Chapter 8 demonstrate the important role that family disruption plays in exacerbating risk for adolescent problem behaviors. These analyses show that the termination of marriage affects the delinquent or antisocial actions of both boys and girls in large part through the adverse influence of the stressful family transition on effective parenting practices. These overt or externalizing problem behaviors represent only one aspect of the many dimensions of developmental difficulties that adolescents may experience when their parents' marriage disintegrates, however. In the following analyses, we turn to an examination of covert or internalizing emotional problems, especially those associated with depressed mood or depressive symptoms.

A first consideration of the distinction between internalizing and externalizing symptoms would suggest that externalizing symptoms should have a significant negative influence on those in contact with the disturbed adolescent, whereas internalizing problems should primarily affect only the distressed youth. Contrary to this view, current evidence suggests that seriously distressed adolescents not only experience a great deal of personal pain but also negatively affect the lives of those around them (e.g., Ge, Conger, Lorenz, Shanahan, & Elder, 1995; Hammen, 1991). Indeed, recent research suggests that adolescent depression has far-reaching implications for the social world of the afflicted youth and that negative perceptions of self affect both interpersonal relations and the instrumental competencies of the depressed adolescent (Petersen et al., 1993). In the following sections, we first consider the definition of adolescent depression and examine findings related to its influence on adolescent development. Then we develop a model that links adolescent risk for depression to marital disruption, test the empirical adequacy of the proposed model, and discuss the implications of the findings.

What Is Adolescent Depression?

We normally think of depressed people as being extremely sad and unhappy, so much so that they seem constantly downhearted and blue. This everyday perspective on the problem, however, captures only a portion of the meaning of the term as it is used in the scientific and clinical literature. A series of recent reviews has shown that the concept of depression refers to at least three empirically overlapping but conceptually distinct phenomena: depressed mood, depressive syndromes, and clinical depression (Compas et al., 1993; Compas & Hammen, 1994; Petersen et al., 1993). These conceptual distinctions regarding depressive phenomena have great importance for the design of studies or models of adolescent depression in that different operationalizations of the construct may produce different results. For example, the causes and consequences of depression may vary as a function of the way it is measured.

In this study, we assess depressed mood, which is evaluated in the same way for both adolescents and adults. Most research on adolescents has measured depression at this level (Petersen et al., 1993). Depressed mood may be determined by no more than a single item on a self-report questionnaire or interview schedule that asks the respondent how sad, blue, unhappy, or depressed he or she has been in the recent past. More typically, and as in the present study, depressed mood is assessed by a self-report checklist of several items that indicate either depressive affect (e.g., feeling sad) or depressive cognitions (e.g., thinking about suicide; Compas et al., 1993). From 15% to 40% of adolescents in community surveys report elevated levels of depressed mood during the past several weeks or months (Compas et al., 1993; Petersen et al., 1993). In a sense, depressed mood is akin to the common cold of emotional afflictions. Almost everyone experiences a significant degree of depression at some time, especially when dealing with difficult or unhappy events such as the loss of a loved one. For most people, these periods of depression are transient and abate without long-term harm.

For most adolescents, however, depressed mood co-occurs with other symptoms of distress, especially anxiety. Compas and Hammen (1994) suggest that anxiety and depressed mood are so highly intercorrelated that they may be inseparable for adolescents. The significant association between depressed mood and other developmental problems led to the creation of several measures designed to assess depressive syndromes, as illustrated by Achenbach's (1991) taxonomy of child and adolescent psychopathology based on questionnaires given to parents, teachers, and youth. Most central for our purposes is Achenbach's measure of an anxious-depressed syndrome that includes questions that capture symptoms of both depressed affect (e.g., unhappy, sad, depressed) and anxious mood (e.g., fearful, anxious). Compas et al. (1993) propose a model suggesting that adolescents scoring high on the anxious-depressed syndrome, about 5% of the population, represent a subset of youth who by definition also suffer depressed mood. Thus, depressed mood and anxious-depressed syndrome can be thought of as two components in a hierarchical sequence in depressive symptomatology. Depressed mood alone would be considered a less severe form of emotional distress that becomes more serious for youth who concurrently demonstrate elevated symptoms of anxiety.

As the final step in this model, Compas and his colleagues (1993) suggest that those scoring highest on the depressed mood and anxious-depressed measures are at greatest risk for developing clinical depression or depressive disorder. They note that, at any given point in time, only about 1% to 3% of the population of adolescents in the community suffer this degree of emotional impairment. Depressive disorder differs from depressed mood and anxious-depressed syndrome because it considers not only the presence of symptoms but also their duration and severity. For example, an adolescent must suffer a number of different symptoms for a minimum amount of time to be diagnosed as depressed. In addition, the diagnosis of depression includes consideration of somatic or vegetative symptoms such as weight gain or loss and sleep disturbances, symptoms not usually included in mood or syndrome scales (Compas et al., 1993). Thus, according to the Compas model, clinical depression represents the most severe form of depressive disturbance. And although the prevalence of depressive disorder is relatively low at any point in time, more than 20% of youth in the community report a major depressive episode sometime during adolescence (Lewinsohn, Hops, Roberts, Seeley, & Andrews, 1993).

As with symptom checklists for anxious or depressed mood, the diagnosis of depressive disorder is essentially the same for adolescents and adults. Because of the similarity in assessments, the prevalence and correlates of adult and adolescent disorder can be directly compared. If diagnosed depression is the most serious form of this problem, however, as suggested by Compas et al.'s (1993) sequential model, one can reasonably ask why is it worthwhile to study depressed mood, as we do in the present analyses? Does it make sense to study seriously an emotional ailment that may be transitory and the mental health equivalent of the common cold? Recent findings suggest an affirmative response to this question.

Why Study Depressed Mood?

A number of recent reviews conclude that adolescent depressed mood, which involves feelings of sadness, unhappiness, or despair, often represents far more than a passing dysphoria or an emotional perturbation consonant with a temporary stage in life (Compas & Hammen, 1994; Petersen et al., 1993). As Petersen and her colleagues (1993) note, psychological problems such as depression during adolescence are frequently precursors of continuing and even more serious difficulties during adulthood. Indeed, findings from the Epidemiological Catchment Area (ECA) studies of the 1980s demonstrate that adults are more likely to report the recurrence of depressive disorders than antisocial or substance abuse disorders (Robins, Locke, & Regier,

1991). These results run contrary to previous thinking that considered antisocial behavior to be a lifelong characteristic and affective disorders to be episodic. Moreover, the ECA studies show that most disorders first occur during adolescence, with a median first onset at 16 years of age.

Current evidence, then, suggests that depressive disorders often first occur during adolescence and they tend to recur in adulthood. Especially important, adolescent depressed mood appears to be a significant subclinical marker for risk of depressive disorder. Thus, identifying the early correlates of depressed mood may help to isolate many of the risk factors that lead to the most serious form of depression, depressive disorder. For example, Gotlib, Lewinsohn, and Seeley (1995) found that adolescents scoring high on a depressed mood scale were several times more likely than low-scoring peers to meet criteria for depressive disorder. Even more important, youth ranking high on depressed mood, compared to normals, were twice as likely to meet criteria for clinical depression within the next 12 months. Our first reason for studying adolescent depressed mood, then, is that it is an important marker variable indicating risk for more serious depressive episodes across time. Understanding the causes of depressed mood should help improve understanding of life conditions and personal characteristics that lead to clinical levels of depression.

A second reason for studying adolescent depressed mood involves its negative influence on adolescent well-being in general. Feelings of sadness and despair reduce the quality of life and lead to a less rewarding and fruitful adolescence (Compas & Hammen, 1994). In addition, depressed mood appears to be just about as disruptive of social and instrumental competence as depressive disorder. From their study of a large community sample of over 1,500 adolescents, Gotlib and his colleagues (1995) conclude that adolescents scoring high on depressed mood are about as likely to suffer impairments in psychosocial functioning as those diagnosed with a depressive disorder. For example, depressed mood is as predictive of problems in family functioning as depressive disorder. In general, then, high scores for depressive symptoms are associated with impairments in social, academic, and family functioning (Compas & Hammen, 1994).

Rather than reflecting a benign and passing condition, elevated depressive symptoms appear to have a disruptive influence on daily functioning and also pose a substantial risk for the development of actual depressive disorder. Once a disorder occurs, it is likely to recur during adolescence and on into adulthood. This evidence supports the view that the study of adolescent depressed mood is important in its own right. Indeed, the depressed mood item from Achenbach's (1991) measures of a broad array of internalizing and externalizing syndromes provides the best predictor of referral for mental health treatment for adolescents living in the community (Compas et al., 1993). If elevated depressed mood represents the common cold of emotional problems, it appears to involve mechanisms that all too often lead to chronic or recurring debilitation of a more serious form and long-term duration. We now consider how adolescents in the present study might come to have high levels of depressive symptomatology.

Family Structure and Adolescent Depressed Mood

As shown in the earlier chapters of this volume, single mothers experience increased risk for depressed mood. Indeed, although adult depressive disorder was not evaluated in the present study, we would expect that the divorced mothers who participated were more likely than their married counterparts to meet criteria for a diagnosis of depression (Hammen, 1991; Robins et al., 1991). Results from a large number of empirical investigations have shown that depression in parents increases developmental problems for children and adolescents, including the likelihood that they too will suffer from depressed mood, syndromes, or disorder (Compas & Hammen, 1994; Downey & Coyne, 1990; Petersen et al., 1993). The exact mechanisms that account for this relationship, however, are not well understood (Compas & Hammen, 1994; Downey & Coyne, 1990).

In an important series of analyses, Hammen (1991) demonstrates that psychosocial factors play an important role in the intergenerational transmission of depressive phenomena. Her results show that a mother's current depressed mood, more than a history of depressive disorder, predicts child and adolescent psychopathology. Moreover, parent depression is strongly correlated with both acute negative life events and ongoing life strains. These stressful conditions also play a significant role in exacerbating risk for adolescent developmental difficulties. In Hammen's work, maternal stress and depression disrupt parenting quality, which, in turn, has a negative influence on the social competence and emotional well-being of the children and adolescents. Similar processes involving negative life events, mother and father depression, disrupted parenting, and adolescent depressed mood have been reported by Ge, Conger, Lorenz, and Simons (1994).

In fact, the history of research on depression in families strongly suggests that the influences are bidirectional (Coyne & Downey, 1991). Life stress affects depression in both parents and children, and depressed mood leads to cumulating family problems and chronic strains (Hammen, 1991). Parent emotional distress increases risk for adolescent developmental problems, which then exacerbate emotional difficulties of parents (Ge, Conger, et al., 1995). Intertwined in this complex web is the adverse influence that chronic family strains have on adolescents (Aseltine, Gore, & Colten, 1994; Hammen, 1991). Adolescent stress then exacerbates the emotional problems of youth (Ge, Lorenz, et al., 1994). All these findings suggest a complex series of causal processes in which distressed families experience greater vulnerability to the sort of life stresses that intensify emotional and behavioral problems.

Although the cross-sectional nature of the present study does not allow for the analysis of the reciprocal influences just described, the data reported thus far strongly suggest their existence in these families. As shown in Figure 10.1 (the conceptual model for the present analyses, most of which is supported by results from earlier chapters, especially Chapter 7), divorce itself is a stressor that is likely a cause, correlate, and consequence of a somewhat risky lifestyle (antisocial behavior). Contemporary research shows that one emotional problem or behavior, such as antisocial conduct, is likely to be highly intercorrelated with a number of other difficulties, such as depression (Robins et al., 1991). That is, it is quite likely that many of the mothers in this study who experienced a divorce and suffered a history of antisocial activities also were depressed at the same time that they experienced other behavioral problems. Thus, if we had a measure of depression during the mothers' childhood and adolescence, it would probably correlate in the same fashion with later divorce and economic pressure, as does the antisocial trait. Indeed, earlier depression would be a strong predictor of current parental depression (Hammen, 1991; Robins et al., 1991).

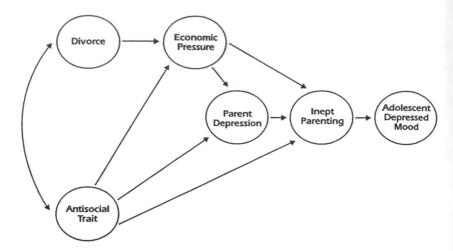

Figure 10.1. The Conceptual Model for the Influence of Family Disruption on Adolescent Depressed Mood

As suggested by earlier research and the previous chapters in this volume, the mediational model in Figure 10.1 indicates that parental predispositions (antisocial trait) and stressors (divorce, economic pressure) increase parental depression, which, in turn, disrupts effective parenting practices (Conger, Ge, et al., 1994; Hammen, 1991). The necessary extension of the model shows the predicted relationship between inept parenting and adolescent depressed mood. Based on the literature just reviewed, we expected that inept parenting would be the primary mechanism through which parent depression would increase risk for adolescent depressed mood.

Although there has been a great deal of support for this mediating pathway in earlier studies, prior research has suffered from inadequate measures of parenting processes (Hammen, 1991). As Compas and Hammen (1994) note, too often information about parent depression, child-rearing style, and adolescent depression has come from a single source, usually the mother. To the extent that a single informant sees the world in a generally negative or positive fashion (negative or positive affectivity), such information tends to be biased by that disposition. This bias tends to inflate the magnitude of correlations among theoretical constructs (Lorenz & Melby, 1994). Thus, an

TABLE 10.1 Mean Scores for Adolescent Depressed Mood

| | Family Type | | | | | | |
| | Divorced | | Distressed Marriage | | Happy Marriage | | |
	X	N	X	N	X	N	F-Test
Boys	18.45[a]	93	16.44[b]	75	15.91[b]	67	5.12*
Girls	21.09[a]	106	20.60[b]	82	17.87[b]	83	5.16*

NOTE: Mean scores with different superscripts are significantly different (Sheffe's Test, $p < .05$).
*$p < .01$

important contribution of the following analyses, which test the empirical adequacy of the model in Figure 10.1, is the use of multi-informant data to evaluate the hypothesized relationships among family stress, parental depressed mood, parenting behaviors, and adolescent depressive symptoms.

Results

DESCRIPTIVE ANALYSES

The measures for the analyses to be presented are described in Chapter 2. The first question to be addressed simply asks whether divorced families differ from intact families in the level of adolescent depressive symptoms. As in earlier chapters, we make a distinction between marriages currently experiencing significant distress and those that seem relatively happy and satisfying. The results, reported in Table 10.1, indicate the expected trends in the data. For boys, the highest average level of depression occurs in divorced families ($M = 18.45$), the lowest in the happily married group ($M = 15.91$), with youth living with maritally distressed parents receiving a score between the two extremes. The only significant differences are between the boys in the divorced families and those in the other two groups. The mean difference between the distressed and happily married groups is not statistically significant.

The exact same pattern of findings applied to the girls in the study. Girls in divorced families are significantly more depressed than those in intact families, and the distressed and happily married families do not differ in terms of the level of girls' depressed mood. Moreover, consistent with earlier research (Petersen et al., 1993), girls experience greater depressed mood than boys. This difference is consistent across the three groups and is statistically significant ($p \leq .01$). These results provide an initial level of validation both for the theoretical model and for the measure of depressed mood. First, given that there is a first-order relationship between divorce and adolescent depression, it makes sense to proceed to an analysis of the mediating linkages proposed in the theoretical model (Figure 10.1) between family structure and adolescent depression. Second, confirmation of the gender difference in depression with the measure used here provides some support that it produces information similar to other checklists for adolescent depressive symptoms. Before proceeding to a test of the theoretical model, however, we examine more closely the specific depression items that appear to distinguish the three types of families.

The percentages reported in Table 10.2 indicate the prevalence of each type of depressive symptom for boys and girls in the intact and divorced families. Each percentage indicates the proportion of respondents from the three types of families that expressed at least some distress for a particular symptom during the past week. An inspection of the results indicates interesting gender and family-type influences. For example, more than 50% of the girls in the divorced and distressed marriage groups reported periods of crying compared with only 33.7% of the girls in happily married families. But even this relatively low prevalence of crying by girls with happily married parents is extremely high compared to boys, fewer than 15% of whom reported this experience regardless of family type. In general, and consistent with earlier findings, girls were more likely to report any of the depressive symptoms than boys.

Regarding specific item differences by family type, boys in the divorced group differed most from boys in the distressed marriage and happily married families, and boys in distressed families differed from those in happily married families in terms of self-blame, feeling hopeless, and feeling that everything is an effort. The more disrupted and distressed the family, the more hopeless and discouraged the boys seemed to feel. Girls differed most across family types in terms of feeling worthless, hopeless, crying easily, self-blame, and feeling trapped. For

TABLE 10.2   Prevalence of Depression Symptoms (percentage of respondents reporting at least some distress for each symptom)

	Family Type					
	Divorced		Distressed Marriage		Happy Marriage	
Individual Symptoms	Boys	Girls	Boys	Girls	Boys	Girls
Low in energy	59.1%	62.3%	46.7%	70.7%	61.2%	56.6%
Thoughts of ending life	10.8	16.0	8.0	15.9	9.0	8.4
Feeling trapped	28.0	38.7	16.0	34.1	16.4	21.7
Blaming self	53.8	57.5	33.3	48.8	28.4	34.9
Crying easily	11.8	56.6	10.7	52.4	10.4	33.7
Feeling lonely	36.6	42.5	29.3	50.0	28.4	39.8
Feeling blue	34.4	54.7	37.3	62.2	26.9	47.0
Worrying too much	50.5	68.9	45.3	78.0	46.3	63.9
Feeling no interest	45.2	44.3	33.3	43.9	31.3	31.3
Feeling hopeless	24.7	34.9	14.7	26.8	11.9	16.9
Everything's an effort	44.1	40.6	30.7	37.8	17.9	31.3
Feeling worthless	22.6	37.7	13.3	28.0	13.4	22.9

both boys and girls, then, marital distress and divorce appear to inculcate a sense of despair.

From these findings, it is not difficult to understand how youth who feel so despondent might reduce their efforts in school achievement, social events, and even family activities, associations between adolescent depression and general well-being reported in previous studies (Compas & Hammen, 1994). Interestingly, in several instances girls from maritally distressed families seemed to do even worse than girls in single-parent homes. For example, girls in maritally distressed families appear to worry more than those from any other group, perhaps anticipating the severity and possible dangers of the family's situation. Hammen (1991) reports that these types of chronic threats or difficulties exacerbate depressive tendencies in both adults and adolescents.

Before proceeding to the test of the theoretical model, it is important to examine the association between family structure and more extreme scores on depressed mood. The findings reported indicate that the average depression score is higher for adolescents in single- compared to two-parent families, but these results do not provide the most compelling evidence that single-parent youth are at significantly greater risk for depressive disorders. In general, the more extreme cases of depressive symptoms best predict current or later disorder

TABLE 10.3 Percentage of Adolescents Scoring in the Top 20% on Depression by Family Type

	Family Type			
	Divorced	Distressed Marriage	Happy Marriage	Chi-Square
Girls	26.4	19.5	12.0	6.03*
Boys	30.1	22.7	9.0	10.31**

*p < .05; **p < .01.

(Compas et al., 1993; Gotlib et al., 1995). For these analyses, we examined the relationship between family type and adolescent placement among the top 20% of the highest scorers on the depression measure.

Table 10.3 shows that 26.4% of the girls and 30.1% of the boys in the divorced families were among the highest one fifth of the adolescents in terms of their scores on depressed mood. Adolescents with happily married parents were unlikely to be in this extreme group—only 12.0% of the girls and 9.0% of the boys. Youth in maritally distressed families were intermediate between the two extremes. As noted, adolescents in this upper end of the depression continuum are at greatest risk for developing serious depression. Clearly, teenagers from families experiencing a divorce are most vulnerable to possibly chronic or recurrent affective disorders. We now consider how well the mediational model guiding these analyses explains these differences in adolescent risk.

TESTING THE THEORETICAL MODEL

We evaluated the structural equation and measurement models using maximum likelihood estimation with LISREL 7 (Joreskog & Sorbom, 1989). As in earlier chapters (e.g., Chapter 7), data were first considered for mothers for whom there was a complete set of measures. Because only incomplete information was available for fathers and because fathers were assessed with a more limited measure of parenting behavior, these results are considered later. Table 10.4 provides the correlations among all constructs in the theoretical model for mothers (see Figure 10.1). Because separate analyses show that these correlations do not differ significantly for boys and girls, they

TABLE 10.4 Correlations Among Study Constructs, Mothers With the Combined Sample of Boys and Girls (N = 506)

Study Constructs	Study Constructs					
	(1)	(2)	(3)	(4)	(5)	(6)
1. Divorce	1.00					
2. Mother antisocial	.40	1.00				
3. Economic pressure	.41	.48	1.00			
4. Mother depression	.24	.47	.43	1.00		
5. Mother inept parenting	.22	.44	.38	.40	1.00	
6. Target depression	.08	.16[+]	.14	.18	.34	1.00

NOTE: All correlations statistically significant, $p < .05$; except $+$ = n.s.

are combined into a single sample. This set of correlations provides the base for determining whether the theoretical model, which proposes several mediated pathways from divorce and antisocial trait to adolescent depression, actually fits the data. For example, the final model indicates no direct path from divorce to adolescent depressed mood; rather, the influence of divorce is expected to be mediated through a series of relationships involving economic pressure, parent depression, and inept parenting.

As Baron and Kenny (1986) demonstrate, for a mediated relationship to be established, the zero-order correlation between the initial predictor variable and the outcome measure must be statistically significant. The results shown in Table 10.4 indicate that, although the zero-order correlation between divorce and adolescent depression is modest ($r = .08$), it is statistically significant. If the findings of the structural equation analysis show that this association with adolescent mood becomes nonsignificant with the hypothesized mediating variables in the equation, then we can conclude that this portion of the proposed mediational model is consistent with the data.

Indeed, all the correlations except one in Table 10.4 are statistically significant. In most instances, then, if the direct paths deleted in the theoretical model are nonsignificant, we can conclude that the proposed mediational model fits the data well. For example, the zero-order correlation between mother's depression and adolescent depression is .18 ($p < .05$). If this relationship becomes nonsignificant, as hypothesized in Figure 10.1, we can conclude that inept parenting explains or mediates the relationship between maternal and youth depression. Similarly, divorced status was expected to predict parent depression through economic pressure. If the zero-order correlation of .24 between divorce and maternal depressive symptoms becomes nonsignificant with economic pressure in the equation, then one can infer that economic pressure is a true mediator in this relationship.

Because maternal antisocial trait is not significantly correlated with adolescent depression (see Table 10.4), however, we cannot infer from the structural analysis that maternal depression and inept parenting are mediators for antisocial trait. In this instance, we use the term *linking variables.* That is, if antisocial trait is significantly related to inept parenting, which, in turn, predicts adolescent mood, we may conclude from the analyses that inept parenting indirectly links anti-social trait to adolescent depression. With these ideas in mind, we turn to the estimation of the theoretical model.

The first step in evaluating the mediational model involved testing it separately for boys and girls. Subgroup analyses showed that there were no significant gender differences in the set of hypothesized relationships among constructs; therefore, the model was next esti-mated with the combined sample of boys and girls. These results, reported in Figure 10.2, show significant consistency between the proposed model and the empirical findings. As expected, mother's inept parenting mediated the influence of all prior variables on adolescent depressed mood. Parenting was significantly related to adolescent depression ($b = .32, p \leq .05$), and there were no significant paths from any of the other variables in the model to the teenagers' depressive symptoms. Other postulated direct paths were statistically significant, as were the loadings of all indicators on their respective constructs. Moreover, the Adjusted Goodness of Fit Index (AGFI) of .95 demonstrates a good fit between the proposed model and the data (Joreskog & Sorbom, 1989).

The final step in the analysis involved estimation of a much simpler model for fathers, for which only a limited amount of data was available. Again, this model was first estimated separately for boys and girls and, again, there were no significant differences between the two groups. The final model is presented for the combined sample in Figure 10.3. The model shows that, although father's parenting pre-dicts adolescent depressed mood and divorce predicts father's parent-

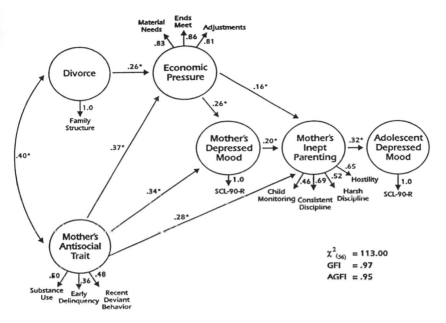

Figure 10.2. Evaluation of the Proposed Model for the Combined Sample of Boys and Girls ($N = 506$, standardized path coefficients, $^*p < .05$)

ing, there is still a direct path from divorced status ($b = .11, p \leq .05$) to adolescent depressed mood. Apparently, the influence of divorce on adolescent depression is transmitted primarily through maternal parenting, even though ineffective child rearing by fathers has its own negative effect on adolescent depressive symptoms. Because the parenting measure for fathers in this study is more limited than that for mothers (i.e., it does not include observer ratings), we cannot be certain whether this result reflects a true substantive difference between parental effects or simply represents an artifact of the poorer measures available for fathers.

Discussion

Adolescent depression is best conceptualized as a range of phenomena of increasing complexity and severity (Compas et al., 1993). At

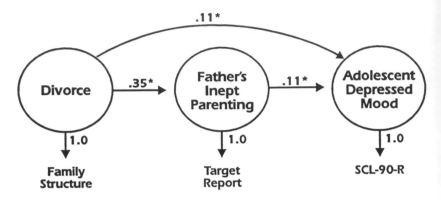

Figure 10.3. Family Structure, Father's Inept Parenting, and Adolescent Depressed Mood for the Combined Sample of Girls and Boys ($N = 506$, standardized regression coefficients, $*p < .05$)

the least problematic end of this continuum rests depressed mood, the focus of the present analyses. Feelings of sadness and demoralization become more serious as they combine with other symptoms, especially anxiety, to form co-occurring syndromes of emotional difficulties. At the most severe end of this spectrum, we find clinical depression, which includes affective, cognitive, and somatic symptoms of some duration and intensity. With increasing frequency, scholars have suggested that these different forms of distress must be studied separately and one must not generalize findings involving one type of depressive phenomena to another (Compas et al., 1993; Coyne & Downey, 1991).

If one accepts this perspective, as we do, then the question arises as to whether the investigation of depressed mood represents a worthwhile expenditure of time and resources. If this form of depression is transient and relatively mild, does the study of its antecedents meaningfully contribute to understanding significant adolescent distress? From the review that began this chapter, we concluded that there is strong evidence regarding the importance of research on adolescent depressed mood. Specifically, adolescents with high symptom scores are far more likely than their low-scoring peers to develop a diagnosis of depression in the near future and they are also more likely to suffer significant impairments in social and instrumental functioning

(Compas & Hammen, 1994; Gotlib et al., 1995). Indeed, in terms of psychosocial difficulties with peers, with family, and in school, adolescents high on depressed mood are quite similar to those meeting criteria for clinical depression (Gotlib et al., 1995).

Adolescent depressed mood, then, is most profitably used as a marker variable indicating increased risk for the onset of more serious forms of depressive disorder. As the evidence reviewed earlier suggests, when such disorder occurs during adolescence, it is likely to recur during adult years and may become a continuing vulnerability for emotional problems throughout the life course (Robins et al., 1991). In fact, current thinking suggests that such mood disorders may be as chronic or more chronic than substance abuse and antisocial behavior, which traditionally have been thought to be highly resistant to change. Thus, our analysis of adolescent depressed mood in this chapter examines a type of emotional distress that, in many instances, marks the beginning of what may become a lifetime emotional disability. What do the findings tell us about the transition to divorce and this form of adolescent distress?

As shown in the earlier chapters involving hostility in sibling relations, conduct problems outside the home, and engagement in early sexual activity, divorce disrupts the environments of youth in predictable ways. Single-parent homes suffer greater economic pressure, which disrupts the emotional health of parents and directly affects child-rearing activities. The mothers in the present study who were under economic pressure and who were demoralized by their situations had difficulty maintaining effective parenting practices. With the distractions created by their financial problems and their own emotional difficulties, they were less likely to monitor the activities of their children or to discipline them effectively when family rules were broken. They were also more likely to treat them in a hostile, derogatory fashion or to use excessive punishment when they responded to rule violations. Along these dimensions, the results were as expected and consistent with earlier findings (e.g., Conger, Ge, et al., 1994).

Mothers' antisocial behaviors did not predict directly adolescent depressed mood. Thus, the relationship between antisocial trait and adolescent distress was not mediated by other endogenous constructs in the model. Because mother's antisocial history did relate significantly to economic pressure, her own depressed mood, and inept parenting, and because these variables directly or indirectly affect adolescent depression, we conclude that antisocial trait is linked to adolescent depressive symptoms through these intervening variables. Taken together, the evidence generated by the test of the mother model suggests that both the transition to divorce and a history of antisocial behavior negatively influence family processes that create increased risk for adolescent depressed mood. Because the boys and girls in the divorced families also were more likely than those from intact families to be among the highest 20% of scorers on the depression measure, we can also conclude that they are at elevated risk for developing a depressive disorder (see Gotlib et al., 1995).

The evidence regarding the more limited father model is not so straightforward. Father's ineffective parenting was associated with higher levels of adolescent depressed mood. Moreover, father's parenting was less effective when divorce had occurred. Father's child-rearing activities did not mediate the relationship between divorce and adolescent mood, however. There seem to be at least two good explanations for the dissimilar findings regarding mothers and fathers. First, the father parenting measure contained a more limited set of items than the mother measure and these reports came only from the target adolescent. If we had the same observer ratings of child rearing for fathers as for mothers, we may have found the expected mediational effects. Second, because these mothers had the primary responsibility for raising these children, the influence of divorce on their parenting practices may be more crucial for their children's well-being. Only future research will be able to determine whether these or other alternative explanations best fit the results of the present study.

Most important, the findings from this and earlier chapters demonstrate that divorce creates risks for children along a number of dimensions, including both internalizing and externalizing symptomatology. For children and adolescents in general, divorce appears to create more threat and loss than growth and self-realization. Certainly in some instances involving significant abuse or neglect by one or the other parent, divorce may be protective for youth. For example, Hammen (1991) reports that children are at less severe risk for mental disorder when dysfunctional fathers leave the home. Nevertheless, the cumulative findings from this investigation suggest that mothers, fathers, and their children may need a substantial investment of services and support to reduce the developmental damage to youth that may follow the termination of a marriage. In the next chapter, we move from investigating emotional and behavioral problems to considering how the transition to divorce influences the academic success of adolescents in single-parent families.

11

Academic Performance
and Future Aspirations

GLEN H. ELDER, JR.

STEPHEN T. RUSSELL

The dramatic growth of single-parent households during the past three decades is generally regarded as an important source of socioeconomic disadvantage and academic failure (Krantz, 1988). When compared to children from two-parent households, the children of single parents are more often characterized by school absences, lower grades and test scores, early school leaving, and weaker or nonexistent intentions of attending college (McLanahan & Sandefur, 1994). Some of this difference is due to the socioeconomic disadvantage of single-parent families, though academic failure is still more common among children from these families when income variations are controlled (McLanahan & Sandefur, 1994; Milne, 1989; Tienda & Kao, 1994). What influences explain the remaining differences and account for the academic success of some disadvantaged youth? Beyond economic disadvantage, the educational adversities of a single-parent family include the life histories that people bring to this new situation from broken marriages. Marital discord leading up to separation may create antisocial tendencies in children that dispose them to teacher rejection and school failure. The residential transience and acute time pressures of conflicted and single-parent households weaken family ties to community institutions and resources (McLanahan & Sandefur, 1994), thereby lessening parental empowerment and personal efficacy. The emotional distress of parents in the time-pressured and resource-deprived households of single caregivers is another handicap to parental effectiveness (Elder, Eccles, Ardelt, & Lord, 1995). This chapter examines the importance of these processes in explaining the link between martial disruption and children's school performance. More specifically, we investigate the extent to which the relationship between family structure and child's academic success is explained by the following factors: family socioeconomic status, mother's personal attributes and social ties, father's and mother's parenting practices, and child characteristics and behaviors.

To obtain a clearer understanding of the relationship between family structure and children's school performance, our analysis includes a comparison of these key influences on children's academic success across three types of families: strong marriage (high on marital satisfaction for both partners), weak marriage (below average on marital satisfaction), and single parent. Such an approach allows us to determine whether it is a weak marriage or marital disruption that is more strongly associated with the processes that undermine children's school performance.

Not all children living in a single-parent family do poorly in school. The negative educational implications of these families have tended to obscure this important fact. Though a good many children from such homes are unsuccessful in school, a number do well and even prosper. Hence, the last part of our analysis consists of a search for factors that account for children who are doing better and worse than one would expect from knowledge of their social background. In closing, we look toward the future, asking how family structure and academic success shape aspirations and plans for adulthood.

Before turning to the analyses and findings, let us consider more fully the various factors likely to explain the relationship between marital disruption and children's school performance.

Influences on Children's Academic Success

The various categories of influences can be arrayed in terms of their theoretical proximity to the academic success or failure of children.

At the most distal end, we have social and economic influences, followed by the personal attributes and social ties of mother, and then by the proximal effects of socialization and child characteristics. Social and economic influences refer to family income level, negative life events, felt economic pressure, mother's education, and residential change. Attributes of mother include characteristics such as emotional depression, antisocial conduct, and social involvement in church, school, and community. Socialization and child characteristics refer to quality of mother's and father's parenting, mother's interest in education, and the behavior of the child, a factor that may well be a prime source of academic failure.

The causal sequence noted above has been described as a general model of family stress processes (Conger & Elder, 1994). The family stress model posits that socioeconomic influences on socialization and child behavior are mediated by parents' emotional well-being and social relationships. Mounting economic pressure is seen as increasing the emotional distress of parents, which, in turn, diminishes the quality of their parenting. A study of 7th grade rural boys obtained empirical support for this causal sequence (Conger et al., 1992). The dependent variable, adolescent adjustment, included a measure of academic success.

Using both observational and family member reports, Conger et al. (1993) found that objective family hardship (including family income and indebtedness) markedly increases the risk of a depressed mood among mothers and fathers through a sense of mounting economic pressure—not enough money to pay bills and cutbacks on consumption costs. Depressed feelings make conflicted relations in marriage more likely and consequently enhance the risk of disrupted and nonnurturing parent behavior. These behaviors, in turn, tend to undermine the self-confidence, peer acceptance, and school performance of boys. A similar process was observed for girls.

The general model presented in Chapter 1 uses this theoretical perspective to explain the association between marital disruption and child adjustment problems. Findings presented in the previous chapters have corroborated various elements of the model. Compared to those who are married, divorced mothers are more antisocial and have experienced greater economic hardship, negative events, and emotional distress. These family structure differences are associated with an increased risk for disrupted parenting. Disrupted parenting, in turn, is linked to a child's affiliation with deviant peers, involvement in delinquent behavior, early sexual intercourse, and psychological distress. We assume that similar processes operate for children's academic success. Mother's personal attributes, level of stress, and quality of parenting are expected to account for much of the association between marital disruption and poor school performance. In addition, however, we expect that there are influences largely specific to children's school success as an outcome.

In addition to the influence she exerts through quality of parenting, a mother might be expected to affect her child's school performance through the educational aspirations and values that she communicates. Past studies have shown that parents' expressed interest in their child's educational progress is a strong force in promoting achievement (Chavkin, 1989; Chavkin & Williams, 1989; Dornbusch & Gray, 1988; Tienda & Kao, 1994).

We also expect that the involvement of mothers in community roles is related to the school performance of their children. In a nationwide survey, Schneider and Coleman (1993) found substantial evidence on the educational benefits of parent social involvement in community, church, and school activities. Other studies show that the participation of parents in parent-teacher association (PTA) meetings and parent-teacher conferences is linked to the academic success of their children (Dornbusch & Gray, 1988; Dornbusch & Wood, 1989; Tienda & Kao, 1994).

Chapter 3 notes that divorced mothers are several times more likely to have moved in the past year than women who are married. The residential instability of divorced mothers suggests that they are less integrated in community and school affairs. As McLanahan and Sandefur (1994) put it, "Moving undermines social capital because long-term relations of commitment and trust cannot develop" (p. 32). Residential mobility in fact has been identified as a significant cause of the academic disadvantages experienced by children living in single-parent families (Astone & McLanahan, 1991).

Consistent with findings from previous research, Chapter 9 reports that children living in divorced families are more likely to exhibit delinquent behavior than those residing in intact families. Past studies have shown that such deviance is associated with academic failure

(Dornbusch, 1989; Dornbusch & Gray, 1988; Dornbusch & Wood, 1989). Indeed, some have argued that academic failure is part of a general syndrome of adolescent problem behavior (Jessor, Donovan, & Costa, 1991). Thus, we expect that, at least in part, the relationship between marital disruption and poor school performance is explained by the fact that parental distress and disrupted parenting lead to antisocial behavior of all sorts, including academic problems.

Findings

The measures used in our analyses are described in Chapter 2. Findings presented in the previous chapters suggest that adolescents living with a divorced mother are more likely to show conduct problems, engage in early sex, and experience psychological distress than those living in intact families. Table 11.1 indicates that this family structure difference also exists for academic performance. The table displays the mean academic performance scores for adolescents living in three types of families: divorced, intact with a strong marriage, and intact with a weak marriage. It shows a gradient across the family types, with children from strong, intact families demonstrating the most academic success and those from divorced families exhibiting the least success. The performance of adolescents living in weak, intact families falls between that of the other two groups. As shown in the table, ANOVA was used to test for differences between groups; the scores for adolescents residing in a single-parent household were found to be significantly lower than for those living with both parents, regardless of marital quality. The difference in means for adolescents living in strong and weak intact families was not significant.

Table 11.1 shows a similar pattern of results for the variable *mastery*. Children living in strong-marriage families have a greater sense of mastery than those with divorced parents, whereas those living in weak-marriage families score between the other two groups. The table indicates that the difference between the divorced and the strong-marriage group is statistically significant, whereas the differences between the weak-marriage and the strong-marriage group and between the weak-marriage and divorced group do not achieve statistical significance.

TABLE 11.1 Academic Success in Relation to Social and Personal Influences; Descriptive Statistics: Means (standard deviations)

Social and Personal Factors	Marriage		Single-Parent Family	ANOVA: Family Type
	Strong	Weak		
Child Variables				
Academic performance	1.3	.6	−1.5	SW > D*
	(5.0)	(5.2)	(5.8)	
Mastery	27.8	26.9	25.9	S > D
	(4.2)	(4.2)	(4.3)	
Mother Variables				
Organization member	.7	.7	.6	S > D
	(.4)	(.5)	(.5)	
Church attendance	.5	.3	−.6	SW > D
	(2.6)	(2.4)	(2.6)	
Attend PTA	3.9	3.6	3.1	S > W > D
	(1.1)	(1.3)	(1.2)	
Interest in education	6.0	6.0	6.0	
	(1.5)	(1.4)	(1.6)	

*S = Strong marriage, W = Weak marriage, D = Divorced.

The results reported in previous chapters indicate that divorced mothers are more likely than married mothers to engage in antisocial behavior, to be depressed, and to experience economic pressure, negative life events, and residential moves. Table 11.1 indicates that they are also less socially involved. The divorced score significantly lower than either the strong- or the weak-marriage group on church attendance and school involvement and lower than the strong-marriage group on organizational membership. Although mothers with weak marriages have lower scores on these variables than those with strong marriages, the differences are not statistically significant. The divorced mothers do not differ from those in intact families regarding interest in education.

MEDIATING EFFECTS

Table 11.2 shows a modest −.22 bivariate association between family structure and academic success; note that it is of approximately the same magnitude as that reported in Chapter 8 for family structure and conduct problems. Table 11.2 presents a sequence of hierarchical

TABLE 11.2 Academic Success in Relation to Social and Personal Influences; Correlations and Regression Coefficients

Social and Personal Factors	r	Models				
		I	II	III	IV	V
Family Type						
Single parent	−.22*	−.17*	−.09	−.06	−.07	−.04
Strong marriage	.17*	.09	.01	−.03	.03	−.03
Predivorce Factors						
Gender	−.18*		−.19*	−.16*	−.15*	−.14*
Income, per capita/1,000	.06		−.004	−.01	.01	.01
Mother's education	.24*		.22*	.17*	.15*	.16*
Social and Economic Influences						
Economic pressure	−.33*		−.25*	−.22*	−.19*	−.18*
Negative life events	−.21*		−.06	−.03	−.02	−.04
Residential moves	−.12*		−.02	.03	.01	.01
Personal Attributes, Mother						
Depression	−.23*			−.10*	−.09	−.08
Antisocial behavior	−.15*			.003	.03	.04
Social Ties, Mother						
Organization member	.21*			.07	.06	.04
Church attendance	.21*			.11*	.10*	.10*
Parents attend PTA	.26*			.16*	.10*	.09*
Socialization, Child Behavior, and Attributes						
Inept parenting, mother	−.31*				−.09	−.01
Parenting, father	−.17*				−.02	−.01
Interest in education, mother	.24*				.11*	.10*
Mastery, target	.23*					.11*
Delinquent behavior, target	−.31*					−.19*
Adjusted R^2		.05	.19	.24	.25	.29

*$p < .05$.

regressions. Variables from our general analytic framework are added in a sequential fashion in an effort to identify factors that mediate the effect of marital disruption on adolescent academic performance.

Table 11.2 shows that family structure drops to insignificant when mother's education and economic pressure are added to the model. Consistent with the literature (Krantz, 1988), girls outperform boys and both do better when the mother is well educated and does not face heavy economic pressure. One might assume from this pattern that family income level, negative life events, and frequent residential moves would also lessen the chances of academic success. None of these factors matters as a direct effect, however.[1]

Residential moves are more common among single parents, but, unlike what other studies have revealed (Astone & McLanahan, 1991), the changes do not entail adverse consequences for the school achievement of children in our sample. This may reflect the extent to which changes in residence derive their meaning from a family's history, whether of socioeconomic well-being or loss and instability.

Mother's emotional depression is predictive of academic troubles to a modest extent, as shown in Model III. More consequential are the social involvements of the mother. Mothers who are involved in social affairs outside the household, whether civic, religious, or educational, tend to have children who are doing well in school, as shown by the correlation coefficients. Only two of the measures emerge as statistically significant in the regression analysis, owing to the degree of shared variance.

Family socialization, child attributes, and negative behavior clearly matter for school success (see Models IV and V). On a correlational basis, success is linked to mothers who are effective in parenting and have an interest in education. Mother's interest in education and the adolescent's feelings of mastery are positively related to academic success, whereas involvement in delinquent behavior has a negative effect. Mother's and father's parenting are correlated with academic success at the zero level, but fail to show significant associations in the regression analysis.

The overall pattern matches well the findings of previous studies. The negative effect of family structure is modest and is largely explained by family and personal factors. The significant influences on academic success in Model V include gender (girls do better), a well-educated mother who is involved in church activities and maintains a keen interest in the child's education, negligible exposure of the mother to economic pressure, and a child who has a sense of mastery and avoids involvement in deviant behavior.

In combination, however, these influences leave two thirds of the variance unexplained. A large number of children are doing well in school despite hard times in the family. There is a looseness, then, in the effect of family and socioeconomic disadvantage on performance in school. We might speak of this connection as a *loose coupling*

TABLE 11.3 Academic Success in Relation to Social and Personal Influences for Strong and Weak Marriages and Single-Parent Families

Social and Personal Factors	Marriage		Single-Parent Family
	Strong	Weak	
Social and Economic Influences			
Gender	−.09	−.09	−.15*
Income, per capita/1,000	−.09	.08	.01
Economic pressure	−.35*	−.18*	.01
Negative life events	.05	−.15	−.08
Residential moves	−.03	.10	.01
Mother's education	.21*	.23*	.16*
Personal Attributes, Mother			
Depression	−.03	−.04	−.09
Antisocial behavior	−.01	−.004	.04
Social Ties, Mother			
Organization member	.07	.06	−.01
Church attendance	.19*	.14	.04
Parents attend PTA	.10	.17*	.05
Socialization and Child Behavior			
Inept parenting, mother	−.03	−.18	.08
Parenting, father	.14	.08	−.02
Interest in education, mother	.13	.03	.13
Mastery, target	.07	.14	.16*
Delinquent behavior, target	.01	−.11	−.33*
N	155	131	196
Adjusted R^2	.24	.39	.21

*$p < .05$.

between actor and social structure (Elder & O'Rand, 1995), a looseness that offers much room for choice and agency in surmounting the limitations of childhood.

Before turning to escape routes from disadvantage, we wondered whether the determinants of academic success are the same in intact and single-parent families. Our analysis to this point investigated the factors that account for family structure differences in children's educational performance. Although we have identified variables that explain differences between types of families, a somewhat different set of factors may explain differences within family types.

Table 11.3 shows the results of regressing academic success on the various explanatory variables for each of the three types of families. The table shows that mother's education is the only variable that has a significant influence on adolescent academic success in all three types of families.[2] Economic pressure has an effect in intact families, regardless of marital quality, but is not related to school success in single-parent families. This suggests that variations in economic pressure may dampen academic achievement most among children who are least likely to be exposed to real economic hardship.

Social ties also show more of an effect in intact than single-parent families. Church attendance is related to school performance in strong-marriage families, and PTA attendance is related to school performance in weak-marriage families. We noted earlier that single mothers are much less involved in civic and school affairs than married mothers. These social factors may fail to predict adolescent academic performance in single-parent households because so few divorced mothers participate in such activities.

Table 11.3 indicates that child attributes and characteristics are the best predictors of academic success in single-parent families. First, the results show that girls tend to experience more success than boys. This finding is consistent with previous studies that have reported that girls adjust better to parental divorce than boys (Krantz, 1988). Second, school performance has a positive association with perceptions of mastery and a negative association with involvement in delinquent behavior. Previous research has linked variables such as family financial hardship and quality of parenting to a child's sense of mastery and involvement in deviant behavior (Patterson et al., 1992; Whitbeck, Simons, Conger, Lorenz, Huck, & Elder, 1991). Thus it appears that the economic pressure and disrupted parenting often seen in single-parent families contributes indirectly to a child's problems in school by undermining perceptions of self-efficacy and by fostering misconduct.

Low involvement in school activities by divorced mothers may partly explain why their children who are in academic trouble are also likely to be engaged in delinquent activity, whereas this is not the case for low achievers from intact families. Single-parent mothers may be less effective as advocates for their children in school. When troubles arise, they may not be able to soften or change the school's judgment and punitive action. In this sense, school for these children represents a less forgiving environment.

EXPLAINING VULNERABILITY AND RESILIENCE

It would be a mistake to focus exclusively on failure because a number of children in single-parent households are doing well in school, better than one would expect considering their background. Rather than focus strictly on causes of academic failure, we focus on factors that facilitate child adjustment regardless of family structure (Richards & Schmiege, 1993). It is also true, however, that some children perform at a level that is lower than one would expect. To select these children, we used both positive and negative residuals from a best prediction equation. This equation included all the statistically significant factors in Model V from Table 11.2: gender, mother's education, economic pressure, church attendance, mother's involvement in school activities such as PTA, mother's interest in child's education, and the child's mastery and delinquent behavior. Two groups of achievers were identified based on quartiles of the residual score: those doing better than expected (highest 25% of residual scores) and those doing worse (lowest 25% of residual scores).

We estimated academic success for each group of achievers by using factors that were not statistically significant in the original prediction equation.[3] Among the achievers in Table 11.4, academic success is predicted by the experience of fewer negative life events and mothers who have organizational ties in the community. Among children who are doing worse than expected, a number of factors predict academic failure: lower family income, fewer community organizational ties of the mother, and inept parenting.

What can we learn from this analysis? Children who do better in school than expected given their family (e.g., economic pressure) and personal characteristics (e.g., gender, sense of mastery, conduct problems) are distinguished by particular social resources or capital and by mothers who are socially engaged in their community and presumably know how to make the best of available options. The children who are doing worse than expected have the added disadvantages of low income, exposure to inept parenting, and a mother with low social capital.

Table 11.5 reports the results of performing this residual analysis using only the single-parent families. School performance for children living in such households was regressed on the statistically significant

TABLE 11.4   Factors That Account for Doing Better or Worse Than Predicted
by Model V in Table 11.2

	Residual Quartiles	
	Top 25%	Bottom 25%
Family Type		
Single parent	–.14	.09
Strong marriage	.03	–.02
Predivorce Factors		
Income, per capita/1,000	.003	–.21*
Social and Economic Influences		
Negative life events	–.18*	.08
Residential moves	–.11	.11
Social Ties, Mother		
Organization member	.16*	–.18*
Socialization and Child Behavior		
Inept parenting, mother	–.13	.35*
Parenting, father	.11	–.05
N	119	126
Adjusted R^2	.16	.23

*$p < .10$.

predictors in Table 11.3 (e.g., gender, mastery, delinquent behavior,
mother's education). Table 11.5 indicates that children from single-
parent families who do better in school than predicted are distinguished by particular social resources or capital—by mothers who are
socially engaged in their community and presumably know how to
make the best of available options. The children who are doing worse
than expected are likely to have experienced a recent residence change
and erratic parenting.

ASPIRATIONS FOR THE FUTURE

Given the different factors that shape academic success for children
in intact versus single-parent families seen thus far, what do these
children expect in their futures? The adolescents were asked about
their expected plans following high school, the importance to them
of having a college education, and the certainty of their college plans.
We created a difference score that indicated the disparity between the
desired level of education and the expected level.

TABLE 11.5 Factors That Predict Doing Better or Worse Than Expected for
Children Living in Single-Parent Households

	Residual Quartiles	
	Top 25%	Bottom 25%
Social and Economic Influences		
Income, per capita/1,000	.19	−.13
Economic pressure	.22	.25
Negative life events	−.13	.05
Residential moves	−.03	.26*
Social Ties, Mother		
Organization member	.28*	.01*
Church attendance	.08	−.17
Parents attend PTA	.22	−.07
Socialization and Child Behavior		
Inept parenting, mother	−.10	.28*
Parenting, father	.08	−.16
Interest in education, mother	.15	−.12
N	49	49
Adjusted R^2	.10	.18

*$p < .10$.

As shown in Table 11.6, future plans and aspirations are clearly
shaped more by a child's academic performance than by family structure. Academic performance is strongly linked to plans for the future.
Not surprisingly, children who are performing above the average
expect to attend a four-year college or university, whereas those with
a lackluster record expect to work full time, go into the military, take
vocational or technical courses, or are not sure. Family structure
affects plans for junior college only; this option is expected more often
by children whose parents are married. College education is most
important to children who perform well academically and have families that are financially secure.

Turning to the relation between desired and expected levels of
education, we find that the difference scores are consistently negative,
indicating that most children do not desire more education than they
anticipate completing. There is no difference between children from
intact and single-parent families; rather, academically competent children are more likely than other youth to feel that they will not achieve
the education that they desire. This may reflect the troubled times

TABLE 11.6 Plans for the Future; Means by High and Low Academic Performance and Family Structure, ANOVA Analyses Controlling for Level of Academic Performance, Family Structure, and Family Income

	High Academic Performance		Low Academic Performance		Significant Effects[a]
	Married	Divorced	Married	Divorced	
Which of the following things do you expect to do the year after you leave high school?					
Work full time in a family business or farm	.02	.00	.09	.04	A:F = 9.02
Work full time, but not in a family business or farm	.13	.14	.22	.25	A:F = 10.57
Enter an apprenticeship or on-the-job training	.07	.00	.07	.10	A:F = 4.26; A*F:F = 3.94
Go into military service	.07	.11	.17	.14	A:F = 7.53
Take vocational or technical courses	.11	.09	.18	.20	A:F = 9.78
Take academic courses at a junior college	.17	.08	.19	.15	F:F = 4.99
Attend a four-year college or university	.83	.90	.48	.49	A:F = 98.49
Not sure	.12	.12	.24	.27	A:F = 17.71
How important is having a college education to you?					
5 = extremely important; 1 = not at all important	4.70	4.80	4.23	4.14	A:F = 62.92; I:F = 4.73
How certain are you of your college plans?					
5 = I am certain I *will* go to college; 1 = I am certain I *will not* go to college	4.63	4.61	3.73	3.86	A:F = 118.47; I:F = 14.70
Difference score: (How much education would you like to have?) (How far do you think you will actually go in school?) 1 = won't graduate from high school 7 = PhD or professional degree Positive scores indicate a desire for more education than one expects	−.39	−.49	−.64	−.84	A:F = 13.78
N	207	93	116	117	

a. A = academic, F = family type, I = income.

189

experienced by many rural families during the Iowa farm crisis (Conger & Elder, 1994).

Overall, these results point again to a loose coupling of family structure and children's academic futures; there is looseness between the experience of family disruption and children's future plans and aspirations. Although our findings and those of others (McLanahan & Sandefur, 1994) clearly indicate that children living in single-parent families suffer academic failure more often than children from intact families, many disadvantaged children perform well in school and intend to continue their academic successes into the future. In fact, future plans and the importance of education for a child are shaped more by academic performance than by family structure. The effect of family structure on future plans is largely indirect through its influence on academic performance.

Discussion and Conclusions

The growth of single-parent households in the United States has many implications, including the presumed inadequacy of this family environment for the development of children's social competence. Consonant with previous research, we found that children with only one parent do not fare as well in school as those with two parents, especially when the married parents get along well. The negative effect of single-parent status on children's academic success was relatively modest, however. A great many of the children residing in single-parent families were succeeding in school.

Previous chapters present evidence that children from single-parent families are more likely than those living with both parents to experience family economic hardship and to be exposed to emotionally depressed and socially isolated mothers who are ineffective as parents. Findings from this chapter suggest that the direct and indirect consequences of these disadvantages account for the increased risk for school problems seen among children of divorce.

Children are most likely to succeed when they come from homes with minimal economic pressure and an educated mother who is effective as a parent, retains an interest in the child's education, and is socially involved in community functions, including the PTA. Economic pressure adversely affects children's prospects for school success by increasing the mother's emotional distress and her ineffectiveness as a parent. Delinquent behavior is the most important correlate of academic failure among children from single-parent households, whereas mother's interest in the child's education represents the only significant positive influence.

The children who were doing better in school than one would expect from these conditions had experienced few negative life events and their mother was actively involved in community affairs. Those who were performing worse than one would expect were distinguished by low family income, exposure to nonoptimal parenting, and a mother uninvolved in community activities.

These findings might be taken as an indication that children from single-parent households are disadvantaged by not having the parental advocacy than is commonplace among children with two parents. Single parents are less involved in school and community affairs and their depressed mental state does not encourage such participation. If this interpretation applies, it may account for why studies have found that children who are reared only by their mothers are likely to perform below expectations based on their IQ. Dornbusch and Gray (1988) conclude that teachers often believe that children living with single parents do poorly in school, and that this expectation negatively affects both teacher evaluations and the child's performance.

What can be said about children living in single-parent families and their ideas about the future? Academic performance for these children does not equal the success of youth in two-parent families; this is why their plans for the future are less positive or definite. Academic performance largely determines educational and occupational goals for the years following high school. The effect of family structure on educational and occupational plans is indirect through its influence on academic performance.

The missing link in this study is the school and its teachers, students, and policies. Schools vary widely in the responsiveness of teachers to the needs of children from disadvantaged families. This variation clearly matters in terms of encouragement for parent involvement (Eccles & Harold, 1994). Even in single-parent households, we find that children do better when their mothers are interested in their schooling. School responsiveness thus has particular significance in the absence of such encouragement from parents. Pathways out of social disadvantage require a more complete understanding of the interlocking influences of family, school, and community.

Notes

1. To test for one source of social and economic influence beyond the immediate family, we examined the child's relationship with grandparents (see Chapter 8) in these models. The results indicate that resources beyond the immediate family do not have significant effects on the child's academic performance.

2. We tested the possibility that mother's education may suppress the effect of inept parenting, but found no evidence that this was the case.

3. We excluded measures of personal attributes of the mother (depression, antisocial trait) because neither was a significant predictor of academic success in our original models.

PART V

SUMMARY AND CONCLUSIONS

12

Theoretical and Policy
Implications of the Findings

RONALD L. SIMONS

This final chapter considers the conclusions and implications suggested by the various findings reported in the previous chapters. I begin by briefly reviewing the methodological advantages and disadvantages of the study. Although the design avoided some of the weaknesses inherent in prior research, it also suffered certain shortcomings. These methodological limitations necessarily qualify the conclusions that can be drawn.

I commence discussion of the results by noting what the analyses suggest concerning the strength of the association between parental divorce and negative developmental outcomes for children. I then turn to a consideration of the findings regarding the processes that link family structure to child outcomes. Next, I provide a short comment on the debate that has raged regarding the merits of research on family structure differences in child adjustment. Finally, I end the chapter by exploring some of the policy implications of the findings.

Methodological Strengths and Weaknesses

It is wise to review the strengths and weaknesses of the current study prior to discussing the results; these methodological considerations determine the confidence that can be placed in the various findings and conclusions.

There are three areas where the present study might be seen as superior to much of the prior research on divorce and child adjustment. First, we used more intensive measures for several of our variables than are often used in studies of families and children. Many of the data sets that have been widely used to assess family structure differences in child outcomes have relied on only two or three items to assess complex constructs such as quality of parenting or financial pressure. Of course, unreliable measures underestimate relationships between variables.

Second, we were able to collect information from multiple sources for many of our variables. Our measures of parenting, for example, included parent self-reports, child reports, and observer ratings. Obtaining data from multiple sources is significant for two reasons. First, some constructs are difficult to measure because no single source is a highly reliable source of information. This is particularly true for family processes because family interaction tends to be so routine and taken for granted that members often have little insight into the patterns that regularly occur. Second, having information from multiple sources allowed us to reduce the problem of shared method variance. Most studies use a single source, usually the mother or the child, to obtain data for all variables. Thus, when the researcher finds an association between two constructs such as parenting and delinquency, some portion of this correlation is likely to be a consequence of the fact that the same person provided information on both variables. For most of our analyses, the parent and child outcome measures included different sources of data.

Third, our study went beyond most research on the effect of divorce on children by comparing the effect of family structure to that of marital distress. Most studies that report a relationship between family structure and child maladjustment are unable to rule out the possibility that the children's problems began prior to marital breakup and are a result of parental discord rather than parental divorce. A rigorous test of this idea requires that the researcher have longitudinal data that include predivorce assessments of the children. Unfortunately, our data are cross-sectional and do not contain such information. We were able to compare the adjustment of children living in maritally distressed, intact families to that of children residing with happily married parents. Although such a test does not rule out the possibility that high rates of maladjustment among children of divorce existed prior to marital breakup, it does provide a crude comparison of the effect of marital discord on child adjustment to that of parental divorce.

Finally, as best we can tell using retrospective data, prior to marital breakup there were no socioeconomic differences between the divorced and intact families in our sample. Prior to divorce, the two sets of families were similar with regard to both income and education. This largely eliminates the chance that the family structure differences that we found are merely a function of class differences that existed prior to marital breakup. Previous research has established that divorce tends to be more common among the lower social classes. Most studies do not collect data on predivorce income; therefore it must be assumed that at least part of any difference in income found between divorced and intact families existed prior to marital breakup (McLanahan & Sandefur, 1994). To the extent that this is true, a reduction in the relationship between family structure and family processes after controlling for income may indicate either that family interaction is negatively affected by decreases in family finances following divorce or that the correlation between family structure and family interaction is spurious due to the association of both variables with social class.

We were able to avoid this confound in the present study because our single-parent families had predivorce income levels comparable to that of our intact families. This fact allows us to rule out predivorce differences in social class or income as an explanation for family structure differences in family processes or child adjustment. In those cases where differences in economic pressure appeared to explain family structure differences in mother's psychological well-being and parenting practices, we can assume that the higher levels of economic pressure seen among the divorced in our sample did not exist prior to marital disruption but are a consequence of the divorce process.

Although our study avoided some of the methodological problems inherent in much of the prior research on the consequences of divorce, our research design also included certain weaknesses. The most prominent limitations relate to the composition of the sample and the cross-sectional nature of the data. All the families in our sample were white and lived in relatively small communities. Although there is no apparent reason to assume that the processes found in our study are specific to families with these characteristics, there is a need to replicate our findings with a more ethnically and geographically diverse sample.

Second, the data used in this study are cross-sectional. Thus, we did not have information on family processes and child adjustment prior to parental divorce. Furthermore, although causal assumptions were made in the path analytic procedures used to perform many of the analyses, the reader is reminded that the relationships found represent covariations between variables. Although cross-sectional data can verify a relationship between two constructs, it cannot establish the causal priority that exists between them. This caveat should be kept in mind as the various findings are discussed.

Parental Divorce and Child Adjustment

With a few notable exceptions (e.g., McLanahan & Sandefur, 1994), most research on the consequences of divorce has failed to provide a clear sense of the size of the effect of family structure on child adjustment. Studies based on samples containing both divorced and intact families typically report correlations between family structure and child outcomes. These correlations are usually statistically significant but of modest magnitude. The coefficients typically range from .15 to .25. Studies with samples that include only divorced families often provide information regarding the proportion of children who develop adjustment problems. The results almost always show that the majority of children of divorce do not develop adjustment problems. These correlations and proportions leave a great deal of leeway for interpretation and can be seen as either supporting or contradicting the idea that divorce contributes to child adjustment problems.

On the one hand, significant correlations between family structure and child outcomes indicate that, on average, children of divorce have more adjustment problems than those living in intact families. This would seem to be evidence that divorce is an important cause of child adjustment problems. On the other hand, the correlations in most cases are small, suggesting that family structure explains little of the variation in child outcomes. This finding, coupled with the fact that the majority of children of divorce show normal adjustment patterns, would seem to indicate that parental divorce poses little threat for children's development. Both positions are logical inferences from the data usually presented in studies of children's response to divorce. Hence such findings have done little to clarify whether parental divorce is a major contributor to developmental problems in children.

A more precise understanding of the magnitude of the effect of parental divorce on child development requires that researchers focus on the extent to which parental divorce increases a child's odds of developing adjustment problems. This is analogous to epidemiological studies concerned with identifying risk factors for various physical illnesses. A condition or circumstance is considered a risk factor for a particular disease if it significantly increases the probability that a person will develop the illness. Smoking, elevated cholesterol, and hypertension, for example, are considered risk factors for coronary heart disease because they have been found to increase the odds that a person will develop this disease.

A factor often shows only a modest correlation with a particular illness even though it doubles or triples the odds of developing the disorder. This is because most illnesses have low base rates and most people who experience the risk factor do not get the illness. In the language of prevention research, a risk factor for a particular problem usually produces a large number of false positives. For example, it is widely recognized that smoking cigarettes produces a severalfold increase in the odds that a person will develop coronary heart disease or lung cancer. Yet, there is only a modest correlation between smoking and these diseases, and most smokers do not develop either disease. Indeed, although smoking is considered to be one of the greatest health risks, two thirds of those who smoke at least a pack of cigarettes a day do not die of any smoking-related disease (Mattson, Pollack, & Cullen, 1987).

The same pattern exists in risk factors for social problems. There is only a modest correlation between exposure to harsh parenting during childhood and harsh treatment of one's own children as an adult (Simons, Whitbeck, Conger, & Wu, 1991; Straus, Gelles, & Steinmetz, 1980). The vast majority of individuals who were abused as children do not grow up to abuse their own children; only about

30% do so (Kaufman & Zigler, 1987). On the other hand, it is estimated that abused children are approximately five times more likely to engage in abusive parenting than individuals who were not the victim of harsh, rejecting parenting (Kaufman & Zigler, 1987). This finding indicates that having been abused as a child is an important risk factor for mistreatment of one's own children.

As these examples make clear, we cannot assume that parental divorce is inconsequential for child development simply because studies report that the correlation between family structure and child adjustment is modest or that the majority of children of divorce do not develop adjustment problems. We need to compare the prevalence of child adjustment problems for divorced families to that for intact families. Such a comparison allows one to identify the extent to which parental divorce increases a child's risk for negative developmental outcomes.

The findings presented in the previous chapters indicate that children of divorce are at least twice as likely as those from intact families to display the problems included in our study (delinquency, early sexual intercourse, emotional distress, and academic difficulties). In some cases, the increased odds are much higher than two. For example, boys living with a divorced mother are four times more likely to display severe delinquency or to engage in early sexual intercourse than those living with both parents. Indeed, although gender is considered a powerful predictor of a child's risk for conduct problems (Gottfredson & Hirschi, 1990), the findings reported in Chapter 9 indicate that parental divorce has a larger effect on the probability of conduct problems than gender. Thus our data suggest that divorce is an important risk factor for child adjustment problems. Although the majority of children show normal patterns of development regardless of their parents' marital status, children of divorce are significantly more likely to develop problems than those living with both parents.

Our finding that marital disruption doubles a child's chances of developing psychosocial problems is consonant with results reported by McLanahan and Sandefur (1994). They used several large data sets involving nationally representative samples to examine the effect of family structure on early childbearing, idleness, and educational and occupational achievement. Their results suggest that adolescents and young adults from single-parent families are approximately twice as likely as those from two-parent families to develop problems in these areas. Indeed, their analyses indicate that the effect of family structure is as strong as that of race or ethnicity. McLanahan and Sandefur found, for example, that a young white woman from a single-parent family has the same risk of becoming a teen mother as a black or Hispanic young woman from a two-parent family. The same pattern of results was obtained for school dropouts. McLanahan and Sandefur note that these findings suggest that "some of the advantages associated with being white are equivalent to the advantages associated with living with two parents" (p. 62).

There has been a substantial increase in many types of adolescent problems since the mid-1960s. The rates of adolescent crime, substance abuse, suicide, school dropout, and teen pregnancy, for example, all have shown dramatic growth during this period. The prevalence of several of these behaviors has continued to climb during the 1990s, especially among African American youth. Between 1985 and 1992, the homicide rate for young white males went up approximately 50%; for young African American males it tripled (Wilson, 1995). Some have noted that the rise in child and adolescent problems parallels the increase in divorce and single-parent families that has occurred in recent decades. Indeed, several studies have reported strong associations between the proportion of female-headed households and adolescent and adult antisocial behavior (Block, 1979; Messner & Tardiff, 1986; Roncek, 1981; Sampson, 1985, 1986; Schuerman & Korbin, 1986; Smith & Jarjoura, 1988). In most of these studies, the effect of family structure is as strong or stronger than variables such as poverty or race. Sampson (1985, 1986), for example, found that rates of violent victimization are two to three times higher among residents of neighborhoods with high levels of family disruption.

As we have noted, at the individual level, there is only a modest correlation between family structure and adolescent problems; this has led many to assume that parental divorce does little to elevate a child's chances of developing problems. This view is at variance with the community-level studies just cited that show a strong association between high concentrations of single-parent families and adolescent deviant behavior. There is no contradiction if, as we argue, correlations between family structure and negative child outcomes fail to reflect accurately the increased risk that parental divorce poses for children. If living in single-parent family increases a male adolescent's risk for delinquency by three- or fourfold, one would expect communities with high concentrations of single-parent families to have significantly elevated rates of juvenile crime.

Many African American, inner-city neighborhoods have experienced a dramatic rise in both single-parent households and in adolescent crime and deviance in the last 15 years (Wilson, 1987). We believe there is a link between the two phenomena. We are not suggesting that family structure is the fundamental cause of adolescent antisocial behavior. We suspect, for example, that neighborhood characteristics (e.g., economic opportunity, gangs, quality of schools) are powerful determinants of adolescent problems. If single-parent families double a child's risk for negative developmental outcomes, however, a large increase in divorce or out-of-wedlock births would be expected to produce a rather substantial rise in the proportion of adolescents with behavioral or emotional problems. Thus the high rate of family disruption in many inner-city, African American neighborhoods probably explains, at least in part, the high levels of adolescent deviance seen in these communities. Consistent with this view, studies using community-level data have found that controlling for proportion of single-parent families largely eliminates the association between race and violent crime (Messner & Tardiff, 1986; Sampson, 1985).

Although in general parental divorce increases the odds that children will experience psychosocial difficulties, information about family structure is not very useful in predicting the course of development for a particular child. Indeed, a teacher or counselor would be ill advised to expect that a child is going to develop emotional or behavioral difficulties simply because his or her parents have divorced. Most children of divorce do not develop problems, hence such an expectation would turn out to be erroneous more often than not. This tends to be true for other types of risk factors as well. A person would be wrong more often than right if he or she predicted that a smoker friend was going to develop lung cancer, that a harshly parented child was going to grow up to be an abusive parent, or that an adolescent nephew living in an impoverished community was going to become delinquent. Although a risk factor increases the odds of a certain negative consequence, most people exposed to it do not suffer this ill effect.

Accurate prediction of which individuals are most vulnerable to a particular risk factor usually requires knowledge of the mechanisms by which the condition produces its deleterious effects. Thus, if we are to identify children of divorce most at risk for adjustment problems, we need information regarding the manner in which family structure increases a child's odds for developmental difficulties. Such knowledge is also necessary if we are to design effective social policies to prevent or reduce the threat to children posed by parental divorce. Results from the present study suggest that stress and family processes mediate much of the effect of family structure on child development. These findings are discussed in the following section.

Explaining the Link Between Parental Divorce and Child Adjustment

There are three general views regarding the relationship between parental divorce and child adjustment problems: the spuriousness hypothesis, the selection perspective, and the stress explanation. Our results are relevant to each of these ideas.

POSSIBLE SPURIOUS FINDINGS

The spuriousness hypothesis posits that there is no causal link between family structure and child outcomes; rather the association between the two constructs is a consequence of the fact that they are both related to some other variable. It is often noted, for example, that marital disruption and child adjustment problems are negatively related to social class, and therefore the relationship between divorce and child outcomes may be spurious due to the association of both with family socioeconomic status.

Consistent with this view, studies generally find that controlling for family income reduces the relation between family structure and child outcomes (Amato, 1993; McLanahan & Booth, 1989). Most studies do not include measures of predivorce family income, however, and hence cannot determine whether family structure differences in income represent social class differences that existed prior to divorce or reductions in income following marital disruption. This makes it difficult to interpret the finding that controlling for family income substantially reduces the relationship between family structure and child adjustment.

The result may be an indication that the correlation between family structure and child adjustment is spurious due to the association of both variables with social class. On the other hand, it might be seen as evidence that financial pressures resulting from marital breakup increase a child's chances of developmental difficulties. In other words, the finding that controlling for income diminishes the relationship between family structure and child adjustment can be viewed as support for either a selection or a strain perspective on divorce. In the present study, we obtained predivorce estimates of income and education; these data suggested that, prior to marital breakup, the single-parent families in our sample did not differ in socioeconomic status from the intact families. Thus it is unlikely that the family structure differences in child outcomes that we have reported can be explained by predivorce differences in social class.

Although discussions of spuriousness usually involve social class, some researchers have noted that the association between divorce and child outcomes may be spurious due to confounds with parental conflict. Persistent marital discord may foster emotional and behavior problems in children (Emery, 1988). In addition, it increases the probability of divorce. Thus parental conflict might be viewed as causing both child problems and marital breakup. We were unable to provide a strong test of this hypothesis because our data set does not contain information on children's behavior prior to parental divorce. We were able to perform weak tests of this hypothesis by comparing adolescent adjustment in three types of families: intact families with a strong marriage, intact families with a weak marriage, and divorced, single-parent families.

We found that adolescents in divorced families are significantly more involved in delinquent behavior and early sex than those living in intact families, whereas there is no difference in these behaviors for adolescents in intact families regardless of the quality of their parents' marriage. Children living in intact families with a weak marriage show more depression and academic problems than those residing in intact families with strong marriages. Children from divorced families, however, demonstrate significantly higher levels of depression and academic problems than those in intact families, regardless of marital quality. Thus our results indicate that the negative effects of parental divorce are greater and more consistent than those of marital discord. This suggests that family structure differences in child adjustment are not simply a continuation of problems fostered by parental conflict prior to divorce.

Furthermore, these findings contradict the popular view that parental divorce is no more injurious to children than living with unhappily married parents. This is undoubtedly true when marital conflict is extreme or involves substance abuse or physical violence. In such instances, marital separation is apt to reduce the child's risk for emotional or behavioral problems (Amato, 1993). In most cases, however, marital conflict, even during the months preceding marital breakup, is probably much less intrusive. Wallerstein and Kelley (1980) found, for example, that children of divorce are usually well aware of the long history of discord between their parents and know that their parents were not happily married. Still, few greeted the divorce with relief and most were surprised and upset by the news that their parents were separating. Children undoubtedly perceive persistent parental discord as frustrating and annoying, but in most cases its effect on the child's emotional and behavioral functioning is probably much less than that of divorce (Cherlin, 1992; Furstenberg & Cherlin, 1991).

THE SELECTION PERSPECTIVE

The selection viewpoint asserts that some adults have characteristics or traits that place them at risk for marital discord and divorce, as well as for other difficulties in functioning (Kitson, 1992; Kitson & Morgan, 1990). In addition to increasing the probability of marital breakup, these vulnerabilities are seen as contributing to a disorganized, stressful lifestyle that includes an ineffective approach to parenting (Simons, Beaman, et al., 1993). This lifestyle and inept parenting would be expected to have a detrimental effect on child development. Thus the selection argument argues that problematic characteristics of the parents account for the finding that marital status is related to child outcomes.

Past research based on the selection perspective has emphasized the consequences of an antisocial orientation. Antisocial behavior involves actions deemed to be risky, inappropriate, shortsighted, or insensitive by the majority of people in society (e.g., fights, substance abuse, sexual promiscuity, minor violations of the law). Lahey et al. (1988) report a higher incidence of antisocial behavior among divorced mothers in their clinical sample than among mothers from intact families, and Patterson and his associates (Capaldi & Patterson, 1991; Patterson & Capaldi, 1991; Patterson & Dishion, 1988) provide evidence that antisocial parents are at high risk for marital disruptions, social disadvantage, and inept parenting practices. Findings from the present study are consonant with the results of these studies.

We found that persons with antisocial tendencies are overrepresented among the divorced. This does not mean that most divorced persons have antisocial tendencies. The percentage who engage in antisocial behavior is small for both divorced and married women. The proportion of women who have recently engaged in antisocial acts is about twice as high among the divorced as the married, however. The analyses indicate that antisocial tendencies exert an indirect effect on child adjustment through their effect on mother's level of stress and quality of parenting. Mother's antisocial behavior increases the probability of family economic pressure, stressful life events, and psychological depression. In turn, high scores on these variables are related to disrupted parenting. In addition, antisocial tendencies have a direct effect on quality of parenting.

These results suggest that part of the association between divorce and child adjustment is a consequence of the fact that antisocial persons are overrepresented among the divorced. Although only about 10% to 15% of the divorced in our sample showed significant antisocial tendencies, these women were much more likely than their more conventional counterparts to suffer high stress, to display ineffective parenting, and to have children with adjustment problems.

Although these findings provide support for the selection perspective, it should be noted that maternal antisocial tendencies account for only a small proportion of the variance in our structural equation modeling. Antisocial orientation accounts for about 20% to 25% of the relationship between divorce and stress variables (family economic pressure, stressful life events, and psychological distress). It explains about a third of the association between divorce and quality of parenting. Thus, although we found some support for the selection perspective, the strain perspective appears to explain the preponderance of the association between family structure and child outcomes.

THE STRAIN PERSPECTIVE

Strain explanations maintain that aversive events and circumstances brought about by family disruption account for the higher rates of maladjustment in single-parent households. Strain explanations generally take one of two forms (Amato, 1993). The economic hardship hypothesis suggests that family structure differences in child adjustment are a result of the severe decline in standard of living experienced by most women and their children following divorce (Demo & Acock, 1988; Duncan & Hoffman, 1985; Weitzman, 1985). The parental adjustment hypothesis contends that children in single-parent families are at risk for poor outcomes because the stress associated with divorce often disrupts a woman's psychological well-being and parenting behavior (Hetherington et al., 1982; McLanahan & Booth, 1989). The model tested in the present study combines these two views (see Figure 1.1). It asserts that the developmental problems seen among children of divorce are in large measure a result of the negative effect of stress on the emotional adjustment and parenting practices of custodial parents. Economic pressure is considered a determinant of family structure differences in child outcomes because of its effect on these variables. The model posits that economic pressure increases stress and psychological distress and reduces quality of parenting. Our findings provide support for the model.

Chapter 3 shows that the divorced women in our sample reported more economic hardship, negative life events, and work-related stress than the married women. This relationship held even after the effects of the women's personal characteristics (e.g., education, antisocial tendencies) were partialled out. The divorced were about twice as likely as the married to suffer economic pressure and they were several times more likely to have experienced negative life events such as a change in residence or criminal victimization. Chapter 4 reports that the divorced women were over twice as likely as the married (28% vs. 11%) to score high on our depression index. Analysis indicates that the elevated psychological distress seen among the divorced is a consequence of their high levels of economic pressure, work stress, and negative life events.

Chapter 5 focuses on quality of parenting. Consistent with other recent studies (e.g., Acock & Demo, 1994), we found that the majority of divorced women are competent parents. Regardless of whether observer ratings, adolescent reports, or mother self-reports are used to assess quality of parenting, the data indicate that only about 20% to 25% of the divorced women were engaging in dysfunctional parenting practices. Taken by itself, this statistic suggests little reason for alarm, as more than three quarters of the divorced mothers are doing a good job of parenting their children. On the other hand, although the percentage of divorced women who are failing to provide adequate discipline and control is relatively small, it is about double that for married mothers.

We tested the hypothesis that the relationship between divorce and quality of parenting is a function of the stress and poorer adjustment of the divorced compared to the married. Much of the association between family structure and parenting practices is mediated by economic pressure, negative events, and depression. About a third of the relationship is also explained by antisocial tendencies. These findings suggest that the inept parenting sometimes seen among divorced mothers is largely a consequence of the frustration and preoccupation produced by financial difficulties and stressful events and by the negativity and irritability that accompanies depression. Secondly, it is a function of the fact that persons with antisocial tendencies are overrepresented among the divorced, and such individuals tend to lack the motivation and social skills necessary for competent parenting. There is a small but significant association between family structure and parenting after controlling for the strain and selection variables. Some researchers argue that absence of a second parent within the home tends to produce a blurring of generational boundaries and a weakening of parental authority (Knok, 1988). The small direct effect between family structure and quality of parenting might be interpreted as evidence for this contention.

Social scientists often speculate that the emotional distress and disrupted parenting seen among divorced women is explained, at least in part, by their having less access to social support than married women. Our results are inconsistent with this idea because the divorced women reported more access to social support than the married women. This is consistent with Kitson's (1992) finding that divorced women spend more time visiting friends than married persons. We believe that people have overestimated the extent to which marital breakup reduces access to social support. Certainly, there is likely to be a decline in the size of friendship networks following divorce, but this is largely a matter of dropping relationships where social ties were between couples rather than individuals or of decreasing interaction with persons identified as more the former spouse's friend. We expect that most women maintain ties with their closest friends following divorce, plus they establish new relationships with other single women. Thus they have as much access to social support from friends and relatives as married women. Of course, the divorced, by definition, do not have access to one type of support available to married persons: support from a spouse.

Having established that economic pressure and stressful events following divorce have a disruptive effect on parental discipline and control, we examined the extent to which this decline in quality of parenting accounts for family structure differences in child adjustment. The results provide strong support for this view. Chapter 7 shows that quality of mother's parenting mediates the association between parental divorce and sibling conflict. Findings from Chapter 8 indicate that quality of mother's parenting accounts for much of the association between parental divorce and adolescent affiliation with deviant peers and involvement in delinquent behavior. Chapter 9 presents evidence that quality of mother's parenting mediates the association between parental divorce and boys' early sexual intercourse. Affiliation with deviant peers was found to be the best predictor of girls' early sex. Quality of mother's parenting indirectly explains much of the association between parental divorce and girls' early sex through its effect on affiliation with deviant peers. Analyses presented in Chapter 10 indicate that quality of mother's parenting explains most of the association between parental divorce and adolescent depression. Results reported in Chapter 11 suggest that involvement in delinquent behavior is a strong predictor of school problems. Quality of mother's parenting explains part of the relationship between parental divorce and school problems through its effect on delinquency.

Thus, quality of mother's parenting is directly or indirectly related to each of the child outcomes included in our study. Furthermore, the analyses presented in the various chapters indicate that the effect of family economic pressure, negative life events, and mother's psychological adjustment on adolescent problems is largely indirect through quality of parenting. This pattern of findings suggests that, in large measure, the relationship between parental divorce and adolescent problems is explained by the following causal sequence: marital disruption increases the probability that a woman will experience economic pressures, negative life events, and psychological depression. This strain and emotional distress tend to reduce the quality of her parenting. Reductions in quality of parenting, in turn, increase a child's risk for emotional and behavioral problems. These findings provide strong support for the model presented in Chapter 1 (see Figure 1.1), which identifies increased stress and disrupted parenting as the primary avenue whereby parental divorce increases children's risk for poor developmental outcomes.

Although our results identify quality of mother's parenting as an important mediator of the effect of divorce on child adjustment, some studies have found only weak support for this perspective (e.g., Astone & McLanahan, 1991; Thomson, Hanson, & McLanahan, 1994). We believe that this inconsistency is a function of differences in measures of parenting. Studies that find small effects often have used short, self-report instruments to measure parental behavior or have examined parents' educational aspirations for their children or amount of time spent talking with children rather than the quality of parental supervision and control. Researchers tend to find parenting effects comparable to those obtained in the present study when they focus on parental monitoring and discipline and use in-depth procedures, including observational ratings, to assess parenting practices (e.g., Hetherington, Cox, & Cox, 1978).

Although our findings provide strong support for the idea that quality of mother's parenting mediates the association between parental divorce and adolescent problems, they also point to additional avenues by which divorced mothers may increase their children's risk for developmental problems. Results reported in Chapter 11 show that divorced women are less likely to participate in school-related events than married women. The lower involvement of divorced mothers is probably a consequence of the fatigue and time pressures they experience as a single adult trying to meet work, household, and parenting responsibilities. Unfortunately, our analyses also indicate that adolescents are more likely to display academic problems when their mothers are uninvolved in school activities. Thus it appears that a portion of the association between parental divorce and adolescent school performance is a consequence of the tendency for divorced mothers to be less involved in school functions than married women.

Findings presented in Chapter 8 indicate that divorced mothers are more apt to engage in antisocial behavior than married women and that such actions increase the chances that adolescent daughters will participate in delinquent activities. Chapter 9 reports that divorced mothers possess more sexually permissive values than married women and that such value commitments increase the probability that daughters will engage in early sexual intercourse. These two findings suggest that part of the association between parental divorce and girls' increased risk for conduct problems is explained by modeling.

We also found evidence that a positive relationship with grandparents can counter negative modeling by the mother. Our analyses indicate that daughters are strongly influenced by their mother's deviant behavior when there is little involvement with grandparents, but that the mother's antisocial characteristics exert little influence when the daughter has a strong relationship with her grandparents. Apparently a close relationship with grandparents can reduce the extent to which girls accept antisocial mothers as role models.

THE ROLE OF FATHERS

The discussion up to this point has emphasized the avenues whereby mothers mediate the effect of family structure on child adjustment. Although the model presented in Chapter 1 (Figure 1.1) identifies maternal functioning as the primary explanation for the link between parental divorce and negative child outcomes, it also posits that the behavior of fathers contributes to family structure differences.

Effective parenting involves activities such as providing encouragement and emotional support, establishing and explaining standards for conduct, and administering consistent discipline (Maccoby & Martin, 1983). Fathers do not need to live with their children to engage in these behaviors. Fathers who engage in such parenting practices would be expected to have a positive influence on child development regardless of whether they share a residence with the son or daughter. Social scientists have noted that there is little empirical support for the contention that divorced fathers influence child development because most studies find that frequency of visitation by nonresidential fathers is unrelated to child adjustment (Amato, 1993; Emery, 1988; Furstenberg & Cherlin, 1991). There is no reason to expect, however, that simply having contact with the nonresidential father would significantly influence a child's development. We believe that it is the quality, rather than quantity, of interaction with this parent that is the key to understanding his influence on child adjustment. Nonresidential fathers must engage in effective parenting behaviors if they are to influence the development of their children. We found support for this idea in a recent paper (Simons, Whitbeck, Beaman, & Conger, 1994).

Unfortunately, studies indicate that nonresidential fathers often behave toward their children more as an adult friend or relative than as a parent (Arendell, 1986; Furstenberg & Nord, 1985; Hetherington, Cox, & Cox, 1976). Much of the time with their children is spent joking and roughhousing, watching TV, attending movies, going out to eat, and the like. Past research indicates that fathers in intact families also show low involvement in parenting (Parke & Sterns, 1993). Interaction between fathers and their children in intact families, like that in divorced families, tends to be focused around play and mutual entertainment (Parke & Sterns, 1993). Thus, regardless of whether they live in the home, fathers are less likely than mothers to engage in parenting activities that have been shown to be crucial for the positive psychosocial development of children (e.g., setting standards, providing encouragement and emotional support, administering consistent discipline). However, while the frequency of these parenting behaviors is low regardless of family structure, fathers in intact families would be expected to be more involved in these activities than nonresidential fathers.

Based on this line of thought, we posited that differences in the parenting practices of fathers explain part of the association between parental divorce and negative child outcomes. Our findings largely corroborate this hypothesis. Quality of father's parenting is inversely related to sibling conflict, adolescent depression, delinquent behavior, and affiliation with deviant peers. Father's parenting is indirectly related to adolescent early sexual intercourse and school problems through its effect on affiliation with deviant peers and delinquency. Furthermore, there is a significant negative relationship between parental divorce and quality of father's parenting. Finally, associations between marital disruption and negative child outcomes are substantially reduced or eliminated when father's parenting is controlled. This pattern of findings indicates that quality of father's parenting accounts for part of the link between family structure and child adjustment.

IMPLICATIONS FOR OTHER FAMILY STRUCTURES

Throughout our discussion, we have referred to "family structure differences." It is important to keep in mind that our study only considered two types of family structures: divorced, mother-headed families and two-parent, never-divorced families. We assume that our theoretical model and research findings also apply to never-married, female-headed households and to divorced, father-headed households. Past research has shown that children living in such families demonstrate more adjustment problems than those living in intact families. We expect that this is because never-married mothers and single-parent fathers are more likely than married, never-divorced parents to experience economic pressure, negative life events, psychological distress, and disrupted parenting. This possibility needs to be investigated in future studies.

Past research has also established that children living in stepparent families show more emotional and behavioral problems than those in intact families (Cherlin, 1992; McLanahan & Sandefur, 1994; Zill, 1988). Our model cannot be used to explain the increased risk for problems seen among children living in such families. Remarriage usually results in a significant increase in family income (McLanahan & Sandefur, 1994; Zill, 1988). Thus stepparent families are less apt to experience the disruptive consequences of financial hardship than one-parent families. Based on our model, the enhanced economic well-being of stepparent families should result in a lower prevalence of negative life events, psychological distress, and inept parenting relative to one-parent families. So what accounts for the elevated risk for psychosocial problems among children in stepparent families?

We expect that the answer involves quality of parenting. Although economic pressure, negative events, and psychological distress may be less evident following remarriage, new threats to parenting may emerge in stepparent families. Marriage is a stressful life transition. Constructing a mutually satisfying marital life usually involves a good bit of time and energy. A parent's attention to this task may distract from the role of parent (McLanahan & Sandefur, 1994). Furthermore, children are often slow to accept the authority of a stepparent. Thus, although the biological parent's parenting may be compromised by the demands of a new spouse, there is a limit to how quickly the new stepparent can take on parenting responsibilities. To the extent that such processes operate, children in stepparent families are apt to receive less monitoring, support, and discipline than those in two-parent, never-divorced families.

Family Structure Versus Family Process

In recent years, several family scholars have contended that researchers concerned with the link between family factors and child adjustment should devote less attention to family structure and concentrate more on family processes (Acock & Demo, 1994; Allen, 1993; Demo, 1992, 1993). We are sympathetic to the concerns these social scientists have expressed regarding research on family structure, particularly their worries that such studies may have a pejorative effect on single mothers or be used by politicians to pursue an antifeminist political agenda. On the other hand, we believe there is overwhelming evidence that family structure is related to child outcomes and that it is in the best interest of women and children, as well as the broader society, to face up to this finding. Furthermore, we believe that researchers who argue for a focus on family process to the exclusion of family structure have incorrectly interpreted the implications of the research they use to bolster their position. In this section, I briefly discuss research findings often cited as support for the idea that it is family process, not family structure, that is important for understanding child development.

First, some researchers have noted that family process variables, such as quality of parenting, are more strongly related to child development than family structure (Acock & Demo, 1994; Demo, 1992, 1993). Although we agree with this reading of the literature, we do not take this pattern of findings as an indication that family structure is an unimportant variable. The effect of family structure is not trivial simply because it is less than that of family process. Although quality of family interaction may be a more powerful determinant of child development than family structure, a factor that doubles a child's risk for negative outcomes cannot be dismissed as unimportant.

Second, it has been suggested that the effect of family structure is minimal because there is much overlap in the distribution of problems for children living in single- and two-parent families. As Acock and Demo (1994; Demo, 1993) have observed, children from two-parent as well as single-parent families develop problems, most children adjust well regardless of family type, and there is greater variation in child outcomes within than between various types of families. It is certainly important that policymakers and the general public be made aware of these points. Children of divorce are not a homogeneous group that inevitably develops problems. As our findings and those of others make clear, there is great variability among children whose parents divorce, and most children of divorce do not develop long-term difficulties in functioning. And, a child is not immune to problems simply because he or she lives with two parents. A significant proportion of children living with both parents develops psychosocial problems.

These findings should not be taken to mean, however, that family structure is inconsequential for child development. Such a conclusion involves confusing differences in dispersion with differences in central tendency (Amato, 1993). Although there may be a good bit of overlap in distributions of outcomes for children in single- and two-parent households, with the majority of children in both types of families showing positive development, there are also important differences in central tendencies for the two groups, with the single-parent children, on average, showing poorer adjustment.

In this sense, family structure is no different than other circumstances viewed as risk factors for negative child outcomes. Most social scientists view abusive or alcoholic parents, family poverty, or living in a disadvantaged neighborhood as conditions that increase a child's chances for poor adjustment. Yet, most children do not develop problems regardless of whether they have experienced these conditions, and within group differences in outcomes are generally greater than between group differences for children who have or have not experienced these risk factors. In this respect, the effect of family structure is similar to that of other circumstances that have been identified as increasing a child's probability of developmental difficulties.

Finally, some family scholars have argued that family processes are more fundamental and worthy of study than family structure because they are critical to the development of children in both single- and two-parent families and because they appear to mediate or explain the link between family structure and child adjustment (Acock & Demo, 1994; Demo, 1992; Demo & Acock, 1988). We certainly agree that family processes are vitally important in understanding child development. Indeed, the investigators on this project have spent much of their careers investigating the manner in which family processes (e.g., quality of parenting, marital conflict) influence adults and children. We believe, however, that the strong evidence that has accrued regarding the salience of family processes naturally leads to questions regarding the determinants of variations in family processes. Why do parents differ, for example, in the quality of their parenting? The results that we have presented, as well as those reported by others, suggest that family structure is one of several variables that influences family interaction.

Family structure does not become an unimportant construct simply because family relationships, such as quality of parenting, mediate their effect on children. Social structures always exert their influence through their effect on social interaction. In this sense, social structures and social processes are interconnected and inseparable phenomena. Community structure, for instance, influences child development, at least in part, through its effect on the types of relationships that adults and children establish with each other (Sampson & Lauritsen, 1994). Few would suggest that community structure is an insignificant determinant of child behavior because its influence is indirect through social interaction between residents. Rather, living in a disadvantaged community is considered to be a risk factor for children precisely because it impedes social interaction necessary for the collective socialization of children. Similarly, family structure is an important risk factor for child adjustment problems because it is related to family processes known to increase a child's chances for developmental difficulties.

Thus it is our position that research on child development should strive to include both social structure and social process variables. Our study emphasizes the link between family structure and parent-child interaction. Certainly, other social structures also influence child adjustment. The ethnic, class, neighborhood, school, and occupational structures of an area, just to name a few, would be expected to affect child outcomes. A comprehensive understanding of the forces that shape child development requires that we investigate the connection between such structures and the types of relationships that children form with family members, other adults, and peers in their social environment.

Policy Recommendations

The social sciences have been reasonably successful in terms of providing insights into the dynamics of various social problems. Unfortunately, they have been impotent when it comes to generating effective solutions to these problems. This book is no exception. Our strong suit is basic research; we are much less comfortable in the public policy arena. Nevertheless, we feel compelled to discuss what we perceive as the policy implications of our findings. As we see it, society might take two basic approaches in an attempt to reduce the number of children who experience emotional or behavioral problems as a consequence of parental divorce. The first is to design social policies that encourage couples with children to stay together; the second involves identifying strategies for reducing the stress and disrupted parenting often experienced by divorced families. Our discussion considers both of these tactics.

CAN THE INCIDENCE OF DIVORCE BE REDUCED?

In recent years, the United States has seen much public discourse regarding its high rate of marital disruption. As noted in Chapter 1, approximately 50% of all marriages end in divorce. This high rate of marital breakup is often attributed to a decline in family values. We disagree with this interpretation. Surveys show that the vast majority of Americans are committed to the institution of marriage. One recent study (Thornton, 1989) found, for example, that 93% of young women and 86% of young men feel that it is extremely important or quite important to have a good marriage and family life. The same study reports that 87% of women and 81% of men think it very likely or fairly likely that they will stay married to the same person for life. Thus, people want to marry and they assume their marital relationship will last a lifetime. Even people who divorce tend to remarry within a relatively short period of time, suggesting that it is their former spouse, and not the institution of marriage, that they perceive as defective.

If most people are committed to the idea of a lifelong marital partner, why do marriages so often fail? We believe the answer involves complex changes in the social circumstances and reward structures of society. It is not that people have stopped believing in the goal of long-term marital relationships; it is that advanced industrialized societies make this ideal very difficult to achieve. This is why several of the politicians who have exposed a political agenda of restoring family values are themselves divorced (e.g., Ronald Reagan, Newt Gingrich, Bob Dole, Phil Gramm, Pete Wilson). Apparently these individuals' devotion to family values did not prevent their marriages from dissolving.

What social changes have contributed to the high rates of marital disruption? Most family sociologists point to socioeconomic conditions and structural arrangements that naturally emerge as societies modernize. People migrate from rural areas to cities, where the traditional household division of labor is no longer functional. Both boys and girls receive public education and women begin to join men in the labor force. Rationality replaces social custom and religious ideology; this new perspective, combined with the availability of birth control techniques, frees people from the constraints of engaging in sexual intercourse outside of marriage. These changes produce a shift in the rewards provided by marriage.

Although marriage continues to furnish some monetary advantages, especially for women, it is no longer an economic necessity. Single women are able to survive financially, even when they have children. Furthermore, marriage is no longer necessary to satisfy sexual appetites. Sexual intercourse is open to single as well as married adults. Concomitant with this decline in the economic and sexual benefits associated with marriage is an increase in the social support function provided by the marital relationship. Periodic moves and life in large cities are barriers to close relationships with extended family and friends. As a result, individuals become more dependent on their spouses for emotional support. People seek marital partners who will be their best friend; it is this mutual support and intimacy that is the primary glue of marriage in modern societies.

This shift in the rewards associated with marriage necessarily increases the likelihood of divorce. As McLanahan and Sandefur (1994) observe, "Once sex and childrearing were 'liberated' from marriage and once women could support themselves on their own, two of the most important rationales for marriage were gone" (p. 143). The intimacy function remains a rationale for marriage, but love is volatile (Collins, 1985). Although partners may experience each other as a friend and confidant at the point of marriage, it is difficult to sustain such a relationship over the life course. Factors such as dissimilar values or interests, disagreements over children and finances, and differing occupational priorities reduce attraction, enhance conflict, and push people apart. If the raison d'etre for marriage is mutual love and support, it is difficult for people to justify staying in a relationship where this is no longer present (Bellah, Sullivan, Swidler, & Tipton, 1985).

As a result, marriages in modern societies are terminated at a much higher rate than in more traditional societies. Although the largest increase has been in the United States, virtually all the industrialized countries showed a dramatic rise in the incidence of marital disruption between 1960 and 1990 (McLanahan & Sandefur, 1994). In some respects, these increased rates signal positive social change. Certainly, they indicate greater freedom for women and children to escape from domineering or abusive relationships. And they suggest that love and mutual affection have become more important in marriage (Collins, 1985). Unfortunately, these achievements come at a price. As Cherlin (1992) notes,

> Even those who would applaud the gains in autonomy and opportunity for women and in greater emphasis on love and companionship must acknowledge that the benefits have been achieved at a substantial cost. . . . Adults are freer to end unhappy marriages but do so through a

process that is often emotionally and economically draining for parents and traumatic for children. (p. 139)

The benefits of a high divorce rate apply almost exclusively to adults. Whereas adults experience greater freedom and autonomy, this is not the case for children. It is true that parental divorce allows some children to escape from an alcoholic or abusive parent. But in the majority of cases, the child is likely to have a reasonably good relationship with both parents prior to marital breakup. The resulting economic distress, negative life events, and disrupted parenting increase the child's risk for emotional or behavioral problems. Although increases in divorce may signal certain positive social changes, divorce is dysfunctional for society to the extent that it significantly increases the number of troubled individuals.

Regardless of whether one chooses to emphasize the social benefits or the social costs of divorce, it is clear that, for the most part, the social conditions and reward structures of modern societies that promote high rates of marital disruption are here to stay. Women's economic independence is likely to show further increases in the coming years; there is little reason to believe that there will be an end to sex outside of marriage. Does this mean that society has no choice but to accept high rates of divorce? Probably, although we believe that there are measures that might be taken to achieve a small reduction in marital disruption. These steps involve implementing policies that reduce the strain and marital discord in two-parent families.

There is substantial evidence that economic pressures are a major cause of marital conflict (Conger et al., 1990; Elder, 1974). Insufficient money to meet expenses fosters arguments over spending priorities and strategies for increasing family income. Economic strain contributes indirectly to marital and family conflict by increasing the frustration and irritability of parents. In large measure, the inverse relationship between social class and divorce is probably a function of the deleterious effects of economic hardship on marital interaction. This suggests that social policies that reduce the financial difficulties of low-income two-parent families will likely diminish marital discord and divorce. McLanahan and Sandefur (1994) discuss two policy changes that might help such families. First, they note that the United States is the only Western industrialized country that does not furnish a child allowance. Instead, the United States provides an income tax deduction that is worth quite a bit to middle-income families but is of little benefit to low-income families. McLanahan and Sandefur recommend that this income tax deduction be replaced with a child allowance of $500 per child.

Second, McLanahan and Sandefur (1994) suggest that the United States expand the Earned Income Tax Credit (EITC) program. The EITC provides a specified amount of governmental match for each dollar earned by low-income persons. Under this plan, a two-parent family with two children and an income below $28,000 would receive a match of 40 cents for every dollar earned, up to a maximum of $3,200 per year. McLanahan and Sandefur cite the example of a two-parent family in which each parent works 30 hours a week at $5 per hour. The annual income for this family would be just over $14,000, a figure that places the family slightly above the poverty level for a family of four. Under the EITC program, this family would have an income of $20,000.

The limitation of the EITC is that it assists only individuals who are working. McLanahan and Sandefur (1994) argue that the program needs to include a job guarantee for all mothers and fathers who are willing to work. They note that the EITC match could be less for government-created jobs so that parents would have an incentive to seek employment in the private sector.

Availability of high-quality, affordable day care and medical services would greatly benefit poor families. Day care costs often consume much of the money earned by low-income parents. Poor families usually have better access to health care if the parents are divorced and the mother is on welfare. Thus, it is important that policies designed to buoy and strengthen economically deprived two-parent families include provisions for affordable day care and medical services.

In addition to these income-enhancing policies, family stress and discord might be reduced by work-related policies that make it easier for couples to coordinate work requirements with the demands of marriage and parenthood. Examples of such policies are leave for parents of infants, flexible work hours, and company day care centers. Such practices make it easier for parents to organize their work schedules around the role of parent. This reduction in stress would be expected to enhance the psychological well-being of parents, with the result being an increase in quality of marital interaction and parenting.

HELPING DIVORCED FAMILIES

Although the measures discussed in the previous section might produce a slight reduction in marital disruption, the primary causes of divorce are endemic to advanced industrialized societies. Hence divorce rates in the United States are likely to remain relatively high. Given this fact, we need to identify steps that might be taken to help single-parent families avoid the circumstances that increase their children's risk for poor adjustment. There are several ways in which society might do a better job of assisting divorced women and their children.

First, our analyses suggest that much of the emotional distress and disrupted parenting seen among divorced mothers is a consequence of economic hardship. The financial situation of these women would be improved considerably if the strategies for strengthening two-parent families that were discussed in the previous section were made available to single-parent families as well. Thus, divorced women should have access to an EITC program that includes a job guarantee and affordable day care and medical services.

In addition, the economic pressures of divorced mothers might be reduced by implementing a more stringent child support policy. Studies indicate that only about half of all noncustodial fathers make the full support payments mandated by the court, and evidence suggests that many fathers could pay much higher dollar amounts than they are asked to provide (Garfinkel & Ollerich, 1989). Furthermore, awards often do not change with increases in the cost of living or the father's salary (McLindon, 1987; Morgan, 1991). Thus, we need a system that specifies realistic awards, is indexed to the cost of living, makes adjustments based on changes in the father's income, and monitors payments to ensure that they are made in a timely fashion.

McLanahan and Sandefur (1994) argue that we should go one step further and strive to assign a child support award for all children, even those born out of wedlock. They state that such a policy is based on the premise that the responsibilities of fathers to their children are nonnegotiable, even if the father has never been married to the mother. Fathers cannot decide to end their obligations to their children. If a man fathers a child, he must help support the child until the child is at least 18 years of age. Of course, some fathers do not pay child support because they are unemployed or make very low wages. McLanahan and Sandefur suggest that this problem can be addressed by guaranteeing minimum wage work and eligibility for EITC to noncustodial fathers, as they recommend for residential fathers.

In addition to these measures for reducing financial distress, society should pursue policies calculated to strengthen the quality of parenting provided by single parents. Earlier, we noted that employers could make it easier for couples to coordinate the demands of work with those of parenthood by permitting leave for parents of infants, providing flexible work hours, and establishing company day care centers. These practices are even more critical for single parents, who have sole responsibility for parenting and household management. It would be much easier for parents to organize their work schedules around their family obligations if employers would adopt these work-related policies.

One of the problems faced by single parents (and many two-parent families as well) is that their child is left unsupervised from the end of the school day until the parent arrives home from work. Parents cannot leave their place of employment during the middle of the afternoon to transport their children to day care, plus many single parents cannot afford to pay for this after-school service. Consequently, many children are left unattended for several hours every school day. There is a need for programs that structure a child's after-school time and provide adult supervision. Schools and local recreation centers should be encouraged, for example, to provide after-school activities involving sports, art, and music.

Finally, McLanahan and Sandefur (1994) contend that single parents might benefit from educational programs designed to help them avoid the risks to children posed by divorce. They argue that parents should be made aware that divorce elevates the chances that children will develop problems and information should be provided regarding the factors that appear to account for this increased danger. We endorse this novel proposal. The format for educating parents about these matters could vary from public service announcements on radio and TV to mandatory counseling at the time of divorce. Regardless of how it is presented, divorced parents need to be informed of certain facts.

We believe it is important that parents understand the nature of the association between parental divorce and child adjustment. They need to be assured that the majority of children from divorced families do not experience long-term problems. But they must also face the reality that divorce doubles the probability of many types of adjustment problems and that the best way to help one's children avoid such difficulties is to be a conscientious parent.

Divorced mothers should know that the stress and conflicting demands of life as a single parent often result in a loosening of behavioral standards, a reduction in monitoring, and a relaxation of discipline. They need to be encouraged to resist the blurring of generational boundaries and the weakening of parental authority that sometimes take place between divorced parents and their children. As a result of the role overload associated with single parenthood, single mothers are less likely than married women to attend school-related activities such as parent-teacher conferences, open house nights, and parent-teacher association meetings. Single mothers need to be prompted to participate in such activities to the extent possible because this decreases the probability that their child will display academic problems. Finally, single mothers need to be conscious of the connection between their behavior and that of their daughters. Our results suggest that daughters are influenced by the antisocial behavior or permissive sexual attitudes of their mothers. Thus, single mothers need to be careful about the behavior they model and emphasize to their daughters that some actions are appropriate for adults but not for adolescents.

Nonresidential fathers also need to be educated. They need to know that frequency of visitation has little effect on child adjustment. Nonresidential fathers facilitate positive child development to the extent that they engage in parenting activities such as monitoring academic progress, emphasizing moral principles, discussing problems, providing advice, and supporting the parenting decisions of the custodial mother. It is important that fathers understand that they can make a difference in the lives of their children even though they do not live in the same household. Nonresidential fathers can exert a positive influence on the development of their children to the extent that they go beyond being a friend and enact the duties and responsibilities of a parent.

Finally, we all need to recognize that parental divorce is not someone else's problem. Virtually every family and friendship network contains a significant proportion of divorced persons. It is our children and those of our friends and relatives who are being placed at risk by parental divorce. This means that we all have a stake in the formulation of social policies that reduce the adverse consequences of marital breakup for children. Furthermore, we must face the fact that in all probability, high divorce rates are here to stay. They are a natural consequence of the structural and cultural changes that accompany modernization. Just as the high incidence of marital disruption is rooted in macrosocietal processes, so broad-based social policies need to be established that promote the positive development of children who experience parental divorce.

References

Abramson, L., Seligman, M., & Teasdale, J. (1978). Learned helplessness in humans: Critique and reformulation. *Journal of Abnormal Psychology, 87,* 49-74.

Achenbach, T. M. (1991). *Integrative guide for the 1991 CBCL/4-18, YSR, and TRF profiles.* Burlington: University of Vermont, Department of Psychiatry.

Acock, A. C., & Demo, D. H. (1994). *Family diversity and well-being.* Thousand Oaks, CA: Sage.

Allen, K. R. (1993). The dispassionate discourse of children's adjustment to divorce. *Journal of Marriage and the Family, 55,* 46-49.

Allport, G. W. (1937). *Personality: A psychological interpretation.* New York: Holt, Rinehart & Winston.

Amato, P. R. (1987). Family processes in intact, one-parent, and step-parent families: The child's point of view. *Journal of Marriage and the Family, 49,* 327-337.

Amato, P. R. (1990). Family environment as perceived by children. *Journal of Marriage and the Family, 52,* 613-620.

Amato, P. R. (1993). Children's adjustment to divorce: Theories, hypotheses, and empirical support. *Journal of Marriage and the Family, 55,* 23-38.

Amato, P. R., & Keith, B. (1993a). Parental divorce and adult well-being: A meta-analysis. *Journal of Marriage and the Family, 53,* 43-58.

Amato, P. R., & Keith, B. (1993b). Parental divorce and the well-being of children: A meta-analysis. *Psychological Bulletin, 110,* 26-46.

American Psychiatric Association. (1987). *Diagnostic and statistical manual of mental disorders, III-R.* Washington, DC: Author.

Anshensel, C., Rutter, C., & Lachenbruch, P. (1991). Social structure, stress and mental health: Competing conceptual and analytic models. *American Sociological Review, 56,* 166-178.

Arendell, T. (1986). *Mothers and divorce: Legal, economic, and social dilemmas.* Berkeley: University of California Press.

Aseltine, R. H., Jr., Gore, S., & Colten, M. E. (1994). Depression and the social developmental context of adolescence. *Journal of Personality and Social Psychology, 67,* 252-263.

Astone, N. M., & McLanahan, S. S. (1991). Family structure, parenting practices, and high school completion. *American Sociological Review, 56,* 309-320.

Bachrach, L. L. (1975). *Marital status and mental disorder: An analytic review* (DHEW Publication No. ADM 75-217). Washington, DC: Government Printing Office.

Bakeman, R., & Adamson, L. B. (1984). Coordinating attention to people and objects in mother-infant and peer-infant interaction. *Child Development, 55,* 1278-1289.

Bakke, E. W. (1940). *Citizens without work.* New Haven, CT: Yale University Press.

Bandura, A. (1977). *Social learning theory.* Englewood Cliffs, NJ: Prentice Hall.

Bandura, A. (1986). *Social foundations of thought and action.* Englewood Cliffs, NJ: Prentice Hall.

Bane, M. J. (1976). *Here to stay: American families in the twentieth century.* New York: Basic Books.

Bank, L., Dishion, T., Skinner, M., & Patterson, G. R. (1989). Method variance in structural equation modeling: Living with "GLOP." In G. R. Patterson (Ed.), *Aggression and depression in family interactions* (pp. 247-280). Hillsdale, NJ: Lawrence Erlbaum.

Bank, S. P., & Kahn, M. D. (1982). *The sibling bond.* New York: Basic Books.

Baron, R. M., & Kenny, D. A. (1986). The moderator-mediator variable distinction in social psychological research: Conceptual, strategic, and statistical considerations. *Journal of Personality and Social Psychology, 51,* 1173-1182.

Baucom, D. H., Sayers, S. L., & Duhe, A. (1989). Attributional style and attributional patterns among married couples. *Journal of Personality and Social Psychology, 56,* 596-607.

Beck, A. T. (1976). *Cognitive theory and emotional disorders.* New York: International Universities Press.

Bellah, R. N., Sullivan, W. M., Swidler, A., & Tipton, S. M. (1985). *Habits of the heart.* Berkeley: University of California Press.

Block, R. (1979). Community, environment, and violent crime. *Criminology, 17,* 46-57.

Boer, F., & Dunn, J. (Eds.). (1992). *Children's sibling relationships: Developmental and clinical issues.* Hillsdale, NJ: Lawrence Erlbaum.

Boer, F., Goedhart, A. W., & Treffers, P. D. A. (1992). Siblings and their parents. In F. Boer & J. Dunn (Eds.), *Children's sibling relationships: Developmental and clinical issues* (pp. 41-54). Hillsdale, NJ: Lawrence Erlbaum.

Bollen, K. (1989). *Structural equations with latent variables.* New York: John Wiley.

Bossard, J. H. S., & Boll, E. S. (1956). *The large family system.* Philadelphia: University of Pennsylvania Press.

Brody, G. H., & Forehand, R. (1988). Multiple determinants of parenting: Research findings and implications for the divorce process. In E. M. Hetherington & J. D. Arasteh (Eds.), *Impact of divorce, single parenting, and stepparenting on children* (pp. 117-133). Hillsdale, NJ: Lawrence Erlbaum.

Brody, G. H., Stoneman, Z., & McCoy, J. K. (1994). Contributions of family relationships and child temperaments to longitudinal variations in sibling relationship quality and sibling relationship styles. *Journal of Family Psychology, 8,* 274-286.

Brooks-Gunn, J., & Furstenberg, F. (1989). Adolescent sexual behavior. *American Psychologist, 44,* 249-257.

Bumpass, L. L. (1990). What's happening to the family? Interactions between demographic and institutional change. *Demography, 27,* 483-498.

Bumpass, L. L., & Sweet, J. A. (1989). Children's experience in single-parent families: Implications of cohabitation and marital transitions. *Family Planning Perspectives, 21,* 256-260.

Capaldi, D. M., & Patterson, G. R. (1991). Relation of parental transitions to boys' adjustment problems: I. A linear hypothesis. II. Mothers at risk for transitions and unskilled parenting. *Developmental Psychology, 27,* 489-504.

Caplow, T., & Chadwick, B. A. (1979). Inequalities and life-styles in Middletown, 1920-1978. *Social Science Quarterly, 60,* 367-368.

Caspi, A., & Elder, G. H. (1988). Emergent family patterns: The intergenerational construction of problem behavior and relationships. In R. A. Hinde & J. Stevenson-Hinde (Eds.), *Relationships within families* (pp. 218-240). New York: Oxford University Press.

Caspi, A., Elder, G. H., & Bem, D. J. (1987). Moving against the world: Life-course patterns of explosive children. *Developmental Psychology, 23,* 308-313.

Chavkin, N. F. (1989). A multicultural perspective on parent involvement: Implications for policy and practice. *Education, 109,* 276-285.

Chavkin, N. F., & Williams, D. L., Jr. (1989). Low-income parents' attitudes toward parent involvement in education. *Journal of Sociology and Social Welfare, 16,* 17-28.

Cherlin, A. J. (1992). *Marriage, divorce, remarriage.* Cambridge, MA: Harvard University Press.

Cherlin, A. J., Furstenberg, F. F., Chase-Landale, P. L., Kiernan, K. E., Robins, P. K., Morrison, D. R., & Teitler, J. O. (1991). Longitudinal studies of effects of divorce on children in Great Britain and the United States. *Science, 252,* 1386-1389.

Chiriboga, D. A., Catron, L., & Associates. (1991). *Divorce: Crisis, challenge or relief.* New York: New York University Press.

Christensen, A., Phillips, S., Glasgow, R. E., & Johnson, S. M. (1983). Parental characteristics and interactional dysfunction in families with child behavior problems: A preliminary investigation. *Journal of Abnormal Child Psychology, 11,* 153-166.

Cohen, S., & Hoberman, H. (1983). Positive events and social supports as buffers of life change stress. *Journal of Applied Social Psychology, 13,* 99-125.

Cohen, S., & Wills, T. A (1985). Stress, social support, and the buffering hypothesis. *Psychological Bulletin, 98,* 310-357.

Collins, R. (1985). *Sociology of marriage and the family: Gender, love, and property.* Chicago: Nelson-Hall.

Compas, B. E., Ey, S., & Grant, K. E. (1993). Taxonomy, assessment, and diagnosis of depression during adolescence. *Psychological Bulletin, 114,* 323-344.

Compas, B. E., & Hammen, C. L. (1994). Child and adolescent depression: Covariation and comorbidity in development. In R. J. Haggerty, L. R. Sherrod, N. Garmezy, & M. Rutter (Eds.), *Stress, risk, and resilience in children and adolescents: Processes, mechanisms, and interventions* (pp. 225-267). New York: Cambridge University Press.

Conger, K. J., Conger, R. D., & Elder, G. H., Jr. (1994). Sibling relations during hard times. In R. D. Conger & G. H. Elder, Jr. (Eds.), *Families in trouble times: Adapting to change in rural America* (pp. 235-252). New York: Aldine.

Conger, R. D., Conger, K. J., Elder, G. H., Lorenz, F. O., Simons, R. L., & Whitbeck, L. B. (1992). A family process model of economic hardship and influences on adjustment of early adolescent boys. *Child Development, 63,* 526-541.

Conger, R. D., Conger, K. J., Elder, G. H., Lorenz, F. O., Simons, R. L., & Whitbeck, L. B. (1993). Family economic stress and adjustment of early adolescent girls. *Developmental Psychology, 29,* 206-219.

Conger, R. D., & Elder, G. H., Jr. (1994). *Families in troubled times: Adapting to change in rural America.* Hawthorne, NY: Aldine.

Conger, R. D., Elder, G. H., Lorenz, F. O., Conger, K. J., Simons, R. L., Whitbeck, L. B., Huch, S., & Melby, J. N. (1990). Linking economic hardship to marital quality and instability. *Journal of Marriage and the Family, 52,* 643-656.

Conger, R. D., Ge, X., Elder, G. H., Lorenz, F. O., & Simons, R. L. (1994). Economic stress, coercive family process, and developmental problems of adolescents. *Child Development, 65,* 541-561.

Conger, R. D., McCarthy, J. A., Young, R. K., Lahey, B. B., & Kropp, J. P. (1984). Perception of child, child-rearing values, and emotional distress as mediating links between environmental stressors and observed maternal behavior. *Child Development, 55,* 2234-2247.

Coyne, J. C., & Downey, G. (1991). Social factors and psychopathology: Stress, social support and coping processes. *Annual Review of Psychology, 42,* 401-425.

Daniels, P., & Weingarten, K. (1983). *Sooner or later: The timing of parenthood in adult lives.* New York: Norton.

Day, R. (1992). The transition to first intercourse among racially and culturally diverse youth. *Journal of Marriage and the Family, 54,* 749-762.

Demo, D. H. (1992). Parent-child relations: Assessing recent changes. *Journal of Marriage and the Family, 54,* 104-117.

Demo, D. H. (1993). The relentless search for effects of divorce: Forging new trails or tumbling down the beaten path. *Journal of Marriage and the Family, 55,* 50-54.

Demo, D. H., & Acock, A. C. (1988). The impact of divorce on children. *Journal of Marriage and the Family, 50,* 619-648.

Derogatis, L. R. (1983). *SCL-90-R: Administration, scoring and procedures manual II* (2nd ed.). Towson, MD: Clinical Psychometric Research.

Dohrenwend, B. S., Krasnoff, L., Askenasy, A. R., & Dohrenwend, B. P. (1978). Exemplification of a method for scaling life events: The PERI life events scale. *Journal of Health and Social Behavior, 19,* 205-229.

Donovan, J. E., & Jessor, R. (1985). Structure of problem behavior in adolescence and young adulthood. *Journal of Consulting and Clinical Psychology, 53,* 890-904.

Dornbusch, S. M. (1989). The sociology of adolescence. *Annual Review of Sociology, 15,* 233-259.

Dornbusch, S. M., Carlsmith, J. M., Bushwall, S. J., Ritter, P. L., Leiderman, H., Hastorf, A. H., & Gross, R. T. (1985). Single parents, extended households, and the control of adolescents. *Child Development, 56,* 326-341.

Dornbusch, S. M., & Gray, K. D. (1988). Single-parent families. In S. M. Dornbusch & M. H. Strober (Eds.), *Feminism, children, and the new families* (pp. 274-296). New York: Guilford.

Dornbusch, S. M., & Wood, K. D. (1989). Family processes and educational achievement. In W. J. Weston (Ed.), *Education and the American family: A research synthesis* (pp. 66-95). New York: New York University Press.

Downey, G., & Coyne, J. C. (1990). Children of depressed parents: An integrative review. *Psychological Bulletin, 108,* 50-76.

Duncan, G. J., & Hoffman, S. D. (1985). Economic consequences of marital instability. In M. David & T. Smeeding (Eds.), *Horizontal equity, uncertainty, and economic well-being* (pp. 427-467). Chicago: University of Chicago Press.

Dunn, J. (1984). Sibling studies and the developmental impact of critical incidents. In P. B. Bates & O. G. Brim, Jr. (Eds.), *Life span development and behavior* (Vol. 6, pp. 335-353). New York: Academic Press.

Dunn, J. (1992). Sisters and brothers: Current issues in developmental research. In F. Boer & J. Dunn (Eds.), *Children's sibling relationships: Developmental and clinical issues* (pp. 1-17). Hillsdale, NJ: Lawrence Erlbaum.

East, P. L., & Rook, K. S. (1992). Compensatory patterns of support among children's peer relationships: A test using school friends, nonschool friends, and siblings. *Developmental Psychology, 28,* 163-172.

Eccles, J. S., & Harold, R. D. (1994, September). *Family involvement in children's and adolescent's schooling.* Paper presented at the Family-School Links Conference, State College, PA.

Elder, G. H., Jr. (1974). *Children of the Great Depression: Social change in life experience.* Chicago: University of Chicago Press.

Elder, G. H., Jr., Conger, R. D., Foster, E. M., & Ardelt, M. (1992). Families under economic pressure. *Journal of Family Issues 13,* 5-37.

Elder, G. H., Jr., Eccles, J. S., Ardelt, M., & Lord, S. (1995). *Inner city parents under economic pressure: Perspectives on the strategies of parenting.* Manuscript submitted for publication.

Elder, G. H., Jr., Liker, J. K., & Cross, C. E. (1984). Parent-child behavior in the Great Depression: Life course and intergenerational influences. In P. B. Baltes & O. G. Brim (Eds.), *Life span development and behavior* (Vol. 6, pp. 109-158). New York: Academic Press.

Elder, G. H., Jr., & O'Rand, A. M. (1995). Adult lives in a changing society. In K. S. Cook, G. A. Fine, & J. S. House (Eds.), *Sociological perspectives on social psychology* (pp. 452-475). Needham Heights, MA: Allyn & Bacon.

Elder, G. H., Jr., Van Nguyen, R., & Caspi, A. (1985). Linking family hardship to children's lives. *Child Development, 56,* 361-375.

Elliott, D. S., Huizinga, D., & Ageton, S. S. (1985). *Explaining delinquency and drug use.* Beverly Hills, CA: Sage.

Elliott, D. S., Huizinga, D., & Menard, S. (1989). *Multiple problem youth: Delinquency, substance use, and mental health problems.* New York: Springer.

Emery, R. E. (1988). *Marriage, divorce, and children's adjustment.* Newbury Park, CA: Sage.

Eron, L. D., Huesmann, L. R., Dubow, E., Romanoff, R., & Yarmel, P. W. (1987). Aggression and its correlates over 22 years. In D. H. Crowell, I. M. Evans, & C. R. O'Donnell (Eds.), *Childhood aggression and violence* (pp. 249-262). New York: Plenum.

Espenshade, T. J. (1985). Marriage trends in America: Estimates, implications, and underlying causes. *Population and Development Review, 11,* 193-245.

Fincham, F. D., & Bradbury, T. N. (1990). Social support in marriage: The role of social cognition. *Journal of Social and Clinical Psychology, 9,* 31-42.

Forehand, R., Wells, K. C., McMahon, R. J., Griest, D., & Rogers, T. (1982). Maternal perceptions of maladjustment in clinic-referred children: An extension of earlier research. *Journal of Behavior Assessment, 4,* 145-151.

Forgatch, M. S., Patterson, G. R., & Skinner, M. L. (1988). A mediational model for the effect of divorce on antisocial behavior in boys. In E. M. Hetherington & J. D. Arasteh (Eds.), *Impact of divorce, single parenting, and stepparenting on children* (pp. 135-154). Hillsdale, NJ: Lawrence Erlbaum.

Forste, R., & Heaton, T. (1988). Initiation of sexual activity among female adolescents. *Youth and Society, 19,* 250-268.

Furman, W., Jones, L., Buhrmester, D., & Alder, T. (1989). Children's, parents', and observers' perspectives on sibling relationships. In R. G. Zukow (Ed.), *Sibling interaction across cultures: Theoretical and methodological issues* (pp. 165-183). New York: Springer-Verlag.

Furstenberg, F. F., & Cherlin, A. J. (1991). *Divided families: What happens to children when parents part.* Cambridge, MA: Harvard University Press.

Furstenberg, F. F., Morgan, S. P., & Allison, P. D. (1987). Paternal participation and children's well-being after marital dissolution. *American Sociological Review, 52,* 695-701.

Furstenberg, F. F., & Nord, C. W. (1985). Parenting apart: Patterns of child-rearing after marital disruption. *Journal of Marriage and the Family, 47,* 893-904.

Garfinkel, I., & Ollerich, D. (1989). Noncustodial fathers' ability to pay child support. *Demography, 26,* 219-233.

Ge, X., Conger, R. D., Lorenz, F. O., Shanahan, M., & Elder, G. H., Jr. (1995). Mutual influences in parent and adolescent psychological distress. *Developmental Psychology, 31,* 406-419.

Ge, X., Conger, R. D., Lorenz, F. O., & Simons, R. L. (1994). Parents' stressful life events and adolescent depressed mood. *Journal of Health and Social Behavior, 35,* 28-44.

Ge, X., Lorenz, F. O., Conger, R. D., Elder, G. H., Jr., & Simons, R. L. (1994). Trajectories of stressful life events and depressive symptoms during adolescence. *Developmental Psychology, 30,* 467-483.

Glenn, N. D. (1993). A plea for objective assessment of the notion of family decline. *Journal of Marriage and the Family, 55,* 542-544.

Glueck, S., & Glueck, E. (1968). *Delinquents and nondelinquents in perspective.* Cambridge, MA: Harvard University Press.

Gongla, P. A., & Thompson, E. H. (1987). Single-parent families. In M. B. Sussman & S. K. Steinmetz (Eds.), *Handbook of marriage and the family* (pp. 397-418). New York: Plenum.

Gotlib, I. H., Lewinsohn, P. M., & Seeley, J. R. (1995). Symptoms versus a diagnosis of depression: Differences in psychosocial functioning. *Journal of Consulting and Clinical Psychology, 63,* 90-100.

Gottfredson, M., & Hirschi, T. (1990). *A general theory of crime.* Stanford, CA: Stanford University Press.

Gottman, J. M. (1979). *Marital interaction: Experimental investigations.* New York: Academic Press.

Gottman, J. M. (1994). *What predicts divorce? The relationship between marital processes and marital outcomes.* Hillsdale, NJ: Lawrence Erlbaum.

Griest, D. L., Wells, K. C., & Forehand, R. (1979). An examination of predictors of maladjustment in clinic-referred children. *Journal of Abnormal Psychology, 88,* 227-281.

Grossman, F., Eichler, L., & Winickoff, S. (1980). *Pregnancy, birth, and parenthood: Adaptations of mothers, fathers, and infants.* San Francisco: Jossey-Bass.

Halem, L. C. (1980). *Divorce reform: Changing legal and social perspectives.* New York: Free Press.

Hammen, C. (1991). *Depression runs in families: The social context of risk and resilience in children of depressed mothers.* New York: Springer-Verlag.

Hartmann, D. P. (1977). Considerations in the choice of interobserver estimates. *Journal of Applied Behavioral Analysis, 10,* 103-119.

Hayes, C. (Ed.). (1987). *Risking the future: Adolescent sexuality, pregnancy, and childbearing* (Vol. 1). Washington, DC: National Academy Press.

Hernandez, D. J. (1988). Demographic trends and the living arrangements of children. In E. M. Hetherington & J. D. Arasteh (Eds.), *Impact of divorce, single parenting, and stepparenting on children* (pp. 3-22). Hillsdale, NJ: Lawrence Erlbaum.

Herzog, E., & Sudia, C. E. (1973). Children in fatherless families. In B. Caldwell & H. N. Ricciuti (Eds.), *Review of child development research* (pp. 141-232). Chicago: University of Chicago Press.

Hetherington, E. M. (1989). Coping with family transitions: Winners, losers, and survivors. *Child Development, 60,* 1-14.

Hetherington E. M. (1994). Siblings, family relationships, and child development: Introduction. *Journal of Family Psychology, 8,* 251-253.

Hetherington, E. M., & Clingempeel, W. G. (1992). Coping with marital transitions: A family systems perspective. *Monographs of the Society for Research in Child Development, 57,* 1-242.

Hetherington, E. M., Cox, M., & Cox, R. (1976). Divorced fathers. *Family Coordinator, 25,* 417-428.

Hetherington, E. M., Cox, M., & Cox, R. (1978). The aftermath of divorce. In J. H. Stevens & M. Mathews (Eds.), *Mother-child, father-child relations* (pp. 148-176). Washington, DC: National Association for the Education of Young Children Press.

Hetherington, E. M., Cox, M., & Cox, R. (1982). Effects of divorce on parents and children. In M. E. Lamb (Ed.), *Nontraditional families: Parenting and child development* (pp. 233-285). Hillsdale, NJ: Lawrence Erlbaum.

Hirschi, T. (1969). *Causes of delinquency.* Berkeley: University of California Press.

Hobfoll, S. E., & Stokes, J. P. (1988). The process and mechanics of social support. In S. W. Duck (Ed.), *Handbook of personal relationships* (pp. 497-517). New York: John Wiley.

Hoffman, S. D., & Duncan, G. J. (1985). Economic consequences of marital instability. In M. David & T. Smeeding (Eds.), *Horizontal equity, uncertainty, and economic well-being* (pp. 427-467). Chicago: University of Chicago Press.

Hoffman, S. D., & Duncan, G. J. (1988). What are the economic consequences of divorce? *Demography, 25,* 641-645.

Hogan, D. P., & Kitagawa, E. M. (1985). The impact of social status, family structure and neighborhood on the fertility of black adolescents. *American Journal of Sociology, 90,* 825-855.

House, J. C. (1981). *Work stress and social support.* Reading, MA: Addison-Wesley.

House, J. C., Umberson, D., & Landis, K. R. (1988). Structures and processes of social support. *Annual Review of Sociology, 14,* 293-318.

Hughes, M. M., & Gove, W. R. (1981). Living alone, social integration, and mental health. *American Journal of Sociology, 87,* 48-74.

Inazu, J., & Fox, G. (1980). Maternal influence on the sexual behavior of teen-age daughters. *Journal of Family Issues, 1,* 81-102.

Jenkins, J. (1992). Sibling relationships in disharmonious homes: Potential difficulties and protective effects. In F. Boer & J. Dunn (Eds.), *Children's sibling relationships: Developmental and clinical issues* (pp. 125-138). Hillsdale, NJ: Lawrence Erlbaum.

Jessor, R., Donovan, J. E., & Costa, F. M. (1991). *Beyond adolescence: Problem behavior and young adult development.* New York: Cambridge University Press.

Joreskog, K. G., & Sorbom, D. (1989). *LISREL 7: A guide to the program and applications* (2nd ed.). Chicago, IL: SPSS.

Kain, E. L. (1990). *The myth of family decline.* Lexington, MA: D. C. Heath.

Kaufman, J., & Zigler, E. (1987). Do abused children become abusive parents? *American Journal of Orthopsychiatry, 57,* 186-192.

Kessler, R. C., Price, R. H., & Wortman, C. B. (1985). Social factors in psychopathology: Stress, social support and coping processes. *Annual Review of Psychology, 36,* 531-572.

Kessler, R. C., Turner, J. B., & House, J. S. (1988). Effects of unemployment on health in a community survey: Main, modifying, and mediating effects. *Journal of Social Issues, 44,* 69-85.

King, V. (1994a). Nonresidential father involvement and child well-being: Can dads make a difference? *Journal of Family Issues, 15,* 78-96.

King, V. (1994b). Variation in the consequences of nonresident father involvement for children's well-being. *Journal of Marriage and the Family, 56,* 964-972.

Kisker, E. E., & Goldman, N. (1987). Perils of single life and benefits of marriage. *Social Biology, 34,* 135-152.

Kitson, G. C. (1992). *Portrait of divorce: Adjustment to marital breakdown.* New York: Guilford.

Kitson, G. C., & Morgan, L. A. (1990). The multiple consequences of divorce: *Journal of Marriage and the Family, 52,* 913-924.

Knok, S. L. (1988). The family and hierarchy. *Journal of Marriage and the Family, 50,* 957-966.

Krantz, S. E. (1988). Divorce and children. In S. M. Dornbusch & M. H. Strober, (Eds.), *Feminism, children, and the new families* (pp. 149-173). New York: Guilford.

Krein, S. F., & Beller, A. H. (1988). Educational achievement of children from single-parent families: Differences by exposure, gender, and race. *Demography, 25,* 221-224.

Lahey, B. B., Hartdagen, S. E., Frick, P. J., McBurnett, K., Connor, R., & Hynd, G. W. (1988). Conduct disorder: Parsing the confounded relation to parental divorce and antisocial personality. *Journal of Abnormal Psychology, 97,* 334-337.

Lamb, M. E. (1977). Father-infant and mother-infant interaction during the first year of life. *Child Development, 48,* 167-181.

Lamb, M. E., & Levine, J. A. (1985). The role of the father in child development: The effects of increased paternal involvement. In B. S. Lahey & A. E. Kazdin (Eds.), *Advances in clinical child psychology* (Vol. 8, pp. 229-266). New York: Plenum.

Lamb, M. E., & Sutton-Smith, B. (Eds.). (1982). *Sibling relationships: Their nature and significance across the lifespan.* Hillsdale, NJ: Lawrence Erlbaum.

LaRossa, R. (1986). *Becoming a parent.* Beverly Hills, CA: Sage.

LaRossa, R., & LaRossa, M. M. (1981). *Transition to parenthood.* Beverly Hills, CA: Sage.

Laub, J. H., & Sampson, R. J. (1988). Unraveling families and delinquency: A reanalysis of the Gluecks' data. *Criminology, 26,* 355-380.

Levitan, S. A., & Belous, R. S. (1981). *What's happening to the American family?* Baltimore: Johns Hopkins University Press.

Lewinsohn, P. M., Hops, H., Roberts, R. E., Seeley, J. R., & Andrews, J. A. (1993). Adolescent psychopathology: I. Prevalence and incidence of depression and other DSM-III-R disorders in high school students. *Journal of Abnormal Psychology, 102,* 133-144.

Lewis, C. (1986). *Becoming a father.* Milton Keynes, UK: Open University Press.

Lin, N., Dean, A., & Ensel, W. N. (1986). *Social support, life events, and depression.* Orlando, FL: Academic Press.

Lorenz, F. O., Conger, R. D., & Montague, R. B. (1993). Economic conditions, social support and psychological distress among rural husbands and wives. *Rural Sociology, 58,* 247-268.

Lorenz, F. O., Conger, R. D., Simons, R. L., Whitbeck, L. B., Elder, G. H., Jr. (1991). Economic pressure and marital quality: An illustration of the method variance problem in the causal modeling of family processes. *Journal of Marriage and the Family, 53,* 375-389.

Lorenz, F. O., & Melby, J. N. (1994). Analyzing family stress and adaptation: Methods of study. In R. D. Conger & G. H. Elder, Jr. (Eds.), *Families in troubled times: Adapting to change in rural America* (pp. 21-54). Hawthorne, NY: Aldine.

Maccoby, E. (1992). The role of parents in the socialization of children: An historical overview. *Developmental Psychology, 28,* 1006-1017.

Maccoby, E. E., Buchanan, C. M., Mnookin, R. H., & Dornbusch, S. M. (1993). Postdivorce roles of mothers and fathers in the lives of their children. *Journal of Family Psychology, 7,* 24-38.

Maccoby, E. E., & Martin, J. A. (1983). Socialization in the context of the family: Parent-child interaction. In P. Mussen (Ed.), *Handbook of child psychology* (pp. 1-101). New York: John Wiley.

Martin, T. C., & Bumpass, L. L. (1989). Recent trends in marital disruption. *Demography, 26,* 37-51.

Matsueda, R. L., & Heimer, K. (1987). Race, family structure and delinquency: A test of differential association and social control theories. *American Sociological Review, 52,* 826-840.

Mattson, M. E., Pollack, E. S., & Cullen, J. W. (1987). What are the odds that smoking will kill you? *American Journal of Public Health, 77,* 425-431.

McGruder, B., Lorenz, F. O., Hoyt, D., Ge, X. J., & Montague, R. (1992). *Dimensions of parenting: A technical report.* Ames: Iowa State University, Center for Family Research in Rural Mental Health.

McLanahan, S. S., & Booth, K. (1989). Mother-only families: Problems, prospects, and policies. *Journal of Marriage and the Family, 51,* 557-580.

McLanahan, S. S., & Sandefur, G. (1994). *Growing up with a single parent.* Cambridge, MA: Harvard University Press.

McLindon, J. B. (1987). Separate but unequal: The economic disaster of divorce for women and children. *Family Law Quarterly, 21,* 351-409.

Melby, J., Conger, R., Book, M., Rueter, L., Lucy, D., Repinski, K., Ahrens, D., Black, D., Brown, S., Huck, L., Miller, B., & Bingham, C. (1989). Family configuration in relation to the sexual behavior of female adolescents. *Journal of Marriage and the Family, 51,* 499-506.

Menaghan, E. G. (1985). Depressive affect and subsequent divorce. *Journal of Family Issues, 6,* 295-306.

Menaghan, E. G. (1991). Work experiences and family interaction processes: The long reach of the job. *Annual Review of Sociology, 17,* 419-444.

Menaghan, E. G., & Lieberman, M. A. (1986). Changes in depression following divorce: A panel study. *Journal of Marriage and the Family, 48,* 319-328.

Mergenhagen, P. M., Lee, B. A., & Gove, W. R. (1985). Til death do us part: Recent changes in the relationship between marital status and mortality. *Sociology and Social Research, 70,* 53-56.

Messner, S., & Tardiff, K. (1986). Economic inequality and levels of homicide: An analysis of urban neighborhoods. *Criminology, 24,* 297-318.

Michael, R. T., & Tuma, N.B. (1985). Entry into marriage and parenthood by young men and women: The influence of family background. *Demography, 22,* 515-544.

Miller, B., & Bingham, C. (1989). Adolescent sexual behavior, pregnancy, and parenting: Research through the 1980s. *Journal of Marriage and the Family, 52,* 1025-1044.

Milne, A. M. (1989). Family structure and the achievement of children. In W. J. Weston (Ed.), *Education and the American family: A research synthesis* (pp. 32-65). New York: New York University Press.

Mirowsky, J., & Ross, C. E. (1989). *Social causes of psychological distress*. New York: Aldine.

Moffitt, T. E. (1993). Adolescent-limited and life-course-persistent antisocial behavior: A developmental taxonomy. *Psychological Review, 100,* 674-701.

Morgan, L. A. (1991). *After marriage ends: Economic consequences for midlife women.* Newbury Park, CA: Sage.

Morgan, S. P., Lye, D., & Condran, G. (1988). Sons, daughters, and the risk of marital disruption. *American Journal of Sociology, 94,* 110-129.

National Center for Health Statistics. (1988). *Current estimates from the National Health Interview Survey: United States, 1987* (DHHS Pub. No. (PHS) 88-1594). Washington, DC: Government Printing Office.

Nelson-LeGall, S., Gumerman, R. A., & Scott-Jones, D. (1983). Instrumental help-seeking and everyday problem-solving: A developmental perspective. In B. DePaulo, A. Nadler, & J. Fisher (Eds.), *New directions in helping* (Vol. 2, pp. 265-283). New York: Academic Press.

Neville, B., & Parke, R. D. (1987). *Developmental shifts in father and mother play and recreational activities with children.* Urbana: University of Illinois, Department of Psychology.

Newcomer, S. & Udry, J. R. (1987). Parental marital status effects on adolescent sexual behavior. *Journal of Marriage and the Family, 49,* 233-240.

Norton, A. J., & Moorman, J. E. (1987). Current trends in American marriage and divorce. *Journal of Marriage and the Family, 49,* 3-14.

Olson, D. H. L. (1977). Insiders' and outsiders' views of relationships: Research studies. In G. Levinger & H. L. Rausch (Eds.), *Close relationships: Perspectives on the meaning of intimacy.* Amherst: University of Massachusetts Press.

Orraschel, H., Weissman, M. M., & Kidd, K. K. (1980). Children and depressed parents; the childhood of depressed parents; depression in children. *Journal of Affective Disorders, 2,* 1-16.

Parke, R. D. (1981). *Fathers.* Cambridge, MA: Harvard University Press.

Parke, R. D., & Bhavnagri, N. P. (1989). Parents as managers of children's peer relationships. In D. Belle (Ed.), *Children's social networks and social supports* (pp. 241-259). New York: John Wiley.

Parke, R. D., & Sterns, P. N. (1993). Fathers and child rearing. In G. H. Elder, Jr., J. Modell, & R. D. Parke (Eds.), *Children in time and place: Developmental and historical insights* (pp. 147-170). New York: Cambridge University Press.

Parke, R. D., & Tinsley, B. R. (1987). The father's role in infancy: Determinants of involvement in caregiving and play. In M. E. Lamb (Ed.), *The role of the father in child development* (pp. 429-457). New York: John Wiley.

Patterson, G. R. (1982). *A social learning approach: 3. Coercive family process.* Eugene, OR: Castalia.

Patterson, G. R. (1984). Siblings: Fellow travelers in coercive family processes. In R. J. Blanchard (Ed.), *Advances in the study of aggression* (pp. 173-215). New York: Academic Press.

Patterson, G. R. (1986a). The contribution of siblings to training for fighting: A microsocial analysis. In D. Olweus, J. Block, & M. Radke-Yarrow (Eds.), *Development of antisocial and prosocial behavior: Research, theories, and issues* (pp. 235-261). Orlando, FL: Academic Press.

Patterson, G. R. (1986b). Performance models for antisocial boys. *American Psychologist, 41,* 432-444.

Patterson, G. R., & Bank, L. (1987, October). *Some amplifying mechanisms for pathological processes in families.* Paper presented at the Minnesota Symposium on Child Psychology, Minneapolis, MN.

Patterson, G. R., & Capaldi, D. M. (1991). Antisocial parents: Unskilled and vulnerable. In P. A. Cowan & E. M. Hetherington (Eds.), *Family transitions* (pp. 195-218). Hillsdale, NJ: Lawrence Erlbaum.

Patterson, G. R., DeBaryshe, B., & Ramsey, E. (1989). A developmental perspective on antisocial behavior. *American Psychologist, 44,* 329-335.

Patterson, G. R., & Dishion, T. J. (1988). Multilevel family process models: Traits, interactions, and relationships. In R. Hinde & J. Stevenson-Hinde (Eds.), *Relationships within families: Mutual influences* (pp. 283-310). Oxford, UK: Clarendon.

Patterson, G. R., Reid, J. B., & Dishion, T. J. (1992). *Antisocial boys.* Eugene, OR: Castalia.

Pearlin, L. I. (1989). The sociological study of stress. *Journal of Health and Social Behavior, 30,* 241-256.

Pearlin, L. I., Lieberman, M. A., Menaghan, E. G., & Mullan, J. T. (1981). The stress process. *Journal of Health and Social Behavior, 22,* 337-356.

Petersen, A. C., Compas, B. E., Brooks-Gunn, J., Stemmler, M., Ey, S., & Grant, K. E. (1993). Depression in adolescence. *American Psychologist, 48,* 155-168.

Popenoe, D. (1993). American family decline, 1960-1990: A review and appraisal. *Journal of Marriage and the Family, 55,* 527-541.

Radin, N., & Russell, G. (1983). Increased father participation and child development outcomes. In M. E. Lamb & A. Sagi (Eds.), *Fatherhood and family policy* (pp. 191-218). Hillsdale, NJ: Lawrence Erlbaum.

Radke-Yarrow, M., Richters, J., & Wilson, W. E. (1988). Child development in a network of relationships. In R. A. Hinde & J. Stevenson-Hinde (Eds.), *Relationships within families: Mutual influences* (pp. 48-67). New York: Oxford University Press.

Rands, M. (1988). Changes in social networks following marital separation and divorce. In R. M. Milardo (Ed.), *Families and social networks* (pp. 127-146). Newbury Park, CA: Sage.

Raschke, H. J. (1987). Divorce. In M. B. Sussman & S. K. Steinmetz (Eds.), *Handbook of marriage and the family* (pp. 597-624). New York: Plenum.

Reis, H. T. (1990). The role of intimacy in interpersonal relations. *Journal of Social and Clinical Psychology, 9,* 15-30.

Reiss, I. L. (1971). *Family systems in America.* New York: Holt, Rinehart & Winston.

Reiss, I. L., & Lee, G. R. (1988). *Family systems in America* (4th ed.). New York: Holt.

Richards, L. N., & Schmiege, C. J. (1993). Problems and strengths of single-parent families: Implications for practice and policy. *Family Relations, 42,* 277-285.

Robins, L. N. (1966). *Deviant children grown up: A sociological and psychiatric study of sociopathic personality.* Baltimore: Williams & Wilkins.

Robins, L. N., Locke, B. Z., & Regier, D. A. (1991). An overview of psychiatric disorders in America. In L. N. Robins & D. A. Regier (Eds.), *Psychiatric disorders in America* (pp. 328-366). New York: Free Press.

Roncek, D. (1981). Dangerous places: Crime and residential environment. *Social Forces, 60,* 74-96.

Ross, C. E., Mirowsky, J., & Goldsteen, K. (1990). The impact of the family on health: The decade in review. *Journal of Marriage and the Family, 52,* 1059-1078.

Rowe, D. C., Rodgers, J. L. & Meseck-Bushey, S. (1989). An "epidemic" model of sexual intercourse prevalences for black and white adolescents. *Social Biology, 36,* 127-145.

Rutter, M. (1985a). Family and school influences on behavioral development. *Journal of Child Psychology and Psychiatry, 26,* 349-368.

Rutter, M. (1985b). Family and school influences on cognitive development. *Journal of Child Psychology and Psychiatry, 26,* 683-704.

Sampson, R. J. (1985). Neighborhood and crime: The structural determinants of personal victimization. *Journal of Research in Crime and Delinquency, 22,* 7-40.

Sampson, R. J. (1986). Neighborhood family structure and the risk of criminal victimization. In J. Byrne & R. J. Sampson (Eds.), *The social ecology of crime* (pp. 25-46). New York: Springer-Verlag.

Sampson, R. J., & Laub, J. H. (1993). *Crime in the making: Pathways and turning points.* Cambridge, MA: Harvard University Press.

Sampson, R. J., & Lauritsen, J. L. (1994). Violent victimization and offending: Individual, situational, and community level risk factors. In A. J. Reiss & J. A. Roth (Eds.), *Understanding and preventing violence* (Vol. 3., pp. 1-114). Washington DC: National Academy Press.

Santrock, J. W., Warshak, R., & Elliott, G. L. (1982). Social development and parent-child interaction in father-custody and stepmother families. In M. E. Lamb (Ed.), *Nontraditional families: Parenting and child development* (pp. 289-315). Hillsdale, NJ: Lawrence Erlbaum.

Santrock, J. W., Warshak, R., Lindbergh, C., & Meadows, L. (1982). Children's and parents' observed social behavior in stepfather families. *Child Development, 53,* 474-480.

Schneider, B., & Coleman, J. S. (1993). *Parents, their children, and schools.* Boulder, CO: Westview.

Schoen, R. (1987). The continuing retreat from marriage: Figures from the 1983 U.S. marital status life tables. *Social Science Research, 71,* 108-109.

Schuerman, L., & Korbin, S. (1986). Community careers in crime. In A. J. Reiss, Jr., & M. Tonry (Eds.), *Communities and crime* (pp. 67-100). Chicago: University of Chicago Press.

Schwarz, J. C., Barton-Henry, M. L., & Pruzinsky, T. (1985). Assessing child-rearing behaviors: A comparison of ratings made by mother, father, child, and sibling on the CRPBI. *Child Development, 56,* 462-479.

Simons, R. L., Beaman, J., Conger, R. D., & Chao, W. (1992). Childhood experience, conceptions of parenting, and attitudes of spouse as determinants of parental behavior. *Journal of Marriage and the Family, 55,* 91-106.

Simons, R. L., & Johnson, C. (1995). Social network and marital support as mediators and moderators of the impact of economic pressure on parental behavior. In G. Pierce, B. Sarason, & I. Sarason (Eds.), *The handbook of social support and the family.* New York: Plenum.

Simons, R. L., Johnson, C., Beaman, J., & Conger, R. D. (1993). Explaining women's double jeopardy: Factors that mediate the association between harsh treatment as a child and violence by a husband. *Journal of Marriage and the Family, 55,* 713-723.

Simons, R. L., Johnson, C., & Conger, R. D. (1994). Harsh corporal punishment versus quality of parental involvement as an explanation of adolescent maladjustment. *Journal of Marriage and the Family, 56,* 591-607.

Simons, R. L., Lorenz, F. O., Conger, R. D., & Wu, C. (1992). Support from spouse as mediator and moderator of the disruptive influence of economic strain on parenting. *Child Development, 63,* 1282-1301.

Simons, R. L., Lorenz, F. O., Wu, C., & Conger, R. D. (1993). Marital and spouse support as mediator and moderator of the impact of economic strain upon parenting. *Developmental Psychology, 29,* 368-381.

Simons, R. L., Whitbeck, L. B., Beaman, J., & Conger, R. D. (1994). The impact of mothers' parenting, involvement by nonresidential fathers, and parental conflict on adjustment of adolescent children. *Journal of Marriage and the Family, 56,* 356-374.

Simons, R. L., Whitbeck, L. B., Conger, R. D., & Wu, C. (1991). Intergenerational transmission of harsh parenting. *Journal of Psychology, 27,* 159-171.

Simons, R. L., Whitbeck, L. B., Melby, J. N., & Wu, C. (1994). Economic pressure and harsh parenting. In R. D. Conger & G. H. Elder, Jr. (Eds.), *Families in troubled times* (pp. 207-222). New York: Aldine.

Simons, R. L., Whitbeck, L. B., & Wu, C. (1994). Resilient and vulnerable adolescents. In R. D. Conger & G. H. Elder, Jr. (Eds.), *Families in troubled times* (pp. 223-234). New York: Aldine.

Simons, R. L., Wu, C., Conger, R. D., & Lorenz, F. O. (1994). Two routes to delinquency: Differences between early and late starters in the impact of parenting and deviant peers. *Criminology, 32,* 247-276.

Simons, R. L., Wu, C., Johnson, C., & Conger, R. D. (1995). A test of various perspectives on the intergenerational transmission of domestic violence. *Criminology, 33,* 141-172.

Skolnick, A. (1991). *Embattled paradise: The American family in an age of uncertainty.* New York: Basic Books.

Smith, D. R., & Jarjoura, G. R. (1988). Social structure and criminal victimization. *Journal of Research in Crime and Delinquency, 25,* 27-52.

Stacey, J. (1990). *Brave new families: Stories of domestic upheaval in late 20th century America.* New York: Basic Books.

Stacey, J. (1993). Good riddance to "the family": A response to David Popenoe. *Journal of Marriage and the Family, 55,* 545-547.

Stack, S. (1989). The impact of divorce on suicide in Norway, 1951-1980. *Journal of Marriage and the Family, 51,* 229-238.

Stocker, C. M. (1994). Children's perceptions of relationships with siblings, friends, and mothers: Compensatory processes and links with adjustment. *Journal of Child Psychology and Psychiatry, 35,* 1447-1459.

Straus, M. A., Gelles, R. J., & Steinmetz, S. K. (1980). *Behind closed doors: Violence in the American family.* Beverly Hills, CA: Sage.

Thomson, E., Hanson, T. L., & McLanahan, S. (1994). Family structure and child well-being: Economic resources vs. parental behaviors. *Social Forces, 73,* 221-242.

Thomson, E., McLanahan, S. S., & Curtin, R. B. (1992). Family structure, gender, and parental socialization. *Journal of Marriage and the Family, 54,* 368-378.

Thornton, A. (1989). Changing attitudes towards family issues in the United States. *Journal of Marriage and the Family, 51,* 873-893.

Thornton, A., & Camburn, D. (1987). The influence of the family on premarital sexual attitudes and behavior. *Demography, 24,* 323-340.

Tienda, M., & Kao, G. (1994, August). *Parental behavior and the odds of success among students at risk of failure.* Paper presented at the Annual Meeting of the American Sociological Association, Los Angeles, CA.

Travato, F., & Lauris, G. (1989). Marital status and mortality in Canada: 1951-81. *Journal of Marriage and the Family, 51,* 907-922.

Tschann, J. M., Johnston, J. R., & Wallerstein, J. S. (1989). Resources, stresses, and attachment as predictors of adult adjustment to divorce: A longitudinal study. *Journal of Marriage and the Family, 51,* 1033-1046.

Turner, R. J., Wheaton, B., & Lloyd, D. A. (1995). The epidemiology of social stress. *American Sociological Review, 60,* 104-125.

U.S. Bureau of Census. (1993). *Poverty in the United States: 1992* (Current population reports, series P-60, no. 188). Washington, DC: Government Printing Office.

Vanek, M. (1981). Division of household work: A decade comparison—1967-1977. *Home Economics Research Journal, 10,* 175-180.

Wallerstein, J. S., & Kelly, J. B. (1980). *Surviving the breakup: How children and parents cope with divorce.* New York: Basic Books.

Weissman, M. M., & Paykel, E. S. (1974). *The depression of women: A study of social relations.* Chicago: University of Chicago Press.

Weitzman, L. J. (1985). *The divorce revolution: The unexpected social and economic consequences for women and children.* New York: Free Press.

West, D. J., & Farrington, D. P. (1977). *The delinquent way of life.* New York: Crane, Russak & Co.

Wheaton, B. (1990). Life transitions, role histories, and mental health. *American Sociological Review, 55,* 209-223.

Whitbeck, L., Conger, R., Simons, R., & Kao, M. (1993). Minor deviant behaviors and adolescent sexual activity. *Youth and Society, 24,* 24-37.

Whitbeck, L., Simons, R., Conger, R., Lorenz, F. O., Huck, S., & Elder, G. H., Jr., (1991). Family economic hardship, parent support, and adolescent self-esteem. *Social Psychology Quarterly, 54,* 353-363.

Whitbeck, L., Simons, R., & Kao, M. (1994). The effects of divorced single mothers' dating and sexual attitudes on the sexual attitudes and behaviors of their adolescent children. *Journal of Marriage and the Family, 56,* 615-621.

White, L. K. (1990). Determinants of divorce: A review of research in the eighties. *Journal of Marriage and the Family, 52,* 904-912.

Whitehead, B. D. (1993, July). Dan Quayle was right. *Atlantic Monthly,* pp. 8-11.

Willner, P. (1985). *Depression: A psychobiological synthesis.* New York: John Wiley.

Wilson, J. Q. (1995). Crime and public policy. In J. Q. Wilson & J. Petersilia (Eds.), *Crime* (pp. 489-510). San Francisco: ICS.

Wilson, W. J. (1987). *The truly disadvantaged: The inner city, the underclass, and public policy.* Chicago: University of Chicago Press.

Wolchik, S. A., Sandler, I., & Braver, S. L. (1984, August). *The social support networks of children of divorce.* Paper presented at the American Psychological Association meeting, Toronto.

Zelnik, M., Kantner, J., & Ford, K. (1981). *Sex and pregnancy in adolescence.* Beverly Hills, CA: Sage.

Zill, N. (1988). Behavior, achievement, and health problems among children in step-families: Findings from a national survey of child health. In E. M. Hetherington & J. D. Arasteh (Eds.), *Impact of divorce, single parenting, and stepparenting on children* (pp. 325-368). Hillsdale, NJ: Lawrence Erlbaum.

Zukow, P. G. (1989). *Sibling interaction across cultures: Theoretical and methodological issues.* New York: Springer-Verlag.

Index

About the Authors

Jay Beaman worked for several years as Project Director for the Iowa Single Parent Project and currently is Assistant Professor of Sociology at Fox College. Much of his research is concerned with the impact of religion on family processes.

Wei Chao is a doctoral candidate in Sociology at Iowa State University. His research interests include the association between family structure and family processes, the influence of parenting on child antisocial behavior, and statistical techniques for modeling panel data.

Katherine J. Conger is a research scientist with the Center for Family Research in Rural Mental Health at Iowa State University. Her research interests include the effect of sibling relationships on child development and the relationship between marital interaction and the emotional well-being of adults.

Rand D. Conger is Professor of Sociology and Director of the NIMH-funded Center for Family Research in Rural Mental Health at Iowa State University. His research interests include the transition from adolescence to adulthood, family research methods such as the direct observation of family interactions, and the influence of family dynamics and acute stressors on physical and mental health.

Glen H. Elder, Jr. is the Howard W. Odum Distinguished Professor of Sociology at the University of North Carolina. His research interests include the influence of economic hardship and social change on families, the interdependence of people's lives, and the effect of social context on life course development.

Elizabeth Goldberg is a statistician for Life Scan in Sunnyvale, California. Her research interests include intergenerational relations, sexual behavior during adolescence, and life course perspectives on family processes.

Christine Johnson is a doctoral candidate in Sociology at Iowa State University. Her research interests include explanations for domestic violence, life course perspectives on intergenerational relations, and the link between family processes and child adjustment.

Frederick O. Lorenz is Professor of Sociology and Statistics at Iowa State University. His research interests include the relationship between social support and emotional health, the effects of measurement error in modeling family processes, and methodological issues associated with the analysis of panel data.

Stephen T. Russell is a Postdoctoral Fellow with the Carolina Population Center at the University of North Carolina at Chapel Hill. His research interests include the effects of neighborhoods, family structure, and parental behavior on child and adolescent development.

Ronald L. Simons is Professor of Sociology and Associate Director of the NIMH-funded Center for Family Research in Rural Mental Health at Iowa State University. His research interests include domestic violence, the intergenerational transmission of problem behavior, and the influence of community factors and family processes on adolescent development.

Les B. Whitbeck is Associate Professor of Sociology at Iowa State University. His research interests include homeless youth, determinants of adolescent early sexual behavior, variations in family socialization practices, and adult intergenerational relationships.